Dakota War Whoop

HARRIET E. BISHOP McCONKEY

The Lakeside Classics

DAKOTA WAR WHOOP

Indian Massacres and War in Minnesota

By Harriet E. Bishop McConkey

EDITED BY
DALE L. MORGAN

The Lakeside Press

R. R. DONNELLEY & SONS COMPANY

CHICAGO

Christmas, 1965

PUBLISHERS' PREFACE

DURING the five Centennial years of the American Civil War, the Lakeside Classics concentrated on narratives pertaining to the struggle between the North and the South in the several theatres of that war. Not many realize, however, that at the same time other conflicts deeply affected many Americans elsewhere in our country.

This year's Lakeside Classic deals with one of these conflicts—the Sioux Uprising of 1862-3 in southern Minnesota and the nearby Dakota Territory.

Here the struggle was between Indians on the one hand, and settlers and soldiers with widely varying amounts of training on the other. Thus this year we return to the mainstream of the Classics of the past—the opening and development of the West, in which Indians have been encountered so many times before.

While our authoress, Harriet Bishop McConkey, was not, quite fortunately, an eyewitness to all the violent happenings she relates and describes, for almost fifteen years she had very actively participated in the development of the area. Some of the participants she knew or came to know. But, more important, her ability to understand and share the emotions of her Minnesota contemporaries enabled her to record the events of the day with unusual sensitivity.

v

Life on the frontier was hard. But, with the Sioux massacres and atrocities, it became gruesome. One admires the fortitude of those who suffered through this period, defending themselves and their settlements, and finally subduing the enemy. They contributed not only to the development of Minnesota but to the winning of the whole West.

Mrs. McConkey does point out that some Sioux were friendly and did help the settlers. From the perspective of history, we can see the Sioux as players in a grand tragedy, victims as well as transgressors.

Present day travelers from Mankato, up the Minnesota Valley to southeast North Dakota, will be interested to find many of the incidents in this volume well memorialized, and their sites indicated on modern road maps.

We are particularly fortunate in having obtained the services of Dale L. Morgan as editor of this year's Lakeside Classic. A prominent member of the staff of the Bancroft Library at the University of California at Berkeley, he is an outstanding authority on Western Americana. In preparing the manuscript for publication, he has provided in the footnotes considerable additional reference material which is of value to the historian and may also be of interest to those who are not professionals.

THE COMPANY has enjoyed another fine year. This is especially gratifying following a most successful performance in 1964. Sizable additions to our plants at Crawfordsville and Warsaw, Indiana and Willard, Ohio have been completed this year, and considerable new equipment installed at almost every location. Additional equipment is planned and ordered for following years, to accommodate the increasing demands from customers, some of whom we have been serving since long before the founding of the Lakeside Classics in 1903, and others who have more recently entrusted their printing requirements to our care.

Our continued growth and success is due to our many friends, old and new. Among these we number our customers, suppliers, employees and many others. In face of many varied and demanding challenges during the past year, members of our Company have maintained the high standards of quality, service and value which have provided the foundation for our continued growth.

To all our sincere thanks, and best wishes for a Merry Christmas and Happy New Year.

THE PUBLISHERS

Christmas, 1965

CONTENTS

ix

Contents

xi

ILLUSTRATIONS

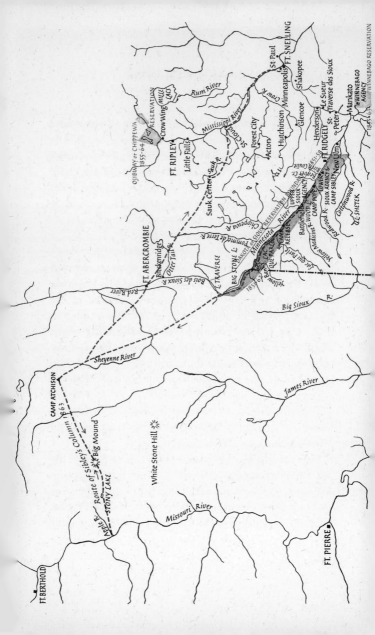

HISTORICAL INTRODUCTION

FOR several years past, the Lakeside Classics have reflected the national interest in the centennial observance of the Civil War. As that centennial drew on to its close, the Publishers began to look for a title which would reflect the convulsion of a hundred years ago, but which also would return the Classics to their preoccupation of many years, personal narratives of the American frontier.

In Harriet E. B. McConkey's *Dakota War Whoop* all agree that such a title has been found, and this work, first published in 1863, becomes the Lakeside Classic for 1965. Mrs. McConkey's account of the Sioux uprising of 1862, and the military campaign that extended into the next year, admittedly is not wholly a record of personal experience. Though she was living in St. Paul at the time of the outbreak, and shared in all the emotions consequent upon the uprising, she was not herself tomahawked, or dragged off into captivity, or otherwise involved in experiences one is glad to be spared at the time, however advantageous to a writer afterward.

Her *Dakota War Whoop* is nevertheless more truly personal in tone than any of the contemporaneously published general narratives of the Sioux uprising, yielding in this respect only to Mrs. Sarah F. Wakefield's contribution to the historic literature of Indian captivities, *Six Weeks in the Sioux Tepees.*[1] She had rivals who competed with her for the hopefully remunerative privilege of getting a book on the Sioux uprising into the hands of curious readers, and we shall give attention to these hereafter. But these rivals were not emotionally involved as was Mrs. McConkey, and for this reason among others, we have given preference to her book in selecting the Classic.

Let us see who our author was, and where she came from.

A biographical sketch by Zylpha S. Morton, "Harriet Bishop, Frontier Teacher," printed in *Minnesota History,* June, 1947, details the principal facts in her personal history. Harriet was born in Paton, Addison County, Vermont, on January 1, 1818, the third daughter of Putnam and Miranda Bishop. She was educated in Vergennes, Vermont, and in the Fort Edward Institute, New York, and taught in Essex, also in New York State. Familiar from childhood with the narratives of Baptist missionaries in Burma, and possessed of an adventurous spirit, Harriet was just the

---

[1] Of the first edition of Mrs. Wakefield's rare narrative, printed at Minneapolis in 1863 (Atlas Printing Company, 54 pp.), only a single copy is known, in the Yale University Library. The second edition, printed at Shakopee in 1864 (Argus Book and Job Printing Office, 63 pp.), is nearly as rare. I have used the copy in the Newberry Library, Chicago. A fictitious work is *Miss Coleson's Narrative of Her Captivity among the Sioux Indians! An interesting and remarkable account of the terrible sufferings and providential escapes of Miss Ann Coleson, a victim of the late Indian outrages in Minnesota* (Philadelphia, Barclay & Co., 1864, 70 pp.; also several later editions).

person to respond when a group of young New England women, meeting at the New York State Normal School at Albany for a preparatory course under Catherine Beecher, were presented with the opportunity to go West as qualified "female teachers."

In the book she published a few years later, *Floral Home,* Harriet relates how it happened that she came to Minnesota. Dr. Williamson of the Sioux Mission addressed a letter to the embryo Board of National Popular Education stressing the great need of "a good female teacher," who could do more to promote the cause of education and true religion than a man. "A teacher for this place should love the Savior, and for his sake should be willing to forego, not only many of the religious privileges and elegances of New England towns, but some of the neatness also. She should be entirely free from prejudice on account of color, for among her scholars she might find not only English, French, and Swiss, but Sioux and Chippewas, with some claiming kindred with the African stock."

That was the first, Harriet says, that she had heard of St. Paul, or even of Minnesota, "and the impression was at once riveted on my mind that *I must go;* and when, after two weeks of prayerful deliberation, the question was asked, 'Who will go to St. Paul?' I could cheerfully, though tremblingly, respond, '*Here am I;* send me.'" Despite the opposition of friends, who considered that she was "tempting Divine Providence," in her innocence she set out for distant

Minnesota. By land and water she traveled from New York State to Cincinnati, thence down the Ohio and up the Mississippi to St. Paul, a 1,700 mile voyage. All nature, she says, conspired to form a glorious day when first she looked upon "Little Crow's Village," or Kaposia, a little below St. Paul, where the boat headed on the morning of July 16, 1847. "The ringing of the bell occasioned a grand rush, and with telegraphic speed, every man, woman, and child flew to the landing."

To an eye so unsophisticated as hers, "the scene on shore was novel and grotesque, not to say repulsive; blankets and hair streaming in the wind; limbs uncovered; children nearly naked, the smaller ones entirely so, while a pappoose was ludicrously peeping over the shoulder of nearly every squaw. In the midst of the waiting throng appeared the Missionary and his sister." The jocular captain observed that the doctor was doing up things in fine style; "he had got the whole village out for an escort."

As soon as she had been presented to Dr. Williamson, she set out to win the hearts of the Indians present, kissing all the babies. Toward evening, she strolled through their village with the Williamsons. "At the lodge of the chief, a skin was placed without the door for my benefit . . . This the mission lady urged me to accept."

A few days later, two Indian girls paddled her upstream to St. Paul, where she called at the home of J. R. Irvine, at which she was to live. The village

was crowded, a Red River caravan having come in
a few days earlier. Accordingly she thought best to
remain at the mission for a time, and several days
passed before Harriet made her formal advent into
St. Paul, receiving "the spontaneous greetings of
the youthful crowd."

The school she opened on July 19, in a "mud-
walled log hovel" once used as a blacksmith's shop,
"covered with bark, and chinked with mud," was the
first in Minnesota, which has made it memorable.
Only two among her first seven pupils were white,
and the complications may be imagined. She gave
instruction in English, interpreted for the children
by a half-breed girl able to speak English, French,
and Sioux.

We shall not follow the history of that school.
Harriet taught there until the fall of 1850, when a
district school was organized in St. Paul. With help
from an Ohio friend, she then opened in St. Paul a
"Female Seminary" or boarding school, fulfilling a
cherished desire to prepare teachers for labor in the
Northwest.

On the frontier, nothing was more certain than
that she would receive proposals of marriage. An
early suitor was an Indian named Oseola, who through
an interpreter promised: "She shall have the best
corner of the lodge, and the dark squaw shall pack
the wood and water, plant and hoe the corn; white
squaw may ride by my side in the hunt, and the
other shall carry the game, set the 'teepee,' and cook

the food and hush the pappoose, while *white squaw eats with me.*" Refused, the gentleman philosophically "begged a dollar to buy a new shirt," and made off.

This courtship Harriet reports in *Floral Home.* Later courtships by more welcome suitors she elected not to describe. Rebecca Marshall Cathcart, who knew her from May, 1849, recalled in 1913:

"Miss Bishop became engaged to Mr. James K. Humphrey, a young lawyer of St. Paul, and some years younger than herself, but not her equal intellectually. She was devoted to him, and during all one summer had planned to be married in the fall; Mr. Humphrey had built a pretty cottage on Irvine Park; the trousseau had been completed, and everything was going smoothly; but, alas, there was a rock ahead which made shipwreck of all these fond anticipations and plans. Mr. Humphrey's sister, Mrs. Selby, came back from the East, where she had been spending the summer, and she forbade the bans; her only reason stated was that Miss Bishop was older than her brother; and he then and there proved our opinion of him, that he was weak, and broke the engagement. Miss Bishop was broken-hearted and decided she could not remain in St. Paul; we all sympathized with her, but thought that she would realize after a time that he had not been worthy of her love. Nevertheless the result was that her life was wrecked and she seemed to lose her fine mental balance. She married a few years after this, and was the author of a historical book entitled 'Dakota War Whoop . . .'; but she had lost her prestige as Miss Bishop, and twenty years later she died in this city, almost unknown. An island in the river was named Harriet after her, and today this island is covered with the Public Baths and Playgrounds, so that in a certain sense her name will always be connected with the education and enlightenment of youth."[2]

Harriet married John McConkey in 1858, and *Dakota War Whoop* was presented under her married name. But eventually she was divorced, and in 1867 the Minnesota legislature by one of its miscellaneous enactments restored her maiden name, "Harriet E. Bishop." Under that name she published a volume of poetry in 1869.

She died in St. Paul on August 8, 1883. A newspaper obituary the following day noted that for several years she had been in poor health, and had in a great measure withdrawn from literary pursuits. She was remarked to have been a lecturer on and a warm advocate of temperance, and to have resided for a time in California. A few years after her death, T. M. Newsom, in *Pen Pictures of St. Paul, Minnesota, and Biographical Sketches of Old Settlers* (St. Paul, 1886)[3], remarked more revealingly: "she was sincere and earnest. She taught, she wrote, she worked—all for the cause of God. She was ambitious; she sought

[2]*Minnesota Historical Collections,* 1915, vol. 15, pp. 531-532.
[3]See vol. 1, pp. 63–64.

fame, and hence she wrote several works—some poetry, and a history of the Sioux outbreak. . . She was angular, positive, determined—such a woman as is necessary for frontier life. She knew no policy. She attacked evils upon their merits; never conciliated or compromised; hence she often antagonized some of her best friends working with her in the same good cause . . . Miss Bishop, once Mrs. McConkey, was a woman of comely appearance; tall, with a good figure; a bright, expressive face; earnest and decided in manners; and quick in speech. She had an air of active business about her, and seemed always in a hurry. Until within a few years she wore curls, and looked much younger than she really was, but back of all her energy and activity and her desire to fill up the measure of her usefulness, there was a sad, broken heart, which at last gave way, and she now rests in peace. Old settlers remember her kindly. . ."

Writing in 1947, Zylpha Morton said that there were still people in St. Paul and Minneapolis "who recall Miss Bishop's graciousness, her hospitality, and her home, where beautiful furniture upholstered in her own needlepoint was admired. As late as 1880 Miss Bishop still wore her hair in curls that framed her face. Her pictures show a beautiful woman with an appealing expression. Though a daughter of Vermont, she readily adopted Minnesota as her home. 'I have known Minnesota from its infancy, and have loved it as a parent does a child,' she said once. But her love extended over the whole western country, of which she wrote, 'I have never so felt my soul flow with enthusiasm, with the fact that I am an American woman, as in scanning the vast field which the West presents, for the exercise of our best faculties, for effort and expansion.' In a note, Mrs. Morton added that some of Miss Bishop's former possessions were inherited by a granddaughter, Mrs. A. B. Wells of Minneapolis, interviewed by her in December, 1944.

From our author, a "strong-minded female," as she might have been characterized in another age, but one whose life is touched with pathos, let us turn to her books. The first, *Floral Home; or, First Years of Minnesota, Early Sketches, Later Settlements, and Further Developments,* was printed in New York by Sheldon, Blakeman and Company, 1857. A work of 342 pages, its first eight chapters detail the early history of Minnesota, after which it becomes a mixed autobiography, history, and commentary on the Minnesota scene, extending to the close of 1856. In style and temper it has much in common with *Dakota War Whoop,* though composed in more tranquil spirit. Her last book, *Minnesota; Then and Now,* printed in St. Paul by D.D. Merrill, Randall & Co., 1869, is a slender, 100-page work of poetry, rather didactic in character, with a few notes at the end to explain factual allusions.

Since, at the time of the Sioux uprising of 1862, Harriet Bishop McConkey was already the author of a published book dealing with Minnesota, she must have felt from the beginning a strong inclination to write an account of these large historic events happening almost under her eye—some, in truth, actually under her eye in St. Paul. She had plenty of rivals, real or potential, and the urge to be first into the bookstores with her narrative must be viewed as a strong factor in the structure of the book. She could not write a wide-ranging personal narrative, in that she was confined to St. Paul during the events of 1862, and as a gentlewoman could expect no invitation to accompany the military columns, that year or the next. But she was deeply involved emotionally, and she had energy, intelligence, and previous literary experience working for her.

Originally it may have appeared that competition would rear its head close to home. The St. Paul *Pioneer* of August 11, 1863, reported: "We learn that the Rev. E. Eggleston of this city has been engaged for some time in collecting materials for a full and complete history of the Indian War, and that it is probable the work will be put to press in a month or two, and will be issued in several numbers, handsomely illustrated. In the meantime Mr. Eggleston solicits contributions from those who are personally cognizant of interesting and important facts connected with the war, that his relation may be made with as much accuracy as possible." Although the *Pioneer* described Eggleston as "a gentleman of scholarly attainments," who would make "a very popular book as well as a truthful one," Edward Eggleston was not then the popular novelist and

historian he became in later years; he was an obscure
pastor of a St. Paul church, a young man in his
middle twenties as much removed from the scenes
of recent violence as was Harriet herself.

In fact, the competition came primarily from two
men engaged in more active pursuits. The most en-
terprising was Isaac V. D. Heard, a lawyer who had
lived in Minnesota for twelve years, been a member of
Sibley's expedition from August to November, 1862,
and "recorder" of the military tribunal which tried
the Sioux prisoners that fall. Heard set about writing,
not a personal narrative, but "a connected and reliable
history," published by Harper & Brothers in New
York as *History of the Sioux War and Massacres of
1862 and 1863*. The preface is dated in New York
City, September 30, 1863, and the book reached the
St. Paul bookshops in late November, just ahead of
Dakota War Whoop. Heard's work was reprinted in
1864, and again in 1865.

The other principal work competing with *Dakota
War Whoop* was Charles S. Bryant and Abel B.
Murch's *A History of the Great Massacre by the Sioux
Indians, in Minnesota, including the personal narratives of many who escaped,* published at Cincinnati
early in 1864. In the preface, dated at Cincinnati
November 25, 1863, the authors explain that it was
Bryant's fortune "to reside at a town in Minnesota,
where, by a law of Congress, a board of commissioners were required to hold their first session for
the adjustment of claims for damages to the pro-

perty of the settlers by the Sioux Indians, in the late massacre. It was his professional duty to prosecute, before that commission, over one hundred claims for damages. In this way he came in daily connection with the sufferers, and was compelled to listen to tales of horror of a character entirely too dreadful to be concealed. Some of these revelations were wholly disconnected with any duties required by the Board of Commissioners, in reducing to writing the necessary testimony relating to the loss of property. It therefore seemed important that some one properly situated and related to these claimants, should save from oblivion many interesting incidents touching the sad and melancholy exit of the innocent sufferers of this cruel and barbarous conspiracy against human life. That duty seemed to fall upon him; and, fully conscious of his inability to execute, to the satisfaction of the public, a task so responsible, he undertook the labor. . . relying confidently upon the generous reader for a justification of the motives by which he was actuated. Unable by his individual efforts to complete the work in the time prescribed for its appearance before the public, he associated with him Mr. A. B. Murch." This book went through several editions, including one of 1868.

One of the earliest intimations of the appearance of *Dakota War Whoop* was given by the St. Cloud *Democrat* on November 26, 1863:

"Book Notice.—Merrill has in press, and to be out in a few days, 'The Dakota War Whoop, or Indian

Massacres in Minnesota,' by Mrs. Harriet E. Bishop McConkey.— Price $1.25.

"It will be beautifully illustrated and full of interest, commencing, as it does, at the very beginning of the Indian troubles, following down to the close of Gen. Sibley's and Gen. Sully's expedition to the Missouri river. Many matters of peculiar interest here find their first mention in print. It is the most readable book that has appeared in a long time. About 400 copies have already been ordered, in this city. Persons wishing to canvass counties or parts of counties, will call on, or address D. D. Merrill, at St. Paul, Minn., immediately."

On December 1 the St. Paul *Pioneer,* in what was obviously another paid notice, began to beat the gongs: "THE NEW INDIAN HISTORY.—The Dakota War Whoop or Indian Massacres in Minnesota, by Mrs. H. E. Bishop McConkey, published by Merrill, St. Paul: price $1.25. This very interesting book is now before the public, and is being distributed to subscribers in this city. Any person, not having had an opportunity to subscribe for it, can procure a copy at Merrill's book, photograph, album and stationery store, on 3d street. Canvassers can do a good thing with this book. Sent by mail (postage paid) on receipt of retail price, to any address." On December 5 the *Pioneer* published a review of sorts: "'DACOTA WAR WHOOP.'—We are indebted to Merrill for a copy of this book. It is written by Mrs. Harriet E. Bishop M'Conkey, a lady who, we believe, established the first school ever opened in St. Paul. It is a narrative of the Sioux massacre, compiled from contemporaneous history, and cannot but prove interesting to the reader. As a specimen of St. Paul workmanship, the book is well bound but poorly printed."

Promptly on publication, Harriet gave a copy of her book to the Minnesota Historical Society, where it is still preserved with her inscription: "To the Minnesota Historical Society, the *first* miscellaneous Book published in the State, is presented by the Author. St. Paul 1 Dec 1863." The title was: *Dakota War Whoop; or, Indian Massacres and War in Minnesota.* By Harriet E. Bishop M'Conkey. Saint Paul: Published by D. D. Merrill, Press Printing Company, 1863. The work ran to 304 pp.

That Harriet was not altogether satisfied with her book is evident from a letter addressed to General Sibley at St. Paul on December 5. (This letter, with others that follow, is preserved in the Sibley Papers, Minnesota Historical Society.)

"Gen. Sibley

"This intrusion is in behalf of Mrs. G. L Haseltine who desires a furlough for her husband about Christmas. If possible I hope her petition may be granted as there are reasons why her request is especially urgent.

"With many thanks for your kind notices of my book, the external of which is a sore disappointment

I am very respectfully

Yours truly

H. E. B. McConkey."

Either because her dissatisfaction grew, or because she felt the spur of competition, Harriet busied herself with a revision of her book, and by October 19, 1864, she was again writing H. H. Sibley from Auburn, N. Y.:

"Dear Sir,

"One long engaged in book business & who employs some 500 agents in their sale desires to enter the 'Dakota War Whoop' on his list. He says at least one hundred of his agents had written him for the book before he saw or heard of it or its Author, there being a call for it in the region where they traveled.

"To facilitate its sale, he suggests that an *introduction of its author from your* pen be added,—a permanent fixture to all *subsequent* editions, & with a little trouble can be added to the unsold copies already issued—not to exceed perhaps a page or two of printed matter. Should this suggestion meet with favor from you, will you please prepare it with as little delay as possible? You will need to see a copy of the new Edition which you can find at Mr. Merrill's.

"I am having a few bound in gilt & morocco, one of which will be sent you. Will you have me *send* the balance of those for which you subscribed now?

"Please write me soon & favor my request if consistent with your conscience, & much oblige

Yours truly

H. E. Bishop McConkey"

She wrote Sibley the following day:

"Auburn, 20 Oct. 1864

"Gen. Sibley
    "Dear Sir
        "It occurs to me that my letter of yesterday was somewhat indefinite as to the *nature* of the request; as suggested by Mr. Stark, the gentleman therin alluded to. An important point was an endorsement of its correctness—a recommendation of the same & a statement as to the facility & ability of the Author for preparing it. With all your burden of cares I regret to make any draft upon your time; but am of course desirous to do all in my power to facilitate the sale of my book, which the best judges think is destined for a wide one, & not to run out in *one* year. The delay for the engravings & other causes has made it a labor of patience for me, but I am now quite satisfied with its mechanical execution. Save those woodcuts of our friends which I hope they will decide to have in steel as it is not yet too late for subsequent editions. Hoping to hear soon I am
                                Very truly
                        H. E. B. McConkey"

R. I. Holcombe, engaged in arranging Sibley's papers at St. Paul in 1894, after the General's death, appended a note that there were "so many errors in Mrs. McConkey's book that Gen. Sibley refused to indorse it by writing a preface or commending it in any manner." But since the volume was dedicated to Sibley, he may have had other motives in not complying with Harriet's request. Simultaneously, or alternatively, she must have written in similar vein to Stephen Miller, then Governor of Minnesota, who under date of November 9, 1864, sent her from St. Paul a statement praising *Dakota War Whoop,* and "commending it to the public, as a faithful and authentic history of the terrible events connected with the outbreak of the Sioux Indians, which involved so many of our border settlers in desolation and ruin." This printed statement is tipped into some copies, including one of those preserved by the Minnesota Historical Society.

Despite Harriet E. Bishop McConkey's hopes and expectations in 1864, a hundred years passed before a new edition of her book was undertaken. It is now republished as the Lakeside Classic for 1965, in somewhat altered form. Since her book was not, as the Classics usually have been, an extended narrative of personal experience, and since the format of the Classics requires a text of no more than moderate length, it seemed desirable to subject it to a slimming process. This has been done by leaving basically intact all statements of fact, while reducing the moralizing, the sentimentalizing, and what must be called the gush, as well as some of the "fine writing." If Harriet shows a man acting the part of a hero, for example, we can do very well without being told what a hero he is. In general, we have given her prose a more muscular character, and to that extent we may misrepresent the work; however, more than enough remains of the original style, and no one is likely to be led astray. Unmistakably, Harriet E. Bishop McConkey emerges from the present text as from the original, in command of the literary situation. The 429-page book that was published in 1864, with paragraphs and a few chapters added, and some corrections of fact made, is the text we have used.

Dakota War Whoop reappears at a time when for various reasons, including centennial observances, fresh interest is being displayed in the Sioux uprising of 1862. In 1959 C. M. Oehler published in New York *The Great Sioux Uprising,* a work that can be described not unfairly as a modern version of Bryant and Murch, since it hews rather closely to the events of 1862, without giving much attention to the Sioux campaigns that followed. In 1961, as a centennial undertaking, the Minnesota Historical Society published Kenneth Carley's *The Sioux Uprising of 1862,* a work comparatively brief, but highly interesting for its numerous contemporary illustrations, and judicious in temper. Quite properly Carley describes the second volume of William W. Folwell's *A History of Minnesota* (St. Paul, 1924), the two volumes of *Minnesota in the Civil and Indian Wars* (St. Paul, 1890 and 1893), and the several volumes of the *Minnesota Historical Society Collections* as the most consistently useful printed sources. The Minnesota Historical Society also devoted the September, 1962, issue of *Min-*

nesota History to the Sioux outbreak of a hundred years before, various aspects of a complex history being examined both thoughtfully and entertainingly.

This heightened attention given to the Sioux uprising in Minnesota is likely to gather momentum and impact. The 1862 outbreak stands as one of the great divides in American history. It was the last of the woodland wars, in which red men would attack forts and whole towns, fighting pitched battles for them. There had been many wars of this kind along the Atlantic coast and inland, over a period of nearly two hundred years. The like would not be seen again. Now the Sioux, expelled as a tribe from the Minnesota homeland where so many of the Dakota peoples had once lived, would enter the era of the Plains wars, different in kind, in temper, and in magnitude from anything that had involved the Sioux in the past. What began in 1862 came to a pitiful end in 1890, and we are still trying to gain an adequate perspective on what happened during those fateful years.

I should like to express my thanks to various friends who have enlarged my own perspective as this book has evolved; to Harry J. Owens, Wright Howes, and Colton Storm in Chicago; to Floyd E. Risvold and Richard B. Dunsworth, who cordially welcomed me to Minneapolis and escorted me on an extraordinary tour of the Minnesota River Valley, with informed comment on sites and battlefields; to Russell W. Fridley and Miss Lucile Kane and others of the Minne-

sota Historical Society who generously extended fa-
cilities for research; to the staff of the National Archives in Washington; and to the Newberry Library
in Chicago, and the University of California and
Bancroft libraries in Berkeley for a wealth of source
books that have helped bring the Sioux era to life for
me.

DALE L. MORGAN

Berkeley, California
March 15, 1965

DAKOTA WAR WHOOP:

OR,

INDIAN MASSACRES

AND

WAR IN MINNESOTA,

OF 1862 --'3.

BY

HARRIET E. BISHOP McCONKEY,

Author of "Floral Homes," &c.

REVISED EDITION.

ST. PAUL:

PUBLISHED FOR THE AUTHOR.

WM. J. MOSES' PRESS, AUBURN, N. Y.

1864.

Dakota War Whoop

Dakota War Whoop

Chapter I

News of the Outbreak

"THREE Hundred Thousand More!" The nation's rallying cry had electrified every telegraph wire and intensified the great heart of the
Northwest. Women with the spirit of the Revolu-
tionary mothers had bidden their loved ones GO,
glad they had husbands or sons to give in the crush-
ing of a rebel foe. Minnesota was thoroughly aroused.
Though as a State she had scarcely seen her first
decade, she had already sent her Fifth Regiment into
the field. Fired with the spirit of the immortal
"First," which won laurels even in defeat,* her
quota was again being filled. Young men, the flower,
vigor, and hope of the State, with musket in firm
grasp, stood ready, impatiently awaiting "orders!"[1]

*At the memorable battles of Bull Run and Ball's Bluff.
[H.M.]

[1]The First Regiment of Minnesota Volunteers embarked for
eastern battlefields June 22, 1861, and served valiantly at
First Manassas (Bull Run) and Ball's Bluff. In 1862 it participated in the Peninsular campaign, was decimated at An-
tietam, and suffered heavily at Fredericksburg. It would again
be decimated at Gettysburg. The Second, Third, and Fourth
Regiments were enlisted by November, 1861, and a Fifth Regiment by the following March. Companies B, C, and D of this
latter regiment were detailed to duty on the Indian frontier,

3

"Home work enough to engage our troops for the present," said the "other half" of myself, excitedly, as he entered from a spirited war meeting. "It is well that they had not received 'marching orders.'"

"Another Indian 'scare,'" I interrogatively replied.

"It is no 'scare,' I assure you, but an earnest and terrible reality."

"To frighten the credulous and the 'new comer'—nonsense!"

"'TRUTH is stranger than fiction.' Facts need no further confirmation. An army of savages are even now sweeping down the Minnesota River valley, swearing destruction to all in their course, and death to every white man!"

"It is not the first time our nerves have been set vibrating by such unpleasant rumors, and I have long since ceased to give credence to these crazy reports. If the Indians would have made trouble, it would have been when we were only a handful, and they strong as now. It is all nonsense."

---

while the other seven companies were sent to join Grant in Mississippi. Lincoln's famous call for "three hundred thousand more" troops was made, by prior arrangement with various governors, early in July, 1862, after McClellan urgently called for large reinforcements. Mustering these additional troops proved difficult, in the Union at large as well as in Minnesota, which led to institution of the draft. See William Watts Folwell, *A History of Minnesota* (St. Paul, 1924), vol. 2, pp. 84–108, 302–327, and the regimental histories printed in the first volume of *Minnesota in the Civil and Indian Wars* (St. Paul, 1890).

Alas! the visions of the night troubled me despite my unbelief. To fancy's ear came the groans of the dying, and to fancy's eye one blood-blinding scene— the dead, in tall prairie grass, or at their own hearth-stones; and above the shrieks and groans of their victims the terrible war whoop of the Dakotas, furious from a taste of blood, and panting for more.

With the celerity for which Gov. Ramsey[2] is noted, he had on the following morning four companies armed and equipped, and moving towards the scenes where hands were already stained with the blood of more than one thousand victims. The demand for action was met by prompt effort, otherwise the savage hordes might have swept through the land, killed or driven off the inhabitants, and repossessed the soil.

It is a dreadful tale; but I have girded for the effort, and the world shall hear what young Minnesota has experienced, how her adopted sons and daughters have suffered from the savage bullet and bloody tomahawk, while yet is undulating the clear prairie air, the terrible Dakota war-whoop.

[2]Alexander Ramsey, born in Pennsylvania in 1815, came to Minnesota as first governor of the Territory in 1849. He negotiated the Sioux treaties of 1851, opening up large areas for settlement, and at the close of his term, in 1853, entered business in St. Paul. As a Republican, he was elected first governor of the State of Minnesota, 1859–1863, then served in the U. S. Senate until 1875. From 1879 to 1881 he was Secretary of War in the Hayes cabinet. He died in 1903.

Chapter II

The Bread Raid

THE Dakota or Sioux Indians number about thirty thousand. These are divided into Bands, and each has its own Chief. They ignore the name of Sioux, by which they are known in the civilized world, and answer only to the name of Dakota. The purchase of the late Reservation secured to the small number of the Bands interested in the sale, the interest annually in gold on $2,000,000 for the ensuing fifty years, together with blankets, provisions, etc., which would place ordinary economists quite above want. On their new Reservation, Government had established two Agencies, the lower at the mouth of the Red Wood, the Upper Agency at the mouth of the Yellow Medicine rivers, both tributaries of the Minnesota. The lower bands, residing mostly at or near the Lower Agency, went there for their pay, while the upper bands, living mostly on the plains, came to the Upper Agency.[3]

Choosing their own time to assemble, or instigated by a secret foe, the upper bands, numbering nearly 7,000 men, women and children, had come to their Agency demanding annuities, the arrival of which was delayed, and in regard to which the Agent,

[3]The agency for the upper Sioux bands was about 30 miles up the Minnesota River from that maintained for the lower bands.

Thomas J. Galbraith,[4] was not advised. They had brought little or no provisions with them, and the small amount of game, with the fish they caught, hardly served to satisfy so many stomachs. They demanded flour, for which orders of distribution had not yet been given—shot an ox belonging to the Agent, which was scarcely a mouthful, among so many. The begging dance would furnish them food for a day or two, and so with the buffalo dance; but they had no idea of seeking any laudable employment, even though some of their children had died, they said, from starvation. But it was a formidable work—knowing the character of the Indians, as they did, that once giving them, you must continue to give—to think of feeding so many, for a period quite indefinite; besides, Government had not provided boarding accommodations at this point, on so grand a scale. But the spirit of unrest became more and more apparent, indicative of hostilities. The tents of their encampment were struck, and removed two miles to the rear. A consultation of the Government officials resulted in sending to Fort Ridgley for an armed force.

[4]By the usual operation of the spoils system, Thomas J. Galbraith succeeded Joseph R. Brown as Sioux agent in 1861. The appointment was unfortunate in some respects, for Brown had a wife of Sioux blood who had borne him several children, and he had considerable influence over the tribe. Galbraith was a party faithful, but had no frontier experience to equip him for his job. No amount of character could make up the difference.

In 1856 [1857] the frontier settlers were thrown into panic by the murder of forty persons at Spirit Lake Settlement in Iowa and southern Minnesota. The leader of the gang was Ink-pa-du-ta, who ever since had roamed at large, the vilest wretch unhung.[5] It had been feared that his going unpunished would embolden the evil inclined — that the leniency would be a precedent on which they might base future deeds. Still, the settlers were unmolested, and those who had known him longest became quite stupid in relation to the red man, so that when the clarion notes rang through the State, one company of volunteers of the Minnesota 5th, at each of the three military posts, was all deemed essential for the protection of Government stores and frontier defense. Capt. Marsh was in command at Fort Ridgley, on the Minnesota, Capt. Hall at Fort Ripley, on the Crow Wing, and Capt. Vanderhock at Abercrombie, on the Red river of the north. The least expectation of these men was that they were to bear the brunt of a home outbreak, and so check the onset as to save the State from general desolation while relief forces were mustering for the conflict.[6]

[5]The tragedy remembered as the Spirit Lake Massacre, though enacted for the most part at the nearby Okoboji lakes, occurred just south of the Minnesota boundary in March, 1857, as described in Thomas Teakle, *The Spirit Lake Massacre* (Iowa City, 1918), and in a novel by MacKinlay Kantor, *Spirit Lake* (Cleveland, 1961). This affair closed the long Sioux era in Iowa, as the 1862 uprising ended that era in Minnesota.

[6]See Note 1. The officers commanding the frontier posts were John S. Marsh, Francis Hall, and John Vander Horck.

The 18th of June, 1862, Lieut. Thomas J. Sheehan, Co. C., Fifth Regiment Minnesota volunteers, a young man, full of patriotic fire, and burning with intense desire to combat a rebel foe, had orders to report with fifty men to Capt. Marsh; and ten days after, loud cheers for their arrival rang through Fort Ridgley. The following morning, June 29, Capt. Marsh issued orders that Lieut. Sheehan, with his detachment from Co. C., and fifty men from Co. B., Fifth Minnesota, with Lieut. Gere, report to Agent Galbraith, at Yellow Medicine, "for the purpose of preserving order, and protecting United States property, during the time of annuity payment."[7]

The Indians would listen to no advice to return home, secure their crops, and await the Agent's call, when their annuities should arrive. Regarding "discretion the better part of valor" in warding the impending blow, Commandant Sheehan waited upon the Agent with the earnest desire that provisions be issued to satisfy the constant demand for "something to eat."

As if to add intensity to kindling fire of desperation, two of their tribe were killed by the Chippewas,

[7]T(imothy) J. Sheehan, whose name has often been misrendered Thomas, as here, figured prominently in the defense of Fort Ridgley chronicled on later pages. Later he won distinction on other battlefields, and attained the rank of colonel. Lieutenant Thomas P. Gere served under him also in the fighting at Fort Ridgley, of which he is one of the principal chroniclers.

a few miles from camp. At early morn the following day an imposing array of mounted and armed Indians, 1500 strong, clad only in moccasins and the breechlet, started on the "war path," but at night returned, crest-fallen, directing vicious glances at the soldier's camp. To avert their minds from the foe, a feast is promised, with the stipulation that they submit to be counted when thus convened, an ordeal essential to payment. Citizens and soldiers, some of whom kept guard, enjoyed the rare fun of the scramble, each for his share, as barrel after barrel of crackers were emptied on the ground. It was a hilarious time, and one of apparent satisfaction to the participants. Some forty barrels of water were served to satisfy the demand of the clamorous crowd for "drink," after which, for an hour or two, the friendly pipe passed from hand to hand, and the counting process was the finale of the day.

On the 27th July, the following order was issued:

"Sir: I have to request that you detail a small detachment of your command, and with it proceed forthwith in the direction of Yellow Medicine river, in search of Inkpaduta and his followers, who are said to be camped somewhere in the region, with stolen horses, &c.

"You will take said Inkpaduta and all Indian soldiers with him, prisoners, alive if possible, and deliver them to me at the Agency. If they resist, I advise that they be shot. Take all horses found in their possession, and deliver them to me.

"A party of reliable citizens will accompany you; they will report to you and be subject to your orders.

"Ten or twelve men will, in my opinion, be sufficient. They should, by all means, be mounted on horses or mules. You should take at least nine days' rations, and should start a sufficient time before daylight to get away without the knowledge of our Indians. While I recommend prompt and rigorous action to bring these murderers, thieves and villains to justice, dead or alive, yet I advise prudence and extreme caution.

"Very respectfully, your ob't servant,

THOS. J. GALBRAITH,

Sioux Agent.

"LIEUT. T. J. SHEEHAN,

"Commanding Camp at Sioux Agency."

Accompanying the expedition as guide was a Christian Indian. He seemed most eager of all to bring the scamp to justice, while he boasted of having killed his son, and was one of the party who rescued Mrs. Nobles and Miss Gardner from their hands, after the Spirit Lake Massacre. After a chase of many a weary mile, finding the deserted camp, their eyes gratified only with the sight of a solitary Indian in the distance, supposed to be a spy of Inkpaduta, whom the best horse could not overtake, and after continuing the search till further pursuit seemed useless, their horses were headed campward, where they arrived on the evening of August 3.

Notwithstanding the drumming and powwow at the Indian encampment during the night, the adventurers rested well after the excitement of the five restless days and nights.

Scarcely had the sun of August 4 gilded the bluffs, when, painted and stripped for the work, the entire body of male Indians, with axes, hatchets and clubs, made general onslaught on the warehouse, the doors of which soon yielded. Then followed an unceremonious seizure of goods, flour and bacon, which the squaws, with wide spread blankets awaited to receive, and convey to their encampment. They had chosen this early hour, before the powers of resistance should be astir, but the alarm was beat, and the little band ready for action. Leaving the rest to guard camp, Lieut. Sheehan with twenty-five men hastes to the scene. The resistance of the immortal one hundred, in Sumter's walls to ten thousand rebels, had less of cool and determined bravery than this. What power have twenty-five men to cope with fifteen hundred infuriated savages, armed to the teeth? But ah! there was a power in the courage of the bearing, in the determined flash of the eye, when he ordered them to "fall back," threatening with instant death any who disobeyed. See them quail— their withering glances change to awe, as they obey. The gun of private Foster was jerked from his hand, discharged, his scalp seized, and about to pass from his head, when arrested by the above order. Mr. Fadden and James Gormon [Gorman], warehouse and trader's clerks, were the only citizens rendering any assistance during this emergency, and are deserving of the thanks of the State.

Now followed a grand stampede for camp. Though awed, they were not subdued. They were rushing to and fro, insulting the soldiers and evidently daring them to unequal contest; but when the howitzer was turned upon them, there was a "scattering in hot haste," for they had no power to cope with this most dreaded monster. The lull was seized by Lieut. Sheehan for an interview with the Agent, in the quiet of his own home. Permission was granted for convening a council with his "red children." The chief speaker shook hands with the commanding officer and made a speech as follows:

"We are the braves. We have sold our land to the great father (the President), and we think that he intends to give us what he has promised, but we can't get it, and we are starving; we want something to eat."

Commandant Sheehan replied: "You should have gone to the agent before breaking open the warehouse, and asked him for something to eat, which he was intending to give you to-day. If your great father heard that you had committed these depredations, breaking open the warehouse and attempting the life of his soldiers, he would not forgive you, for it would make him very mad."

"We have asked the Agent almost every day, but he will give us nothing; now we are starving, and we want you to ask him for us. We know if we kill the soldiers, it will make our great father mad. We held a council last night, and concluded we must have something to eat."

"If I get you a good issue of provisions this afternoon, will you all go back to your teepees, and not trouble my camp, nor come around the warehouse any more?"

"Yes, that is what we want."

The responsibility thrown upon the shoulders of this young officer, with results which followed, may have had its parallel, but has been surpassed by few. The plunder being ordered returned to the warehouse, the execution of the order devolved on him, but it was hauled from the shoulders of the men by the Indians, as often as raised thereto. Matters seemed rife for a general massacre. Guards were set by the savage rebels, and the lowering war clouds again muttered their thunders. Still the determined courage of the man did not forsake him, and in every effort was nobly seconded and aided by his comrade, Lieut. Gere. He again demanded an issue of provisions, for which "they were as eager," he says, "as wolves for blood." This being received, the aggressors retired to feast in their own encampment, regarding themselves, no doubt, victors of the day. This was a fortunate ending, even though but temporary. The following day some of the ring-leaders were put in jail, when came a demand for their release, with a threat to kill every man and blot out the Agency, if not complied with. Agent Galbraith ordered their release.

Capt. Marsh, in compliance with the request of Lieut. Sheehan, arrived in camp August 6th, and gave immediate orders for the issue of the goods and provisions on hand, when quiet returned and seeming satisfaction was restored. The military force having other, and as thought more important posts of duty, withdrew. Alas for limited human foresight![8]

[8]This "bread raid" at the Upper Agency on the Yellow Medicine was described by Agent Thomas J. Galbraith in his annual report, January 27, 1863, printed in 38th Congress, 1st Session, *House Executive Document 1* (Serial 1182), pp. 382–412—a report that embraces the whole of the subsequent uprising.

CHAPTER III

The First Blow

THE first event to confirm that the Sioux had broken truce with the whites, was at Acton, Meeker county, on Sunday the 17th of August, 1862. A party of six or seven young warriors from the Lower Agency, forty miles south, had gone out the previous day on a Chippewa "scalp hunt," but meeting no success in that line, and imbibing largely of "fire water," entered that isolated settlement. The house of Mr. Jones, the postmaster, was first visited, where they were loud in their demand for whisky, but he gave them tobacco, to their apparent satisfaction. They left with no unfriendly demonstrations. Still, Mr. Jones was suspicious that evil was lurking in their hearts, as he an hour after asserted at the house of his step-son, Mr. Howard Baker, where he and his wife had gone, leaving his niece, an adopted daughter, with a child a year old, alone in the house.[9]

[9]Robinson Jones, postmaster at Acton, settled there in 1857, when he and Howard Baker took up preemption claims. In 1861 he married Baker's mother, and the couple adopted a 15-year-old girl, Clara D. Wilson, and her 18-months-old half brother, children of a deceased relative. Although contemporary accounts (like that in the St. Paul *Pioneer and Democrat,* August 20, 1862) say that "seven or eight" Sioux warriors came to Jones's home this day, a Sioux informant, Big Eagle, said they numbered four only (he gave their names, and as of June, 1894, said one was still living). By this ac-

Three weeks previous to this, a "prairie schooner," a mere speck on the horizon, was seen approaching the settlement. It "cast anchor" before the door of Mr. Baker, and its crew was Mr. and Mrs. Webster, who had come to start life in that inviting region.

---

count, the four went over into the Big Woods to hunt and on Sunday, August 17, "came to a settler's fence, and here they found a hen's nest with some eggs in it. One of them took the eggs, when another said: 'Don't take them, for they belong to a white man and we may get into trouble.' The other . . . dashed them to the ground and replied: 'You are a coward. You are afraid of the white man. You are afraid to take even an egg from him, though you are half-starved . . .' The other replied: 'I am not a coward. I am not afraid of the white man, and to show you that I am not I will go to the house and shoot him. Are you brave enough to go with me?' The one who had called him a coward said: 'Yes, I will go with you, and we will see who is the braver of us two.' Their two companions then said: 'We will go with you, and we will be brave, too.' They all went to the house of the white man (Mr. Robinson Jones), but he got alarmed and went to another house (that of his son-in-law, Howard Baker), where there were some other white men and women. The four Indians followed them and killed three men and two women (Jones, Baker, a Mr. Webster, Mrs. Jones and a girl of fourteen). Then they hitched up a team belonging to another settler and drove to Shakopee's camp six miles above Redwood agency), which they reached late that night and told what they had done . . ." (*Minnesota Historical Collections,* 1894, vol. 6, pp. 388–389). Some accounts have it that when the Indians went to Jones's house, they asked for whiskey, and were so surly when refused that Jones fled to Baker's house, where his wife had gone on a Sunday call; but Jones left his two adopted children behind, and when these Sioux made their leisurely way to Baker's place, relations with them were at first friendly. See William Watts Folwell, *A History of Minnesota,* vol. 2, pp. 415–417, for a fuller discussion.

Here a temporary home was given them, while preparations for their own went forward.[10]

A little before noon these same Indians in their usual unceremonious manner entered the house of Mr. Baker, where the friends were in social converse. Save their being drunk, there was nothing to incite suspicion. In such a state they are always to be feared. After much meaningless talk, they proposed to "go out and shoot at a mark."

Mr. Webster, who had never before seen an Indian, stood on the door step, a mere spectator of the game. The Indians made him their first victim. His wife was in the covered wagon unpacking some articles and thus escaped their bullets. Mr. Jones ran a short distance, when an unerring aim brought him down. Mr. Baker rushed into the house, where he and his mother, Mrs. Jones, were soon prostrate in death. His wife, with two children of four and six years, fled to the cellar, and so escaped. The sight of blood infuriated their demon thirst, and hastily they return to Mr. Jones', break down the door the young girl had fastened, and killing her, spared the child, which next day is found lying in the blood of the slain, which is in coagulated pools on the floor.[11]

[10]Vilanus and Rosa Ann Webster were homestead-seekers from Michigan. Mrs. Webster told her story to M. S. Croswell, whose letter was printed in the St. Paul *Press,* September 4, 1862; she also testified next year before the Sioux claims commission.

[11]Folwell finds that the murderers, on turning westward, "shot at the Wilson girl, probably through a door or window,

As soon as it was safe, Mrs. Webster and Mrs. Baker come from their concealment and, survey the dreadful scene. The life-blood of Mr. W. had not yet ceased its flow, and an hour afterwards he dies in the arms of his stricken wife. It was no time for communion with grief, but prompt and decisive action. They call to a white man then passing. He stands in the doorway when with speechless lips they point to their dead. He says, "O, they've got the nose bleed," and turned to go. "But you will not leave us alone with these dead bodies," pleaded the women.

"They're doing well," was the reply of the heartless wretch, and then he followed in the wake of the Indians.

Various were the conjectures as to who this monster might be, some of the more charitable believing him insane. Not so in the neighborhood where the tragic scene transpired. By those, he was believed in league with the enactors, inciting to the bloody deeds.

Three miles away was an intelligent Swede settlement, and thither these women and helpless children wend their way. The sun had sank to rest, ere with sickened hearts and weary feet they are welcomed at a friendly abode—friendly, though the spoken lan-

---

and killed her. Here again they committed no depredation and they left Jones's whisky untouched." The murderers, conscious of the gravity of their crime and its possible consequences, thought of nothing but a headlong return to their village. Folwell also provides a map showing the sites of the Acton murders.

guage of each is not understood by the other. The Indians had been seen; yea, a fine span of horses had been rode off by two of them. The grief-marked faces and blood-bedabbled dresses told the awful tale. Before midnight, the whole settlement was aroused.

The following morning some two hundred in all, every man armed, went out to bury their friends. Mr. Jones, whom the women had supposed instantly killed, concealed from their view by an outbuilding, had had a severe grapple with death, deep holes dug in his struggles by his hands and feet. Already the bodies had become very offensive, and pools of clotted blood were all over the house. The burial party was fired on before the hasty rites were finished; a ball passing through the hat of one, which was returned with even less effect, save in causing them to mount their stolen steeds and fly to the woods[12].

[12]Isaac V. D. Heard, *History of the Sioux War* (New York, 1863), pp. 56–57, gives a similar though slightly variant account; he says Mrs. Jones found her husband agonizingly wounded after the Indians left, that he ordered her to fly and save her child, but she remained until he died, then went into the woods. The same tale is told of a heartless white man passing by. "When the wounded were dead, Mrs. Baker and Mrs. Webster hastened to the house of a Norwegian a few miles distant, and, half dead with fright, narrated what had occurred. There was no man at home, and a boy was dispatched to give the alarm at Ripley, twelve miles distant ... So incredulous were the people ... that they did not credit what the boy said for some little time, but finally they sent a messenger with the news to Forest City, twelve miles distant, where Captain [George C.] Whitcomb had a number of recruits; and twelve or fifteen horsemen rode to Acton, which

That was an anxious night, for those about to abandon their homes for safety. Guards were stationed around the house where the women and children were gathered, while the main body of men were preparing to depart on the morrow. In that vast train of sixty teams was one bright Swede girl, afterward employed as a domestic in the home of the writer. From her these facts were obtained. All was smiling with plenty and homes were becoming attractive, when savage hands wrote desolation on all. Change, how sudden, had come over their earthly hopes! Blight how unexpected had fallen on their prospects! As they wind over the prairie, both ear and eye are alert, lest an ambushed foe lurks; but safely they are guided to a haven of rest. The smitten hearts find sympathizing friends; but no kindness can efface the memory of that Sabbath day. These women evinced rare good sense and genuine intelligence, impressing those who conversed with them of their worth and virtues.

---

they reached at dusk. They placed a wagon-box over Jones, but did not disturb the bodies until next morning, after an inquest was held.

"While the inquest was progressing, [eleven Indians] not knowing what their companions had done, appeared on horseback, and some of the whites who were mounted gave chase. They crossed a slough, and all the whites checked their horses at the edge except a daring fellow from Forest City, who followed over and fired. One of the Indians dismounted and returned the fire, and then mounted his horse again and fled with the others." Heard adds that about seventy-five persons were present at the inquest.

Chapter IV

The Council Fire

THE purpose of Little Crow, chief of the Lower Annuity Indians, was to strike a decisive blow at the Lower Agency as soon as "paid off," before the whites had scattered to their homes, and this to be followed up by extermination and a repossession of the entire State.

A premature blow had been struck at Acton, and with lightning speed some of the fiendish perpetrators hastened on to Red Wood, or Lower Agency, twelve miles above Fort Ridgley and at midnight, stand before their chief, exhibiting their blood-stained hands, recounting in triumph the deeds of the day, and urging an immediate onslaught on the whites. For well they knew the consequences if they were given up to a proper tribunal—if withheld, war was inevitable.

Little Crow had, in several trips to Washington and otherwise, picked up some knowledge of the world, and the nation's power, and he knew well the element with which he had to contend. He had so far adopted the customs of the whites as to wear their apparel, live in a brick house, sleep in a bed, eat at table and drink all the whisky he could get. Being an adept in craft, he hesitates, though his heart thirsts for blood. "Wait till paid off," he said, and then the work should begin. Still, if his young men were going to fight, he coveted the glory of leadership — they could have their own way.

Here let us say that the name by which this bloody Chief is known is only a nickname. His grandfather received it from wearing a crow's skin upon his breast. His true name is Tah-o-ah-ta-doo-ta, meaning "his scarlet people." The band he governed was known as the Lightfoot Band.[13]

The longer that council fire burned, the higher and brighter rose the flame. They urged that the whites, all but the old men and boys, had "gone to the war," and that these, with the women and children, could be easily exterminated. Now was the time for the work of death to begin — to avenge their wrongs.

Here let us pause and investigate those wrongs. Personal wrongs there may be, but national wrongs in relation to them we fail to see. Sloth is their worst and most powerful enemy. Like the care of a provident parent for the children of his love is the government provision to render them useful and happy. To encourage civilization among them, it has used every means that money or influence could induce. To every Indian who will lay aside his blanket,

[13]This paragraph is one of those added to the revised edition. The three preceding paragraphs are now seen to be faulty in their view that a deep-dyed plot had been hatched among the Sioux prior to the Acton affair. The Sioux as well as the whites were swept along by events, and it seems clear that Little Crow became a leader lest he be relegated to the status of follower.

cut off his hair, and put on white man's apparel, is accorded, in addition to his annuities, a farm of eighty acres, prepared and stocked, and farming implements provided; on this a house is built and furnished, and medical attendance guaranteed. In addition, he receives a percentage on every rod of fence built, on every bushel of grain or potatoes raised, and for every acre of new land cultivated, full ownership of the same, so long as he continues to occupy it, or follow industrial pursuits. How would the souls of poor white men expand with ambition, was the same kindly governmental care extended to them! There would be far less poverty and wretchedness in our large cities than now. But in the main, the Indians prefer their own mode of life, and despise the one who sells his tribal birthright (his blanket), and goes to work like a white man. Some have done it in spite of the disgrace, as many small but comfortable brick houses at Red Wood and elsewhere will testify. This, however, is the exception. More generally, you find their chivalrous spirit manifested in lounging and smoking, while the women perform all the labor except fighting and eating.

The decision was made. The remainder of the night was spent in preparations for action. Before dawn, the spirit was deeply imbibed by all, with few exceptions, and the murderous weapon clutched with a desperation never before known. They were eager for the onset.

The signal was to be the firing of a gun by the store where waved the American flag. The assailants, previously divided into squads and stationed at every house, would each discharge a volley, and the people, rushing from their houses to learn the cause, would become an easy prey.

It will be remembered that the Lower Annuity Indians all resided at or near the Lower Agency, and a day was sufficient to bring them all together to payment, whenever the gold and goods should arrive. These they were now willing to exchange for the booty they would obtain, and the glory of wearing a scalp feather.

CHAPTER V

The Outbreak at Red Wood

THAT Monday morning of August 18, 1862, dawned clear and mild, all nature seemed radiant with life and hope. [The Indian] plan was admirably carried out, and had blood alone been their intent, not one would have escaped. The people rushed to the doors to ascertain the cause of the alarm, with no apprehension of evil. Men were indiscriminately shot down, hatchets were buried in the heads of women and children, or they were dragged off into captivity, a fate far worse.[14] Soon arose the smoke of burning buildings—and the shrieks and groans of the sufferers, as the tomahawk cleft their bones and chopped their flesh in pieces, was beyond the power of pen to describe. There were women and children imploring mercy from those whom their own hands had fed, and their own houses, now in flames, had often sheltered from the rain and cold. O the horrors of that first hour! So paralyzed were the people that not a gun was fired, not a hand raised in defense.

The first victim was James W. Lynde, son of an eminent Baptist minister of Covington, Kentucky.

---

[14]Very few women were killed or mortally wounded in the first attacks on the settlements; most were made captives. Some children were slain, others allowed to accompany their mothers.

He was a single man, thoroughly cultivated in all the physical, social, intellectual and refined elements of manhood. His love of nature led him where he could revel amid her beauties. His passion for the muses he had extensively cultivated. He had held the position of editor of the "HENDERSON DEMOCRAT," had served as State Senator, and held many other offices of trust in his adopted State. He with others stepped to the door to learn the cause of the tumult, when he was made a target for seven balls and fell dead.

Andrew Myrick, formerly of Westport, N. Y., when the first gun was fired, ran upstairs, where for a long time he lay concealed under a dry goods box. The Indians, with all their daring, are arrant cowards, and no one dare to be the first up for fear of being a victim to whatever weapon he might have. To bring him down, they in a loud voice proposed to fire the store, when he climbed through the scuttle to the roof, let himself down by the lightning rod to a low addition, and from thence jumped to the ground and ran toward the brush where he might have been safe. Unfortunately, [he was seen] and a shower of arrows pierced him through. He was dragged back to the store, and pelted with the gold coin they had found in his safe, while the vilest imprecations fell from their lips.[15] The burying party of Birch Coolie noto-

[15]The Sioux did not pelt Myrick with gold coin, but stuffed his mouth with grass, ironic response to Myrick's reported remark a few days earlier, "So far as I am concerned, if they are hungry, let them eat grass."

riety, of whom more anon, found his body and buried it, so marking his grave that his brother had him afterward removed to St. Paul.

William Bourat was clerk in the store, and on being wounded, rushed up stairs with another, whose history demands a separate chapter, securely fastened the trap door and prepared for their fate. With a wild whoop of triumph, the Indians had rushed in and taken possession of the store, and while distributing the goods, were concocting their plans to dispatch these hapless victims, and then burn the building. Bourat determined to make a dash for his life, wounded and bleeding as he was, rushed down stairs and through the crowd, clamorous in securing their plunder, and passed out in safety. When two hundred yards from the building, he received a heavy charge of duck shot in the side, and another in his leg. which brought him to the ground. His clothing was stripped from him, and then he was piled with logs to prevent escape till they could return and "cut him up." What a moment was that! To do or die, was the only alternative. He must save himself if saved, and by superhuman effort he removed the logs and went on rejoicing.

Doct. Humphrey, Government physician, had fallen in death, at his own door. His house, in which his wife and children were fastened, was set on fire, and she and her three little girls were burned in it. Several weeks after, their charred and blackened remains were found in the cellar, and with the body of her husband, decently buried. A little boy of this family, eleven years old, escaped from the burning building to the woods, across the river, where he remained concealed till the arrival of troops, when he "fell in," and stood in the thickest of the fight, till conveyed to friends in St. Paul—the sad-hearted remnant of an unbroken happy family of the previous day.[16]

Such was the surprise of the whites that they were as nearly paralyzed with wonder as alarm. Some mistake, thought they, and in some instances, actually gazed at the elevated rifle, threatening to send a bullet to the heart. Many had come out with half made toilets, some of whom were shot down, and others barely escaped with their lives, having no time to return for more clothing. What a scene! burning dwellings, dead men strewing every yard, and for-

---

[16]Heard, *History of the Sioux War*, p. 68, more correctly says that Dr. Philander Humphrey, physician of the Lower Sioux, "fled with his wife and three children, two boys and a girl, the eldest aged twelve years, and reached the house of one [John] Magner [or Wagner], two miles from the river. The doctor sent one of the boys down a little hill to bring some water, as they were very thirsty. While the child was gone the Indians killed his father, and burned his mother and the other two children in the house. Hearing the report of the fatal gun, and seeing the Indians, the child remained concealed until they left. When he emerged from his hiding-place he went and looked at his father, and found that the miscreants had cut his throat. Then he retired to a hiding-place again, and presently some more Indians came along and chopped off his father's head with an axe. All the buildings at the agency but two were committed to the flames."

bidding entrance to every door, women butchered or dragged into captivity, children screaming, till their brains are dashed out against a tree, or the butt of a rifle, and all so sudden, so unlooked-for!

With demoniac yells, they seize upon every treasure. Goods are trodden down, safes broken open and the contents divided, and a scene of such carnage and plunder, modern history does not record. When the sun arose, the smoke of burning buildings darkened its rays, and the earth was drinking the blood of the slain.

Chapter VI

The Slaughter

A FEW had escaped by the ferry, and, the Indians well knew, would carry the news of their dreadful work to the Fort. Retributive justice was sure to follow. To retard this, they secure the ferry-boat, kill the ferryman, disembowel him, chop off his head, hands and feet, which they insert in the cavity, and then dance around him, in hellish triumph.

In some instances, after the first onslaught, persons met their death by slow torture. A boy trying to escape was overhauled, stripped to the skin, and then pierced with sticks and knives, as he was driven along, they meantime mimicking his agonies, hooting and laughing till death ended his sufferings.

One man leaped from the window of the mill to the river, not soon enough, however, to prevent their balls from entering his breast. He was scarcely alive when he reached the opposite shore. For four days, without food, he dragged himself round in swamps and grass more dead than alive, and was at last found by a party of refugees, sixty-five miles from his starting point, and taken to a place of security.

Women were tortured in every imaginable manner. Some, with infants in their arms, had their breasts cut off, others their toes, and some were hamstrung and dragged over the prairie till torn and mangled; from that alone they died. Those who escaped, spread

31

the alarm. The people seemed paralyzed to all but personal safety, and fled precipitately, not knowing whither they went. In one instance, several families, not far away from home, had congregated in consultation as to their course, when they were overtaken by the Indians, at the head of whom was "Cut Nose." The first volley killed the few men. The women and children in their defenseless state, huddled closely together in the wagons, and bending low their heads, drew their shawls tightly over them. Two of the fiends held the horses while Cut Nose jumped into a wagon containing eleven, and deliberately cleft the head of each, while, stupefied with horror and powerless from fright, each awaited their turn, knowing the tomahawk would soon tear through their flesh and bones in like manner. Then kicking these butchered victims from the wagon, they filled it with plunder from the burning houses, leaving them a prey to vultures and wolves.

Forcing an infant from its mother's arms, with the bolt of a wagon they fastened it to a tree, and holding the mother, compelled her to witness its dying agonies. They then chopped off her legs and arms, and left her to bleed to death. And thus they butchered twenty-five, within as many rods.[17]

To serve their base passions, some of the younger

[17]This rehearsal of Sioux atrocities may be overwrought, but it is representative of the tales told at the time. Many more may be found in Charles S. Bryant and Abel B. Murch, *A History of the Great Massacre by the Sioux Indians in Minnesota* . . . (Cincinnati, 1864).

women were saved alive, while perhaps the parents were cut down before their eyes.

One family a few miles out, consisting of the parents, son and daughter, fled from the back door, as the murderers appeared at the front door. The father fired the first gun that had been raised against them, but before he could reload, with fiendish yells the savages sprang upon them. The father, mother and son fell dead, and the daughter, with genuine tact, fell to the ground, holding her breath and feigning death. The monsters, after hacking and mutilating the quivering flesh of the others, seized her feet to drag her off—unconsciously, she attempted to adjust her dress—which these barbarians seeing, and sparing her life for viler purposes, sent her back to swell the company of captives.

On the route between Yellow Medicine and Red Wood, George H. Gleason, Agency Clerk, having in charge Mrs. Wakefield and two children, was surprised by a party of these Red Wood murderers, now ravaging the country in every direction. Gleason was a favorite with all, and they had never received aught but kindness from his hands. But that did not save him. A bullet went to his heart. His person was searched, valuable papers scattered to the four winds, and he left, stripped nearly to the skin, while Mrs. Wakefield and her children were carried into captivity.[18]

[18]Sarah F. Wakefield, wife of the agency physician, Dr. J. L. Wakefield, was captured about two miles above the mouth of

the Redwood River, as described in Bryant and Murch, *A History of the Great Massacre, by the Sioux Indians in Minnesota,* pp. 102–103, and in her own *Six Weeks in the Sioux Tepees* (here cited in the second edition, Shakopee, 1864), pp. 11–14, 54–55. Gleason met two armed Indians in the road, Hapa and Chaska, and after passing, the former shot him. It was to Chaska that Mrs. Wakefield owed her preservation, then and in the weeks that followed, but he was later executed (by mistake) for having acknowledged that he "snapped his gun" at Gleason. "After Mr. Gleason was dead, as we rode away from his body," she says, "I heard Chaska say to Hapa, 'Get out and shoot him again; don't leave him with any life to suffer.' Hapa said, 'You have not shot to-day; you go with me, and I will go.' Then they both got out, giving me the lines to hold, and went to the body, but it was still and motionless. Hapa fired at him; Chaska raised his gun, but it snapped fire. I don't believe his gun was loaded at all."

Chapter VII

George H. Spencer

THE subject of this chapter, who will play a conspicuous part in the tragedy, came to St. Paul in the dawn of manhood, while yet the young city was struggling in swaddling bands. West of the Mississippi river, the Sioux title was not yet extinct. Their villages and encampments were in close proximity to town, and numbers of them daily [paraded] the streets, visiting the stores to trade, and the houses to beg.

Young Spencer, as clerk, found a knowledge of their language essential to success in business. Devoting half the night to study, and being a persevering scholar and good linguist, he soon acquired a perfect knowledge of the Dakota language. This made him a favorite, and strong personal friendships were formed with some of the most deserving of the tribe.

The study our hero most loved was the starry heavens. To perfect himself in Astronomy, was the absorbing desire of his life. And this was the main inducement for forming a co-partnership with Wm. H. Forbes, which would isolate him in the heart of the Indian country for five years. The lumber which entered into the construction of his store, was drawn more than two hundred miles.

Goods were readily converted into furs, and these into gold, which poured into the coffers of the firm like rain from full clouds. True, Spencer was obliged to "risk his scalp"; for though he had many professed friends, those who sought his advice, and offered to him their daughters for wives, yet he knew there was many a secret foe, who would not hesitate to do him any amount of evil.

Once his store was fired in the night time, when, but for timely notice by his Argus-eyed friends, he and all his goods would have been consumed.

Another time, his store had, all the evening, been filled with those who came for trade or gossip, when, at a late hour, he drank from a pail of water. An unusual taste excited his suspicion, in test of which he gave some to a cat, which died in violent convulsions, in less than a minute. Investigation proved the presence of strychnine. His heavy moustache had collected the poison, and thus saved his life. Those more honorable than their fellows tried, in both instances, to find out the guilty, but investigation was a failure. He had learned thereby a lesson of caution, and that as a race the Sioux were worthy of little confidence.

Mr. Spencer was en route to visit his St. Paul friends, where he held membership in the First Baptist Church, and stopped to spend the Sabbath at the Agency. He was at the store of his partner when the attack was made, and thinking there must be some mistake, was looking on in perfect wonder, till recalled by the power of three convincing bullets. But as Mr. Spencer still lives, after being forty days regarded as dead, we shall let him tell his own story, simply adding, that this Chapter was commenced as a biography when there was scarcely a hope of his being alive. That he was shot, and said he must die, was all that his escaped friend knew of him or his fate.[19]

The engraving represents him in the dress in which he was taken captive, the bullet holes being distinctly seen. While a captive, he was obliged to wear the Indian costume, but his clothes, watch, diamond pin and ring, together with his money, were carefully kept by his Indian friend, and returned to him on his release.

[19]George H. Spencer, Jr., made a considerable contribution to Mrs. McConkey's book. A statement apparently written for her personal use provides substance for this and many later chapters. Spencer also furnished a statement to the government, parallel in some respects, printed in 37th Congress, 3rd Session, *House Executive Document 68* (Serial 1163), pp. 4–9.

Chapter VIII

Captivity and Release of George H. Spencer, as given by Himself

"UPON Monday morning, August 18th, 1862, the dissatisfaction which had long been manifested by the Mile-na-kan-toan and Wah-pe-ku-te bands of the Sioux Indians, reached the culminating point, and inaugurated one of the most horrible massacres of which we have any record. . . .

"I had arrived in the place on Saturday evening, the 16th. On Sunday evening, the 17th, I attended the Rev. Mr. Hinman's Church, where I heard a very fine and appropriate sermon.[20] Had the Rev. gentleman known that the events which transpired on the following morning were to have taken place, he could not have preached a more appropriate sermon for the occasion.

"On Monday morning, about six o'clock, on going to the door, I noticed an unusual number of Indians coming down the road into the village, all armed and naked, except the breech-cloth. I knew it was a war party, and upon arriving in the village, they divided into small parties, and stationed themselves around every building in the place, and upon in-

[20]Samuel D. Hinman was established as a missionary for the Protestant Episcopal Church at the lower Sioux agency in 1860. His statement to Isaac V. D. Heard on the Sioux outbreak is printed in the latter's *History of the Sioux War*, pp. 65–67.

quiring of those around our building— (the store of
Wm. H. Forbes) —what the matter was, I was told
that some of the enemy were seen near by, and that
they were going to attack them. Supposing they
meant Chippewas, I thought no more about the matter. Presently, however, I heard the firing of guns,
and hideous yelling outside, when I rushed to the
door, with five or six others, and just had time to
see that the trading house of Messrs. Myrick & Co.,
had been attacked by them, and that they were firing
into it, when a volley was discharged at us. Four
men fell dead, and I received three balls, one through
my right arm, another struck me in the right breast,
and the third in the stomach. One white man, William Bourat, and a half-breed boy, were not hit. I
did not fall, and with these two, rushed up stairs.
Upon reaching the foot of the stairs, I turned to see
if they were following, when I saw the store was
filling with Indians, and one had followed me to
the stairs, where, placing his double-barrel gun
almost against my body, endeavored to shoot me,
but, providentially, both barrels missed fire, and
I succeeded in reaching the upper story, without
further injury.*

"After being up stairs a short time, the half-breed,
looking through the window, saw an Indian, to whom
he called. The Indian told him to come down, and

*This Indian so intent on the life of Spencer was one
whom, with his family, he had kept two winters from starvation. Such is the Indian's gratitude. [H.M.]

he should not be hurt; he thereupon opened the door and went down.

"It was a trap door, secured by two or three boxes of guns, making it quite impossible for the Indians to open from below.

"Bourat also gave himself into their hands, and after getting outside of the house, perceiving a good opportunity, started, and ran for life. The Indians fired upon him, and two charges of duck-shot struck him in the side and hips.

"He fell, and feigned death. Some of them then threw some sticks of wood upon him, but he never moved, and they, supposing him to be dead, left him, saying they would come back and cut him up, when their other work was done. After a while, seeing the coast clear, he succeeded in making his escape.[21]

[21]The St. Paul *Pioneer and Democrat*, August 26, 1862, printed a statement obtained from Bourat, who had come down on the *Antelope* the previous day. "He says that on Monday last the Indians, to the number of 25 or 30, appeared in front of Forbes' store. Four persons were in the store, George Spencer, jr., George Thomas, Wm. Taylor, (barber of this city) and William Bourat. The Indians fired into the store, wounding George Spencer in the arm and sides. The other men ran up stairs, and the Indians took possession of the store. Bourat heard one of them say, 'Let us go up and kill them, and get them out of the way'; and he determined to make a dash for his life. He rushed down stairs and succeeded in getting about 200 yards from the store, when he received a heavy charge of duck shot in the side which brought him to the ground. Another shot was fired at him which took effect in his left leg. They then came up to him, stripped him of his clothing and shoes, and piled some logs

GEO. H. SPENCER

"The half-breed,* through fear, I am inclined to think, joined the Indians in some of their raids, and confessed to having killed a white woman. He was among those who surrendered themselves to Gen. Sibley's command, and was convicted and executed at Mankato, with the others.

"Being thus left alone up stairs, and my wounds becoming painful, I threw myself upon a bed, expecting, if I did not very soon die, that the Indians would come up and dispatch me. While lying there, I could hear distinctly, all that was going on below.

"I soon learned, from their conversation, that they were afraid to follow me up stairs, as they had the impression that I was standing at the head of the stairs, with a gun. There were four cases of double barreled shot guns, and one case of rifles, in the upper story, of which they were aware. They pro-

---

over him, to prevent his escape, promising to come back and cut him up.

"He succeeded in extricating himself from the logs and crawled away, and eluded the search of the Indians. He made his way in the most excruciating torture, to Glencoe, and from thence to Carver and to this city." Bourat thought there was no doubt Spencer, Reed, and Taylor had been killed. He did not see Gleason, "but whenever he met a white man on the road to Glencoe, he was assured that Gleason and the Wakefield family were murdered." Bourat was described as very much exhausted, suffering from his wounds. "He was carried from the boat. With proper care he will probably soon recover."

*His name was Paulite Osier, once a pupil of the writer, and by her taught the first rudiments of education. He was now a clerk in Forbes' store. [H.M.]

ceeded to open the boxes and bales of goods and to carry them out. They appeared very anxious to get at the guns, but would not come up, each one fearing to be the first one up, as they supposed he would be shot. They talked of firing the building. Fearing this, I arose quietly, and took off my shoes, and took a bed-cord and attached one end to the bed-post, and carried the other end to one of the windows, which I raised. I thought if they did apply the torch, I would lower myself to the ground and take the chances of being shot again, rather than to be burnt to death. About this time, an Indian called out to me, from below, to come down, that I should not be hurt, or, as he expressed it, 'you shall live.' I went to the door, but not recognizing him, refused to go down. I had been in tight places before, among the Indians of the plains, but a kind providence had always watched over me, and delivered me safely, and I now put my trust in that same Power, to deliver me from this most dangerous situation.

"Thus matters stood, and things began to look desperate, when I heard a well known, and to me, most welcome voice, shouting my name from below. I recognized the voice at once, and hastened to the door, and called him up. I was saved for the present, at any rate. It was the voice of my Indian comrade, Wa-kin-yan-tu-wa (Chaska). We had been intimate friends and comrades for the past ten years, and he happened to hear that I was wounded, but still living, and hastened to where I was, to save me, if possible.

When he came up, several others followed him, some of whom took me by the hand, and appeared to be very sorry that I had been hurt. My friend asked me 'if I was badly hurt, and if I thought I would die.' I replied, I did not know, but that my wounds were very painful. He then said that he would take me home with him, and cure me, if he could, and if I died, he would bury me like a white man.

"He then assisted me in getting down stairs, when several Indians cried out, 'kill him! kill him! show mercy to none! spare no American!' &c., when my friend, who was unarmed, seized a hatchet that was lying near by, and declared that he would cut down the first one who tried to do me any further injury. Wa-kin-yan-tu-wa had always been noted for his bravery on the war-path against the Chippewas, and they knew that he was not to be trifled with. Said he, 'this is my friend and comrade; we have been comrades for ten years, and if you had killed him before I got here, of course I could have said nothing, but now that I have seen him, I will protect him or die with him.'

"They then suffered him to pass out. After getting out of the house, he gave me in charge of a couple of squaws, and told them to take care of me while he got a wagon to carry me home. His lodge was about four miles above, at Little Crow's village. After putting me in the wagon, he ordered the squaws to take me home, saying that he would be along in a few minutes. We were stopped on the way three or four

times, by armed Indians, on horse-back, who would ride up to the wagon, and demand 'what that meant.' *
Upon being told, by the squaws, that 'this is Wa-kin-yan-tu-wa's friend, and he has saved his life,' we were allowed to pass on, and reached the lodge in safety.

"My friend soon came home with some roots, with which, after washing me, he dressed my wounds, which were, by this time, exceedingly painful. Several of the Indians came in to see me, and to talk over their wrongs, (?) &c., and the reasons why they had declared war.

"Little Crow, with whom I had been personally acquainted for many years, came in to see me frequently, and assured me that I need have no fears, that I should be well treated, and thought that I could be very useful to him as soon as I recovered from my wounds. This professed friendship, however, did not last long, for my friend utterly refused to join in the war against the whites—Little Crow attributed it to my influence over him—and they frequently quarreled in regard to the disposition that was to be made of me."

*This was the first adult male captive whose life was saved, and the only one. [H.M.]

CHAPTER IX

U. S. Troops Cut to Pieces

AT the time of the outbreak, only eighty men garrisoned Fort Ridgley, which was distant from Red Wood twelve miles. At nine o'clock the first breathless refugee had told them of the awful slaughter, and one-half of the command, with Capt. Marsh, post commander, were hastily moving toward the scene of carnage.

At noon they approach the ferry, but all is as quiet as death. Not a red skin is to be seen. The ferry boat is on the other side, and the ferryman killed. There is no means of crossing, and they wait in doubt how to proceed. The ambushed Indians, all stained with blood of the slain, see their dilemma. Crawling through grass and bushes to a bend above, they get across the river in canoes, unperceived by the troops, till sending one forward with instructions to detain them in friendly conversation through Interpreter [Peter] Quinn, whom they beckoned to their aid. Then a galling, a terrible fire is poured upon them from both sides of the river. Twenty-six fell, to rise no more. Capt. Marsh, a brave man, but bewildered by the unexpected onslaught, rushed into the river, sword and pistol in hand, as his only means of escape. Whether his death was occasioned by an enemy's ball or by drowning is not known. He was carried down by the current, and one month later was found among driftwood one mile below, his body in a remarkable state of preservation. He had been stripped of his coat and sword, which had been worn and flourished by the defiant savage, as testified by Spencer.[22]

The remnant of the command, fourteen in number, reached the Fort by different routes during the day, where the wildest alarm now reigned. Refugees, many wounded, and all torn, worn and weary had come in, to the number of five hundred. The stock of ammunition was small; their leader dead, and only thirty men capable of bearing arms. What was to be done in case of attack, which might come, any moment? It was a question to be tested!

With the other events of the day to be chronicled, was the arrival of the long-delayed annuities, but for the delay of which the trouble would have been

[22]Captain John S. Marsh, though a Minnesotan, had fought at Bull Run in a Wisconsin regiment. As W. W. Folwell says (*A History of Minnesota,* vol. 2, pp. 112–113), he was "brave but young, ignorant of Indian warfare, overconfident, and unapprehensive," so that he moved his men in closed ranks directly into the ambuscade at Redwood Ferry. More extended accounts of the "battle" there are those of Lieutenant Thomas P. Gere in *Minnesota in the Civil and Indian Wars, 1861–1865* (St. Paul, 1893), vol. 2, pp. 178–181; Bryant and Murch, *A History of the Great Massacre by the Sioux Indians,* pp. 182–187; Isaac V. D. Heard, *History of the Sioux War,* pp. 71-73; and Oscar G. Wall, *Recollections of the Sioux Massacre* (Lake City, Minn., 1909), pp. 47–76. An account written in 1887 by Sergeant John F. Bishop, who led fourteen of the survivors back to Fort Ridgley, is printed in *Minnesota in the Civil and Indian Wars,* vol. 2, pp. 166–170.

postponed or prevented. It is but justice, however, to say, that the delay was unavoidable, "the powers that be" having had much trouble in purchasing the gold, for such was the treaty stipulation, and with no other funds would they be satisfied. This having been forfeited, their treaty annulled by their own base hands, never went to the Agency.

The reader will recollect that some two weeks previous to the general outbreak, Lieut. Sheehan with one hundred men had been ordered to Yellow Medicine, that their armed presence might awe the hordes of Indians awaiting "payment." From thence he had been ordered to attend Commissioner Dole, in efforts to make a treaty with the Red Lake Indians.[23] So, when the blow was struck, the match ignited to produce a conflagration, he was forty miles away in rapid march northward.

Orders were dispatched for his return. His men hurried most of the way on "double quick," and arrived at the Fort on Tuesday noon, Aug. 19, having made the distance in 9½ hours. The command now, by the death of Capt. Marsh, devolved on Lieut. Sheehan.

The morning previous to the outbreak, Maj. Galbraith, government agent, who had left his family and post to raise the company of Renville Rangers, had reached the Fort, fifty strong. They were on the way to Fort Snelling, to be mustered into the volun-

[23]The Red Lake Indians were a band of Chippewas. See Chapter XXXIX and Note 77.

teer service of the general government, in response to the first three hundred thousand call. Thus in one day was that little handful re-enforced by one hundred men, ready for action. Without these, the Fort must have fallen, and an unparalleled massacre ensued.[24]

For days Maj. Galbraith continued in the active discharge of duty. His family he had little doubt had shared in the general massacre. This gave intensity to his efforts to meet the foe, and vigor to his arm when the siege had commenced. He would avenge their death! But fortunately they had made their escape, the husband and father hears of them in St. Paul.

[24]In his annual report, January 27, 1863, Thomas J. Galbraith tells of recruiting the Renville Rangers—young Frenchmen, mixed-bloods, employees about to be discharged at the agency, and sojourners, a total of about fifty good fighting men. Hearing of McClellan's repulse before Richmond and other Union reverses, they expressed a wish to volunteer. Galbraith agreed to lead them to Fort Snelling when it seemed that contentions over leadership would break up the group. On August 12, he says "some thirty men enlisted at Yellow Medicine, and with them, on the 13th, I proceeded to Red Wood. Some nineteen or twenty enlisted there on the 14th. I remained at the lower agency putting things in order, and on the afternoon of the 15th we proceeded to Fort Ridgley ... on the 16th, Captain Marsh having placed at our disposal sufficient transportation ... we started for New Ulm, to get some recruits who were there, and on the morning of the 18th we started for and arrived at St. Peter in the afternoon." About sundown that day, J. C. Dickinson arrived from the lower agency "in a state of excitement bordering on insanity" to report what was happening upriver.

Chapter X

Yellow Medicine

THE settlement at Yellow Medicine is a farming community, the country for miles being laid off in eighty acre farms, on which are comfortable houses and other buildings. The owners are "farmer Indians." Here at Hazelwood, was the Mission station of Rev. Mr. Riggs[25]; and here, in their little chapel, on Sunday, while the Acton tragedy was being enacted, was celebrated the supper of our Lord and Savior, of which several Indians partook.

One mile below this point was the Mission house of Rev. Dr. Williamson; and, three miles below this, the Agency, with all the government buildings and the dwellings of other citizens. Here the "upper Indians" came annually to payment, and in addition to those residing here were now gathered, to the number of several thousand, for this purpose.

Secure, as in months agone, the people had slept

[25]Stephen Return Riggs had come with his wife as a Presbyterian missionary to the Sioux in 1837, as described in his *Mary and I, Forty Years with the Sioux* (Chicago, 1880; new edition, with added chapter, Boston, 1887). He might easily have gone to China, he says. "But Dr. Thomas S. Williamson of Ripley, Ohio, had started for the Dakota field the same year that I graduated from college [1835]. His representations of the needs of these aborigines, and the starting out of Whitman and Spalding with their wives to the Indians of the Pacific coast, attracted me to the westward." Riggs's papers are preserved in the Minnesota Historical Society.

that night, and the morning dawned bright and beautiful, full of hope and promise, for there were no premonitions of danger. They knew not that all day long the council fire in the Dakota encampment burned with fearful brilliancy; that their great captain, the Devil, had instigated them to strike the blow of extermination, and duped them into the belief that they were adequate to the task. Then they should be a great and mighty people, like the "big knives" (Americans). Other tribes would see and admit their greatness and they would have no need of war.

John Other-Day, the Christian name of one seated in that council, was, four years before, a miserable drunken Indian; now his very presence seemed a terror to those inclined to evil. What had wrought the change? "It is the religion of Jesus Christ alone; but for this, I should have been the bloodiest of the murderers."

His dress was now the white man's, and by his side sat a white woman, whom he had brought from Washington to be "the Indian's bride," his home, transformed from a bark lodge to a comfortable brick house. He urged them to heed no more the muttering war thunders, but listen to the good spirit rapping at their hearts, patiently await their annuities, and then return to their homes, adopt the customs and industrious habits of the whites, and the religion which the missionaries preached, so would they be prosperous and happy. Though he could not prevent, he evidently delayed the decision.

[At] sunset a horseman with flashing eye, flowing hair and blood-stained blanket rode up to the council circle. Intuitively they understand. Every warrior springs to his feet and clutches his musket. The work of destruction has commenced. Red Wood is a heap of smouldering ruins. Other-Day waits to hear no more. Taking his wife by the arm, he moves in the direction of the Agency, warning all of their danger. In obedience to his directions, sixty-two persons flee to the Agency warehouse, a strong brick building. Around this building, with four others, he keeps faithful watch all that anxious night.

Outside a hostile guard was set, with the supposed intent of dispatching them and attacking the building at the signal for general attack. But the Almighty Ruler thwarted their purposes and permitted these sixty-two persons to escape.

At dawn the sharp crack of musketry was heard, followed by loud and triumphant yells. The hostile guard yell in response, and run for their share of the booty. The attack was on the government stores. At the two Agencies, during these two days, they took some twenty tons of ammunition to aid in their deadly work.[26]

Seeing the coast clear, Other-Day and his party hastily prepare for evacuation. The sixty-two persons were crowded into five wagons, and before the sun had arisen, they looked their last on their pleasant homes and the scenes which association had rendered dear.

[26]This figure seems exaggerated.

From Tuesday morn till Friday noon they wandered over the prairie with little rest, when they found themselves opposite the Lower Agency, only thirty-eight [*i. e.* thirty] miles in advance of their starting point. They had desired, on crossing the river, to take the main road to the Fort, to which Other-Day would not listen, and refused to act as their protector unless they yielded to his wish. Events proved the wisdom of his choice.

We regard John Other-Day as one having this especial mission to fulfill, one the Lord had prepared to act this part in the bloody drama. A full week had passed before all were safely housed with friends at the lower settlements, grateful for their escape, and anxious for the future.[27]

Mr. [Stewart B.] Garvie, for several years a trader at Yellow Medicine, inclined not to credence of the reports brought to him at an early hour, resolved to stay and defend his property to the last; but before

[27]Folwell, *A History of Minnesota,* vol. 2, p. 118, discusses this council and its aftermath, primarily on the basis of a statement by John Other-Day, a letter by Dr. Williamson dated August 26, and a communication from A. J. Ebell in St. Paul *Press,* August 28, 29, 30, 1862, and a letter by Stephen R. Riggs, August 24, 1862, in *Missionary Herald,* October, 1862, p. 299. Riggs described John Other Day before his conversion as "a peculiarly abandoned and fierce savage." The St. Paul *Pioneer and Democrat,* August 24, 1862, remarked that "'Other Day,' the noble Indian . . . can never return to the Indians again. He will be here in a few days, and should receive a suitable reward for his fidelity." Among those he escorted to safety at Hutchinson were the wife and children of Agent Galbraith.

many hours he found reality in the alarm, and all night vigorously defended himself and his barricaded building. He was finally hit by a ball fired in at a window. He escaped from the rear of the building and reached the warehouse about a half a mile distant, where Other-Day and his party were convened. His wounds aroused them to a keener sense of their danger. Before the terminus of their journey, the sufferings of Mr. Garvie became so great they were obliged to leave him in the care of a friend, where death came to his release.[28]

[28]According to the St. Paul *Pioneer and Democrat,* August 24, 1862, Garvie, after being wounded, got across the Minnesota River and overtook the refugees being guided by Other Day at Cedar, 8 miles from Hutchinson. There he died.

Chapter XI

The Family of an Old Settler
Taken Captives

JOSEPH R. BROWN was one of the earliest adventurers in Minnesota. Understanding the language perfectly, he had often been an important agent in the adjustment of Sioux matters. His wife is a full-blood Sioux, whose mother still lives with her tribe. His residence is a few miles below Yellow Medicine, and his family, at the time of the outbreak, numbered fourteen. Most of his children had been pupils of the writer when he resided in St. Paul, and it was with no ordinary emotion that we received tidings of the massacre of the entire family. Mr. Brown himself, returning from the East, read the same in a St. Paul daily, while on board a steamer, and knew not to the contrary, till he learned they were in savage hands.[29]

[29]The alarming tale of the deaths of the Brown family, eighteen in all, was printed in the St. Paul *Pioneer and Democrat*, August 23, 1862, on the authority of Antoine Frenier, who claimed to have visited both the upper and lower agencies after the murders, and to have seen also the dead bodies of the Galbraiths, Wakefields, Williamson, and Riggs. The report was happily contradicted the following day.

Born in Maryland in 1805, Brown came with the troops to Fort Snelling in 1819, and was identified with the area until his death in New York, November 9, 1870, while on a business trip. Long engaged in the Indian trade, and with an unmatched knowledge of the Sioux, Brown had served as Sioux Agent from 1857 until replaced by John Galbraith in 1861. Many

On Monday the 18th Miss Ellen Brown went to see her grandmother at Yellow Medicine, and was by her warned of the bloody intent. She returned home in alarm, but the family discredited it till the following morning. It was earnest and hasty work then. Two teams were got ready, and they started for the Fort. Angus Brown, Charles Blair, his brother-in-law, and hired man, remained to see the way things were going, and follow on horseback. They were joined by two men who had crossed the river and come upon them unawares. Apprehensive that the enemy might approach them in the same way, they turned the cattle loose and started on after the family. Blair rode ahead, and overtook them at Patterson's Rapids, where they were prisoners in the hands of about twenty Indians. This savage party averred they had as yet shed no blood, and did not wish to begin there, as all except Mr. Blair were allied to them by blood. They shook hands with him and ordered him to dismount, appropriating his horse to their own use. The balance of the party, re-enforced by other refugees, were also taken prisoners, and the men allowed to go on with the rigid

---

thought that the 1862 uprising would never have occurred had Brown been in charge during the critical weeks before the outbreak. His Sioux wife is said to have been a quarter-, rather than full-blood; this alliance gave him additional influence. "What Joseph R. Brown could not do with and for the Sioux Indians," W. W. Folwell remarks, "could not be done." A brief biographical sketch is published in *Minnesota Historical Collections*, 1870–1880, vol. 3, pp. 201–204.

injunction "to speak to no one on the way"—the first instance men in their power were left unharmed, which was owing to Sioux blood.

As the captive party proceed, half bewildered by events, and half doubting the reality of their experience, they are startled by the sight of three dead mangled bodies. They, too, might be awaiting a like fate!

After various movements on the part of their captors, they were taken to the top of Red Wood hill, and compelled to listen to a discussion as to the disposition to be made of them. An old Indian woman got off the Browns to Little Crow's village, and into an upper room of the chief's house.

Here they remained, trembling, till late in the evening, when Little Crow himself came up, and shook hands with all. Evidently on his part there was no hostile design. But he shook his head when Mrs. Brown spoke of ransom, and would not encourage the hope.

He, however, assured them they should all, except Blair, be safe from hostile hands. He evidently wished his escape, and to facilitate this blew out the light before going down stairs. Little Crow went off into the village, and a young Indian soon came, commissioned to aid Blair in escaping. Hasty preparations left him "shaven and shorn," as well as blackened and blanketed. Several times suspicious ones tried to pull his blanket from his face, as he followed his guide through their village. When two rods beyond its limits, he was told to "go," and needed not a second bidding.

That night he went into a marsh, where, for half a day, he floundered in the mud, then lay in the tall grass for four days, eating only two crackers the old squaw had given him. Whenever he raised his head to reconnoitre, he held grass before his face—an Indian trick, but for which he would have been seen, for the woods around were filled with them. On the fifth day he crossed the river, under cover of a log pushed before him, and at night reached the Fort in safety.

CHAPTER XII

The Panic

DESPITE the unbelief evinced in the introductory chapter, the reader has seen it was not all a "scare." In every direction men, women and children with streaming hair, *en dishabille*, or garments rent and torn, in wild confusion fly from the theatre of danger. Horsemen are flying through the country giving the alarm, perhaps when there is no cause for it, and the people "flee for their lives," as if Indians were at their heels, tomahawks raised above their heads. Mothers go one way, children another, while perhaps the husband and father hides himself from sheer fright. Some hide in the tall prairie grass; some seek the woods; some rush to the river and take to the nearest water craft they see, and others fly to the nearest village, to find it evacuated, and feel themselves comparatively safe in the deserted houses they enter.

One instance we know of where a mother, alone with four children, was preparing them for bed. A messenger called that "the Indians would soon be upon them, and were murdering all in their way." The children were almost nude at the moment; the mother little in advance of them and barefooted, threw one child over her shoulder, took her babe in her arms, bade the others hold to her skirt, and thus, though raining hard, she ran eight miles, never laying down her burden or stopping for breath, while she saw an Indian on every stump, and a blanket in every bush; and there was not then an Indian within a hundred miles.

"I myself" confess to a feeling akin to this, even though a citizen of St. Paul, a hundred miles or more away. I knew the Indian from an acquaintance of fifteen years, and knew no good of him. Now the least street alarm would bring my quivering body to the window, for the Indians might even come here, the town half destroyed before an alarm was sounded! Many families actually went "below," while those from "above" were rushing here for safety. [30]

But it was not everywhere thus. Far up the valley the alarm started, and like a tornado it rushed on till every house was filled in all the villages; every strong building was barricaded, and put in the best possible state for defense. Arms and ammunition were concentrated with all speed, and men, yes MEN of will and purpose, resolved to do or die.

Still they come, those worn refugees: One mother has dropped her darling infant by the wayside, and being hotly pursued, could not stop to recover it. A child has seen its parents fall beneath a murderous bullet or tomahawk, and barely escape with life. In

[30]The panic spread far beyond the borders of Minnesota; see Milo M. Quaife, "The Panic of 1862 in Wisconsin," *Wisconsin Magazine of History*, December, 1920, vol. 4, pp. 166–195, and Frederick T. Wilson, "Fort Pierre and Its Neighbors," *South Dakota Historical Collections*, 1902, vol. 1, pp. 297–298.

many hamlets, every house is an inn, and every woman a nurse, and not a few are obliged to turn to the covert of bushes, and the protection of Him who "carries the lambs in his bosom."

As if to add to horror, a storm of thunder and lightning, wind and rain, fell on those shelterless ones. Vivid flashes made the darkness visible, felt almost, as in Egypt in the day of the plagues. It is no fiction, nor a single instance, that when the sun again rose on these mothers, it rose, also on a new existence. Yes, during surroundings like the above, many a child was born; many a mother prayed the angels would take her child before it should die from starvation and want, or fall into the hands of the savage.

Much of the panic occurred where there was no cause for it; yet it cannot be wondered at. Fresh excitement was constantly imparted by continual arrivals. With all who participated in the panic, the cause was real. They suffered equally, in mind, with those flying from the actual murderous scenes. They believed them to follow close in the wake of those who told the tale. In short, to be just upon them.

During that memorable Monday, Aug. 18, the Indians ranged over Brown county, carrying death and carnage wherever they went. Those who escaped their murderous hands rushed to the charming little town of New Ulm, and, added to the population, made about 2,000 souls.

Gov. Ramsey, in his message to the Legislature soon after convened, says, "Brown county, adjacent to the Sioux Reservation, has felt the worst effects of this calamity. It was peopled chiefly by Germans, and their neat cottages and fine farms gave evidence of the superior thrift and industry which distinguish this class of our foreign-born citizens. Driven from their homes, their property destroyed or plundered, robbed even of their household goods—many mourning wives, husbands, children and parents—their beautiful town of New Ulm and their own homes a blackened heap of ruins:—these poor fugitives, many of whom cannot speak our language, are especially deserving our sympathies.

"In all probability, not less than 30,000 are involved, directly or indirectly, in the loss of life or loss of property, from pillage, destruction, or abandonment," and each individual experience would make a volume of thrilling interest.

Chapter XIII

Attack on New Ulm

FIFTEEN miles below Ridgley, on the opposite side of the Minnesota river at the mouth of the Cottonwood, was New Ulm, containing about 1,500 inhabitants.[31] Sad to say, infidel Germans were first attracted by its beauty—first to build here. The original proprietors had stipulated that no church edifice should ever "disgrace its soil," under penalty of returning to the former owners. With no religious restraints, they became strong in wickedness, defiant of the restraints of the Gospel, and resolved that no minister should be allowed among them. One they drove from the place, and another was annoyed in every possible way. Even private Christians could not live in peace. They built a dancing hall, and the Sabbaths were spent in drinking and dancing. Wealth had rolled into their coffers, and they said, "our own hands have gotten it." As the crowning act of ungodliness, some of the "baser sort" paraded the

[31]New Ulm, the first settlement in Brown County, was founded by the German Land Association of Minnesota, on a site selected in 1854. The first buildings were erected in 1855. Since many of the intending colonists had migrated from Württemberg, the most important city of which was Ulm, the choice of name was natural. See Mrs. Clark Kellett, compiler, *History of Brown County* (New Ulm, 196–?). Mrs. McConkey's view of the townsfolk and their ways must be discounted somewhat in the light of her personal bias.

streets one bright Sabbath day bearing a mock figure purporting to represent our blessed Savior and labeled with blasphemous mottoes; and the closing scene of the day was burning him in effigy.

Scarcely had the smoke of their unholy doings ceased to rise when the enactors hide themselves as from the wrath of the Almighty. The pleadings of women to protect their homes were unavailing. New Ulm was doomed. The dance hall escaped the general conflagration, being afterward used for worship by the troops stationed there. Yes, He who was here so lately derided was worshipped and adored.

Some of its citizens found on Monday afternoon several dead bodies, horribly mutilated, a few miles back of town. Hastening to give the alarm, this party was fired upon by Indians, some of their number and two horses killed. The panic, increased by the constant arrival of refugees who had barely escaped the bullet, the knife or tomahawk, became terrible.

No man for the emergency was near. A few brave, God-fearing men stood firm and unscared, ready to confront the danger, with a suitable leader.

Midway between St. Peter and Traverse, which are separated only by a school section, is the mansion of Judge Flandrau, forty miles from New Ulm. On Tuesday morning, while it was yet dark, the Judge was aroused by a violent rapping at his door. The startling news needed no repetition. By noon, with a company of one hundred and fifty men, true as steel, and of the best mettle, he was ready to march to the "seat of war." [32]

At four o'clock the same day, the dreaded assailants, three hundred strong, besieged the town. The entire population were huddled together in houses inside of two squares, utterly powerless from fright, when the first volley was fired. Eighteen men had preceded the main body from St. Peter, but vain were their efforts to rally the panic-stricken citizens. The Indians had first fired with long range guns from

[32] W. W. Folwell has summed up Charles E. Flandrau: "Someone has said that Judge Flandrau was the best-known man in the state after Governor Ramsey. Certainly he was so known in the Minnesota Valley. After leaving school at the age of thirteen he went to sea for about two years and then gave three years to a mechanical trade. Next he studied law and, after two years' practice at the bar in New York, his native state, he came to Minnesota in 1853 at the age of twenty-five. Not long after he settled at 'The Traverse,' which was soon to become a city of great expectations, but nothing more. His enterprise, physical vigor, wit, and bonhomie soon gained him friends, and his influence with juries rapidly extended his reputation. In 1856 his neighbors sent him to the territorial Council and in the same year President Pierce appointed him agent for the Sioux Indians. While holding that office he sat in the constitutional convention, where . . . he was a conspicuous figure. Still in the same year, 1857, President Buchanan permitted him to exchange his Indian agency for a seat on the supreme bench of the territory. At the first state election, which was held in that year, he was elected to the same position, from which he resigned in 1864, before the expiration of his term . . . The arena and the forum were congenial to his nature. A colleague said of him: 'He was not of the ordinary type of man. He was original, unique, picturesque, versatile, adventurous; and his career is illuminated by the light of an heroic spirit.'"

the top of the table-land. While they were advancing, this brave little body hastily organized to meet the foe, who were now intrenched behind buildings, pouring their murderous volley into the town. The sure aim and true steel of these defenders of those who would not defend themselves, was made to tell, and several red skins "bit the dust." A man and woman, running through the street to seek better security, were killed, and these alone met death in this encounter. To increase the panic, several buildings were on fire, some fired by the enemy and others by friends, in order to get a better shot.

At six o'clock, Judge Flandrau arrived, to the great joy and relief of those who preceded him. His cavalry charged at once, killing twelve or fifteen. The Indians, seeing they had encountered more than their match, gather up their dead, and retire from the field.[33]

[33]On the issue sharply debated since 1862, "Who saved New Ulm?" Mrs. McConkey clearly votes for Charles E. Flandrau. W. W. Folwell examines this complicated question in an appendix to his *A History of Minnesota,* vol. 2, pp. 361–374. The German people of New Ulm have always considered that the defense measures taken, and the fight put up, under Jacob Nix on August 19 primarily wrought the salvation of the town. A squad of men from Swan Lake arrived in time to have a part in the battle, and so did the vanguard of Flandrau's force from St. Peter, under Sheriff L. M. Boardman. Folwell wonders whether Mrs. McConkey did not have the Swan Lake group in mind (erroneously giving St. Peter as their starting place) in saying that eighteen men arrived in advance of Flandrau's main force. The St. Peter *Minnesota Statesman,* August 22, 1862, related that the party of eighteen from Swan Lake and the town of Nicollet arrived at New Ulm to find the people huddled in two squares of the main street,

At the end of these two memorable days, in which the soil of Minnesota drank the blood of more than one thousand of her citizens, eighty of these were in New Ulm and the immediate vicinity.

---

in utter confusion. The new arrivals elected A. M. Bean captain, then took shelter behind a house from which they could fire to good effect; four or five pressed on to another house but had to retreat. Such execution was done by six good rifles that the Indians finally fell back. "Just at this time" Boardman and eleven others arrived from St. Peter, whereupon the Indians disappeared.

Flandrau's report to Governor Ramsey, New Ulm, August 20, 1862, printed in *Minnesota in the Civil and Indian Wars,* vol. 2, pp. 165–166 says in part: "We . . . raised 90 men and started for this point, where we arrived last night, between 9 and 10 o'clock. As we approached the town we found the upper part of it in flames, and the citizens, together with the advance guard of horsemen, sent out by us, engaged in a brisk battle with the Indians, which lasted about two hours and resulted in the repulse of the Indians . . . Our timely arrival saved the town and inhabitants from a night attack which might have proved fatal . . . To-day about 70 men arrived from South Bend, and we look for a detachment from Mankato hourly. We feel now confident of our ability to hold the town against any force they can bring to bear upon us . . ."

Flandrau wrote "Ex-Governor Sibley" from New Ulm on August 22 to say he thought he could hold the town until Sibley arrived, if not attacked by a large force. This letter was printed in the St. Paul *Pioneer and Democrat,* August 24, 1862, and again in *Minnesota in the Civil and Indian Wars,* vol. 2, pp. 197–198. Flandrau's further dispatch of August 27, recounting the battle of August 23, is printed herein as Chapter XVI. Flandrau later published a reminiscent account in his *The History of Minnesota and Tales of the Frontier* (St. Paul, 1900); and yet another reminiscent narrative of the events of 1862, which he wrote in the 1890s, is printed in Russell W. Fridley, Leota M. Kellett, and June D. Holmquist, eds., *Charles E. Flandrau and the Defense of New Ulm* (New Ulm, 1962).

Chapter XIV

Attack on Fort Ridgley

THE thrilling events at Yellow Medicine, the weary prairie marches 'neath a burning sun, the rapidly varying change of programme, did not abate the zeal of the young officer on whom, now that Capt. Marsh had fallen, devolved the salvation of the post, and the hundreds who had sought refuge there. Rest was forgotten, food scarcely taken into account, while active preparations to resist an attack went on. No little assistance was rendered by Mr. Wycoff [C. G. Wykoff] of the Indian department, accompanied by J. C. Ramsey, A. J. VanVorhes and Maj. E. A. C. Hatch, since commissioned with the celebrated Hatch's battalion.[34]

[34] The Secretary of War, on June 12, 1863, authorized the raising in Minnesota and adjacent Indian territories of Hatch's Independent Battalion of Cavalry, under Major Edwin A. C. Hatch. It was to consist of two companies of infantry and two of cavalry, to serve three years or the duration of the war. The order was later revised, eliminating the infantry and providing for five companies of cavalry, of which, however, only four were organized in 1863, between August and November. Neither Sibley nor Pope cared for the formation of such an independent body in their military jurisdiction. Sibley arranged for it to be ordered to Pembina, and it was en route there when the first edition of *Dakota War Whoop* appeared. The Battalion patrolled the northern frontier until mustered out in 1866. See W. W. Folwell, *A History of Minnesota,* vol. 2, pp. 289–294, and the more extended account by C. W. Nash in *Minnesota in the Civil and Indian Wars,* vol. 1, pp. 594–611.

So crowded was the garrison that rigid discipline had to be kept over the citizens as well as the soldiers, and the men were armed, or set to work on the defenses. Those were anxious hours, greatly embarrassed by the presence of women and children. But the energy of their leader never failed; everywhere present, he cheered the men in their work, infusing throughout the ranks his indomitable spirit. No knowledge could be obtained from the outer world. They knew not of the fearful work in progress at New Ulm, but were sure that this calm was no precursor of good tidings.

Foiled in their first attack on the city, and thirsting for blood, these besiegers design a grand surprise of the fort. Very guarded was their approach, with flowers and grass fastened to their heads, that they might not be detected. But sentinels discovered them on the west side of the fort at noon on Wednesday, Aug. 20. At one o'clock, with horrid yells, they poured a volley into the garrison. Several crawled to the walls of a building, raised the windows, and fired at Mrs. John Jones, wife of the Ordnance officer, who was rescued by a squad from Co. C., one of whom, Mark Grere [Greer] lost his life in the act, for which the lives of three Indians at once paid the forfeit.

The excitement was intense. Men rally to the conflict—women and children scream in uncontrollable panic—the big guns fail to work, and investigation finds them stuffed with rags, the work of four half-breed soldiers, who had gone over to the Indians and were now encouraging them in their work of death.[35] Had the courage of the assailants been equal to the opportunity, they might have rushed in at this moment and carried off the scalp of every person there.

But God overruled. The calm presence of mind which characterized the commandant through all this siege never for a moment forsook him; reckless of personal safety, even when bullet showers were thickest, he passed from post to post, cheering and encouraging his men, and had the satisfaction of seeing one savage fall by his own aim. The leader's spirit was soon diffused through the ranks, and every man stood firmly at his post. A six pound howitzer being ranged upon the foe, in the hands of Sergeant Jones, did deadly work. Some were seen to bound into the air, from its effects, and

[35]Tales of misconduct by the Renville Rangers were widely current; Isaac V. D. Heard, *History of the Sioux War,* p. 83, tells much the same story. However, Oscar G. Wall, not one of their number, who fought beside them at Fort Ridgley, admits only that one of the Rangers, a three-quarters blood Indian, "deserted to the enemy in the night, first succeeding in plugging the parked cannon with rags, to render them ineffective for quick service. The Renville Rangers, who were brave and loyal men, felt keenly the disgrace brought upon them by this traitor to the cause they were upholding." It was the Rangers, enlisted for service on distant battlefields and diverted to the Sioux frontier without even being formally mustered in, who fought in support of Sergeant Jones's artillery. Wall describes several noteworthy exploits. See his *Recollections of the Sioux War,* pp. 95, 151.

all scattered like autumn leaves in a strong wind. As darkness fell, the foe gathered in council so near that the clamor of voices was heard, all that weary, working night. The day's battle had been sharp, determined and persistent on the part of the assailants; as sharp, more cool and decided, on the other. Two soldiers and two citizens had been killed, and one wounded.[36]

The Fort buildings are mainly of wood, erected more for the purpose of storage than military defense, hence in constant danger of being fired, as were also the citizens' buildings without. Several ignited arrows were shot into the roofs, fortunately without effect. A timely rain, with thunder and fearful tempest, checked the night work, and gave the handful of men within the Fort time to rally their failing strength and courage.

With no lightning speed had the news of the outbreak gone to the Executive department, The Eden Valley of the Minnesota had not yet seen its first decade since it passed from savage to civilized hands, and telegraph posts had not had time to grow. But messengers disguised as Indians had crept forth

[36]One enlisted soldier only, Mark M. Greer, was killed in this day's battle, with six others of the Fifth Minnesota Infantry wounded. Two enlisted men are reported to have been killed, and four wounded, among the Renville Rangers; but the reference apparently is to refugees, insofar as deaths are concerned. Robert Baker was killed, and a youth, Heinrich Rieke, died (of a heart attack, it was thought), when one of the soldiers was badly wounded. Compare Oscar G. Wall, *Recollections of the Sioux War*, pp. 120, 150–151.

and gone, with swiftest horse speed, demanding re-
enforcements.

Impatient of delay, and distrusting their own
powers of endurance, this struggling band daily, during the five days they were besieged, sent forth a
"hurry up" for relief. Every hour was full of the most
intense anxiety. If the battle ceased, it was only to be
renewed with greater vigor.

Women huddled together in almost breathless fear,
children clung to their mothers in terror, and those
too young to understand seemed conscious of impending danger. Sentinels stood on the "watch tower"
keenly alert, and ever and anon a spyglass surveyed
the direction whence re-enforcements were expected; officers and men stood at their posts all that
night, not doubting but the attack would be renewed.
At daylight on Thursday, 21st, the attack came but
less bold than on the previous day.[37] The numbers
seemed depleted, probably owing in part to losses of
the previous battle, but more to parties being out,
plundering the country and extending the work of
death. The Indians retired, after about four hours'
hard fighting, until six, when they renewed their
work of death, continuing it for an hour and a half,

[37]August 21 was uneventful, as observed by both Oscar
Wall and Lieutenant T. P. Gere, the latter writing in *Minnesota in the Civil and Indian Wars*, vol. 2, p. 184. The attack
described came about noon on Friday, August 22. Meanwhile
the garrison had taken advantage of the reprieve to construct
barricades for the better protection of the gunners, Sergeant
Jones in particular.

when, being warmly repulsed, again retired, leaving the struggling, heroic band to another night of anxiety. Aside from an occasional alarm, nothing broke upon its quiet. It is surprising how long and how much, in the face of danger, men can endure without rest. O, how eagerly they waited re-enforcements.

On Friday morning the Indians seemed resolved on one more desperate assault. In anticipation of this, strong breastworks had been commenced, and though incomplete, afforded some protection.

At mid-day, the enemy were seen advancing at a distance of two miles, in increased numbers, and all mounted. The ravine surrounding the Fort gave them protection till ready for action. For five hours bullets flew like hail, the guns one continuous rattle; the battle was bitter and persistent. In one room thirty-two balls were picked up, which had perforated the walls. One who was there says, "All our previous engagements were as boys' play, in comparison with this. It was evidently expected to be the last, on the part of the enemy for they confidently designed a charge and a capture. The first volley, discharged from the woods, the high reeds and out-buildings, was perfectly terrific. It seemed that all the incarnate fiends of hell were concentrated and let loose upon this little band, with all the fierceness of infuriated demons, crazed for blood and plunder. The fire was received with coolness, by our men, and returned in the same spirit. The officers and gunners were most exposed, yet only one man was killed, and but four wounded." [38]

Too much praise cannot be awarded the officers and gunners; yea, every man in that seven days' engagement deserves a commission of high rank. Sergeant Jones, doing deadly execution with his big gun, really saved the post. At one time a charging party was placed very near the fort, and the half-breeds within distinctly understood the order "to charge on and seize the cannon." But they had not the courage.

Early in the engagement, they cut loose the mules and horses in the government stables, and attempted to fire some outside buildings.

The writer above alluded to, A. J. Van Vorhes, further says under date of 25th, "After seeing themselves foiled in taking the post, their next game was to burn the barracks, in which are the government stores, the families of citizens seeking protection, &c. A number of fire arrows were found on the roofs of these buildings, but, fortunately, they failed in their mission. Every preparation was made for a night attack, but the severe lesson of the afternoon, or a care for their plunder, prevented.

[38]The quoted eyewitness, as is soon seen, was A. J. Van Vorhes, whose letter of August 25 from Fort Ridgley was printed in the St. Paul *Pioneer and Democrat*, August 29, 1862. Mrs. McConkey more correctly would have ended her quotation, "three or four slightly wounded." In her further quotations from Van Vorhes in following paragraphs, Mrs. McConkey takes liberties with his text, as shown by bracketed additions.

"About six o'clock, Saturday morning, this body of demons was seen approaching by the same route, but continuing along the ravines, and under cover of hills and woods, they passed by, most probably on their way to New Ulm, or vicinity, from which direction the fires of burning buildings were seen, all of Saturday night . . .

"Since the battle of Friday, we have been undisturbed, but are in momentary expectation and preparation. The weather, perhaps, has had something to do with it, as we have had rain most of the day and a good portion of last night.

"Some three hundred women and children are here, for support and protection. This is a great embarrassment to the officers and soldiers. With them out of the way, a great point would be achieved. When the hospital becomes filled with them, as will be the case, unless removed soon, our position will be distressing indeed.

"What is the matter at St. Paul and Fort Snelling? Have re-enforcements been sent and cut off, or are we to be sacrificed to indifference and apathy? Let help be sent in such force that it cannot be impeded. With this point in the hands of the enemy, the Mississippi will share the universal desolation."

There was prompt response to the first alarm, and yet they knew it not. Lieut. Sheehan had written on the 21st: "We can hold out but a little longer, unless re-enforced. We are being attacked almost every hour. Our little band is being decimated. We had hoped to be re-enforced to-day, but as yet, hear of none coming." [39]

Gov. Ramsey had hastened to Fort Snelling, where the new regiments were, and ordered four companies of the Sixth to march at once to the scene under Hon. Henry H. Sibley, whose long residence on the frontier and thorough acquaintance with Dakota character especially qualified him for the command. Seven other companies soon followed under Col. William Crooks, with orders to report to Col. Sibley.

We do not wonder that in this severe siege, with no rest save, as every man occasionally slept on his arms a few moments at a time, they should feel themselves neglected. Hours were magnified into days, and days into weeks, while relief troops were moving up the Minnesota valley.

'Twas a foot-sore march. The men, many just from the counting-room or law office, were not inured to hardness. Besides, there were unavoidable delays. To meet the foe unprepared would be to rush to unbidden death, and the rifles were found to be useless, even in the hands of those most skillful in their use;

[39]Mrs. McConkey seems to have permitted herself even greater liberties with this text than remarked in the preceding note. As printed in the St. Paul *Pioneer and Democrat*, August 28, 1862, Sheehan's letter read: "We can hold this place but little longer, unless reinforced. We are being attacked almost every hour, and unless assistance is rendered we cannot hold out much longer. Our little band is becoming exhausted and decimated. We had hoped to be reinforced to-day, but as yet, hear of none coming."

they must camp at St. Peter, till the defect could be remedied, or others brought from St. Paul. Two mounted companies under command of Col. Samuel McPhail went forward and reached the Fort August 28, after the walls of the wooden buildings were perforated "like the lid of a pepper-box," greatly to the relief of the worn-out men, which enabled the half starved refugees to go to a place of greater security. The night of the 30th was the first of rest, to the besieged party, for ten days.

The Minnesota Third, a brave and gallant band as ever "sighted" rebels, was surrendered by their officer in command, to which they never assented, at Murfreesboro, Tenn., in July, 1862.[40] They were at once paroled, the officers remaining prisoners of war. This well-disciplined regiment was deemed a desirable force for frontier emergency; hence, a request from the Executive Department to the War Department, resulting in prompt "orders" to report at Fort Snelling. On the day of their departure from the south, an "exchange" was effected with the rebel powers, and so they entered the field untrammeled by the shackles of parole.

To the Third was added the Seventh, which re-

[40]Modern historians concur in the contemporary judgment that condemned Colonel Henry C. Lester for surrendering the Third Minnesota at Murfreesboro, Tenn., on July 13, 1862. He and other officers who voted to surrender were dismissed from service by order of the President on December 1, 1862. The Third welcomed the opportunity presented by the Sioux campaign to retrieve its reputation.

ported as before mentioned, so that Col. Sibley moved on to the fort with a force of fifteen hundred men. He arrived August 31, but found not an Indian to oppose him, though tokens of their doings everywhere met the eyes, and dingy smoke wreaths had not ceased to rise from the ruins. Dead men lay here and there on the prairies, their bodies far advanced in decomposition, torn and fed on by hogs and prairie wolves, and tainting the air. That night they were saluted by a few shots from the foe, with no serious effect.

We close this chapter with the record of Lieut. Sheehan's promotion to a captaincy of the Company he so gallantly led in the seven days of peril—a merited honor awarded by Governor Ramsey, 26th Sept.; and thereafter his military skill found wider scope on the fields of the South, in combat with a rebel foe. May his well-won laurels ever be green.

CHAPTER XV

Second and Final Attack on New Ulm

DURING those fearful days while the engagement was going on at Fort Ridgley, this doomed village was unmolested. The time was appreciated in intrenching, burying their dead, and sending out scouting parties in various directions. One brought in thirteen persons who had secreted themselves in a slough.

The route of the Indians from the Fort was marked by burning buildings, seen at New Ulm, and intimating their approach to those preparing for their reception. When four miles in the distance the foe were seen, and soon drove in the pickets, but all save the still panic-struck inhabitants rallied for defense. From twelve to five o'clock the battle raged in the most approved style of savage warfare. They dodged from house to house—fifteen of which, in less than half an hour, were in flames—picking their man as they went. Their arms were the best, and their aim deadly.

The commander-in-chief, Judge Flandrau, was during all these terrible hours in a shower of leaden hail, cool, discreet and determined, constantly among "the boys" cheering them on, and these performed their part equally as well. More and more desperate the enemy become! Captain William B. Dodd, well known in the State, makes an effort to drive them back. Riding forward of the breastwork, shouting to his comrades, "come on," he becomes the target. His body is pierced by five balls, but he keeps his saddle till he fell in the arms of his own people.

"At five o'clock was the turning point in the struggle. Now it seemed as if the Indians would capture the town. The remarkable gallantry of Judge Flandrau alone prevented this result, and a massacre, which for magnitude would have been without a parallel in the history of Indian warfare. He rallied his men, and charging at their head, drove them out of the brush at the lower end of the town, the point whence they had inflicted the greatest injury upon the garrison.

"All night the burning of houses continued. Occasional guns were fired till ten, when they fell back, formed into three great parties, and had war dances, shouting and singing during the night."

During the fight, ten men were killed, and nearly fifty wounded. Theirs were carried from the battlefield, the number not known—supposed to be not less than forty killed.[41]

[41]The "second battle of New Ulm" on August 23, 1862, was as bitterly fought as Mrs. McConkey indicates. In his *A History of Minnesota*, vol. 2, p. 142, W. W. Folwell comments: "This was no sham battle, no trivial affair, but an heroic defense of a beleaguered town against a much superior force of infuriated savages alive to the strategic advantage of a capture and keen for scalps and plunder. It cost the lives of twenty-six citizen soldiers and wounds for many more. Seven of the total number killed were members of Captain John Belm's company of New Ulm—good proof that there were Germans in New Ulm who could fight. Six belonged to Captain Flandrau's St. Peter

"As morning dawned, the enemy again came dashing over the prairie, 'spoiling for a fight,' and great indeed was their chagrin and surprise to find their breastwork but a few smouldering ashes. They gathered at the east end of the town, and seemed to be consulting what course to pursue. Finally, they collected a large drove of cattle, of which there were plenty all around them, and moving these as a breastwork, again advanced. But the cattle were not to be allied to such chaps, and soon commenced to make tracks for other parts, and the enemy, finding himself perfectly thwarted, skedaddled."

As these took up their line of march, they formed a train four miles long, of cattle, farm horses, wagons loaded with valuable booty, and several elegant "turn-outs." No wonder that they had made the night hideous with dance and song.

Now came the evacuation of New Ulm. The entire region above, and on either hand, was desolated, depopulated, one-half of the town destroyed, and had it been safe to do so, there was no inducement for the people to remain.

It was a mournful cortege which, on Monday morning, Aug. 25, took up its line of march for Mankato, twenty-five miles distant. Instead of ambulances for

---

Frontier Guards." Had Fort Ridgley and New Ulm fallen, the Sioux war in Minnesota would have been much more widely extended; and as some 1,200 noncombatants were cooped up in New Ulm during the fighting, the extent of the disaster, had Flandrau been overwhelmed, may be imagined.

the eighty wounded persons, some of whom were little children[42] hacked and mangled in a most shocking manner, they were conveyed in hard running farm wagons, while Indians watched from a distance.

Such another company, perhaps, the world has never seen. Here were mothers whose children had been slaughtered before their eyes — strong men "shorn of their strength," who in one day had passed from wealth to poverty — homes in ashes, wife and children gone, some of whom had crept away into sloughs or bushes to die — wives bereft of husbands, children of parents, the heads of all bowed down in overwhelming grief and a sense of utter destitution. For their protection, the bayonet gleamed, yet a sense of comparative security was no relief. In two instances actual insanity occurred.

[42]None of the wounded seem to have been children.

CHAPTER XVI

Battle of New Ulm—Official Report of Captain Flandrau

St. Peter, August 27th, 1862.[43]

His Excellency, Governor Alex. Ramsey:

SIR:—Events have transpired so rapidly, and my time has been so taken up since my last communication, that I cannot with certainty recall the condition of things existing at its date, but believe I wrote you almost immediately preceding the second attack upon New Ulm, which occurred on Saturday last.

During the morning we discovered a succession of fires on the Nicollet county side of the river, very near the bluffs, approaching us from the direction of Fort Ridgley. Our supposition was that the Fort had fallen, and the Indians were moving down upon the town, on that side of the river, to unite with another party on the side we were occupying.

As they increased in numbers very rapidly, I thought it best to send a detachment over to ascertain the design of the enemy, and if possible give him a check on that side of the river. Lieut. William Huey, of Traverse des Sioux, volunteering to per-

[43]Mrs. McConkey appears to have taken characteristic liberties in printing Flandrau's letter, with additions, deletions, and some changes in phraseology—which, however, do not alter the sense. An official text is printed in *Minnesota in the Civil and Indian Wars*, vol. 2, pp. 203–207.

form the service, I detailed seventy-five men with him, and they crossed at the ferry opposite the town, about nine o'clock, A. M. Very shortly after departure, the Indians were discovered issuing from the woods above the town, in large numbers, and assembling upon the prairie.

I at once posted all my available force upon the open prairie, outside the town, about half a mile at some points, and at a greater distance towards the point at which I conceived the attack would be made, determining to give them battle in the open field, where I conceived would be our greatest advantage.

At nearly ten A. M. the body began to move towards us, first slowly, and then with considerable rapidity. The men were encouraged by their officers to stand firm and meet the attack, and all promised well. We had in all, about two hundred and fifty guns, while the Indians were variously estimated at from four to five hundred. I fixed the number at not over three hundred and fifty.

Their advance upon the sloping prairie, in the bright sunlight, was a very fine spectacle, and, to such inexperienced soldiers as we all were, intensely exciting. When within about one mile and a half of us, the mass began to expand like a fan, and increase in the velocity of its approach, and continued this movement until within about double rifle shot, when it had covered our entire front. Then the savages uttered a terrific yell, and came down upon us like the wind. I had stationed myself at a point in the rear, where communication could be had with me easily, and awaited the first discharge with great anxiety, as it seemed to me that to yield was certain destruction, as the enemy would rush into the town and drive all before them. The yell unsettled the men a little, and just before the rifles began to crack, they fell back along the whole line, and committed the error of passing the outer houses without taking possession of them, a mistake which the Indians immediately took advantage of by themselves occupying them in squads of two, three, and up to ten. They poured into us a sharp and rapid fire, as we fell back, and opened from the houses in every direction. Several of us rode up to the hill, endeavoring to rally the men, and with good effect, as they gave three cheers and sallied out of various houses they had retreated to, and checked the advance effectually. The firing from both sides then became general, sharp and rapid, and it got to be a regular Indian skirmish, in which every man did his own work after his own fashion.

The Indians had spread out till they had got into our rear, and on all sides, having the very decided advantage of the houses on the bluffs which commanded the interior of the town, with the exception of the windmill which was occupied by about twenty of the Le Sueur Tigers, and held them at long range. The wind was from the lower part of the town, and this fact directed the larger part of the enemy to that point, where they promptly commenced firing the houses, and advancing behind the smoke. The conflagration became general in the lower part of the town on both sides of the street, and the bullets flew very thickly, both from the bluff and up the street. I thought it prudent to dismount and direct the defense on foot. Just at this point, Capt. William B. Dodd, of St. Peter, and some one else whose name I do not know, charged down the street, to ascertain (I have since learned) whether some horsemen seen in the extreme lower town, were not our friends coming in, and were met about three blocks down with a heavy volley from behind a house, five bullets passing through Capt. Dodd, and several through his horse. They both turned, and the Captain got in sufficiently near to be received by his friends before he fell. He died about five hours after being hit. Too much cannot be said of his personal bravery, and general desire to perform his duty manfully.

Capt. E. C. Saunders, of the Le Sueur company, was shot through a part of his body shortly after, and retired, placing his rifle in effective hands, and encouraging the men. The fight was going on all around the town, during the whole forenoon and part of the afternoon, sometimes with slight advantage to us, and again to the Indians, but the difficulty that stared us in the face, was the gradual but certain approach, up the main street, behind the burning buildings, which promised our destruction. We frequently sallied out and took buildings in advance, but the risk of being picked off from the bluff, was unequal to the advantage gained, and the duty was performed with some reluctance by the men. In the lower part of the town I had some of the best men in the State, both as shots and for coolness and determination. It will be sufficient to name two as types of a class of the fighting men—Asa White and Newell Houghton, known to all old settlers. They did very effective service in checking the advance, both by their unerring rifles and the good examples their steadiness placed before the younger men.

We discovered a concentration of Indians on the side of the street towards the river, and at the rear of the buildings, and expected a rush upon the town from that position, the result of which I feared more than anything else, as the boys had proved unequal to it in the morning; and we were not disappointed, for in a few moments they came, on ponies and on foot, furiously, about sixty in number, charging round the point of a little grove of oaks. This was the critical point of the day, but four or five hours under fire had brought the boys up to the fighting temperature, and they stood firmly, and advanced with a cheer, routing the rascals like sheep. They received us with a very hot fire, killing Houghton, and an elderly gentleman, whose name I did not know.[44] As they fled in a crowd at very short range, we gave them a volley that was very effectual, and settled the fortunes of the day in our favor, for they did not dare try it over. I think, after once repulsing them in a fair fight, we could have successfully resisted

[44]Later identified as John Summers, of Nicollet County.

them, had they returned a second time, as the necessary confidence had been gained.

White men fight under great disadvantage the first time they engage Indians. There is something so fiendish in their yells, and terrifying in their appearance when in battle, that it takes a good deal of time to overcome the unpleasant sensation that it inspires. Then there is a snake-like stealth in all their movements that excites distrust and uncertainty, which unsteadies the nerves at first.

After this repulse, the battle raged until dark, without sufficient advantage on one side or the other to merit mention in detail, when the savages drew off, firing only an occasional shot from under close cover.

After dark, we decreased the extent of our lines of barricades, and I deemed it prudent to order all the buildings outside to be burned, in order to prevent their having come from behind which, to annoy us. We were compelled to consume about forty valuable buildings, but as it was a *military necessity*, the inhabitants did not demur, but themselves applied the torch cheerfully. In a short time we had a fair field before us, of open prairie, with the exception of a large square brick building, which we held, and had loop-holed in all the stories on all sides, which commanded a long portion of our front towards the bluff. We also dug a system of rifle pits on that front, outside the barricades, about four rods apart, which completed our defenses.

That night we slept very little, every man being at the barricades all night, each third man being allowed to sleep at intervals.

In the morning, the attack was renewed, but not with much vigor, and subsided about noon.

During the day, a body of men appeared in the lower town, and turned out to be a detachment of one hundred and fifty volunteers from Nicollet and Sibley counties, under Capt. E. St. Julien Cox, which had been forwarded to our relief by Col. Sibley. They had about fifty Austrian rifles, and the rest were armed with shot guns and hunting rifles. Their appearance inspired us with gladness, as things were becoming doubtful.

I held a council of the officers, and we determined to attempt an evacuation of the town, carrying off all the inhabitants, women, children, sick and wounded, to the number of about two thousand. This movement was a very perilous one to undertake, with the force at our command, but the confined state of the town was rapidly producing disease among the women and children, who were huddled up in cellars and close rooms, like sheep in a cattle car, and we were fast becoming short of ammunition and provisions. I feared the result of another attack by a larger force, and all the people decided that they would abandon the town the first opportunity, as residence there was impossible under the circumstances.

At daylight next morning the barricades were broken, and the wagons taken out and put in motion.

The scene was one of indescribable confusion and destruction. The poor people, naturally desirous of carrying off all they could, filled their wagons with boxes and baggage, to the exclusion (as we found before the train was complete) of many of the women and wounded. I was, therefore, compelled to order all articles of a bulky nature to be tumbled out, and their places supplied by more valuable freight. It was hard, but necessary, and the inhabitants yielded with less reluctance than I had anticipated.

About nine o'clock A. M., we moved with one hundred and fifty-three wagon loads of women, children, sick and wounded, and a large company on foot. Lieutenant Cox took the general disposition of the escort, and the various commands were posted so as best to protect the whole in case of attack. It was a melancholy spectacle to see two thousand people, who a few days before had been prosperous and happy, reduced to utter beggary, starting upon a journey of thirty miles, through a hostile country, every inch of which we expected to be called upon to defend from an attack, the issue of which was life or horrid butchery. Beggary, starvation, and probable destruction were at one end of the road; a doubtful escape from the latter at the other. We took the latter alternative, and, under Providence, got through.

During the battle, we lost, as near as I can ascertain, about ten killed and fifty wounded. I can give you no accurate detail of either, as the casualties occurred among citizens, soldiers, and strangers. The physicians, of whom, fortunately, we had a good supply, may have kept some hospital lists, but I have been too much occupied to ascertain. I was satisfied to know the wounded were well cared for, without knowing who they were.

I was seconded, ably and bravely, by all the officers and most of the men of the companies, and many citizens from different parts of the State, and strangers who were present, so uniform was their good conduct, and valuable their services, that one could not be mentioned without naming all. There were several cases of abandonment immediately preceding the attack, which, if designed to evade the struggle, were disgraceful in the extreme, and unworthy of Americans. But as they may have arisen from other causes, I will not report the names of the parties.

Many narrow escapes occurred during the protracted fight. Several persons were shot through the hat. One young man received three bullets through the pantaloons in rapid succession, without being hurt in the least.

We did not burn the town on leaving, thinking possibly that the Indians might not return and destroy it, and not deeming it much of a defense for them, should they occupy it on our return.

It was my design that the country between New Ulm and Mankato, should be immediately reoccupied by our troops, and the ground temporarily lost by our withdrawal, regained at once by fresh troops, well equipped and capable of remaining on the field, and I looked for material of that sort for the business on my arrival; but not a soldier from the regular service, except Captain Jerome Dane, with one hundred horses, has yet reached that part of the country, which is at this moment utterly defenseless, except so far as he is capable of holding it.[45] The citizen volunteers that went to the assistance of New Ulm, disbanded pretty generally on their return, being barefooted, overworked, and required at their homes.

I wish your Excellency would turn the tide of soldiers flowing into the valley, to the Blue Earth region, from which the whole southern portion of the State can be protected, and efficient co-operation afforded the column advancing upon the north side of the Minnesota.

Hoping my operations meet your approval, I am Truly your obedient servant,

CHARLES E. FLANDRAU,
Commanding West of the Minnesota.

[45] Jerome Dane was the captain of Company E of the Ninth Regiment, which he recruited at Mankato on August 19, 1862. He continued in service until January 14, 1865.

Chapter XVII

The Mission Party

D R. Williamson, unwilling to believe there was anything but a "scare," yet fearing all things, sent away from Yellow Medicine on Tuesday morning the younger members of his family, while with his wife and sister he remained. For thirty years he had labored among this people—had a perfect knowledge of their language, and was wholly engrossed for their good—in short, had been a faithful, self-sacrificing missionary. His influence was under some circumstances very great. Why not now? He had seen individual dissatisfaction, but never a general uprising, and was unwilling to interpret aright the demonstrations before him.

Mr. Riggs, under the guidance of a Christian Indian had started with his family from Hazlewood early on Tuesday morning, but was met by a hostile party and his team taken from him. They escaped to a bushy island in the river, where they were nearly devoured by mosquitoes. The first detachment of Dr. Williamson's household hunted them out, and with them went on their way, numbering in all some forty persons, and not over six armed men in the company. Providentially, the terrible storm which caused the battle at the fort to cease obliterated their tracks, so that they were not followed and murdered by the war party which crossed their trail.

The Doctor remained until Wednesday, when, assured it was no longer safe to do so, they started in an ox cart guided by a Christian Indian to overtake their family and other friends. Passing Beaver Creek Settlement, they found it entirely deserted. Some Indians, asked where the white people were, replied:

"All gone to the fort, and you go, too, or you will be shot."

Nearly all had been killed or made captive. In one instance, a war party started out of the Big Woods,[46] with the design of crossing the trail of these parties. "His-big-fire," a Christian Indian known as Robert Hopkins, kept with them until their intended victims had passed beyond reach when he left the war path and returned to find the people of his choice—the Christian Missionaries.

On, the separate mission parties journeyed, scarcely knowing their whereabouts, or caring, so that they kept out of the way of the savages, occasionally seen in the distance. It was woman's patience and faith which buoyed up the spirits of the men, during those days and nights, suffering for food and often drenched to the skin with the cold rain. Even the children endured with a fortitude which shames complaining manhood.

[46]The Big Woods, as noted by Isaac V. D. Heard, *History of the Sioux War*, p. 52, was a "large and remarkable forest, commencing about eighty miles above the Falls of St. Anthony, and extending south at a right angle across the Minnesota River to the branches of the Mankato, or Blue Earth River."

At last the two mission parties, each increased by wounded fugitives, together make for the fort where, unknown to them, the battle raged with the greatest violence. All were eager to enter its walls, thinking all danger would be over.

Now they pass a sight which makes all quail, and thank God for their deliverance thus far. A mother and three children lay by the roadside (the first time they had dared take to the road), weltering in their own gore. And near by a sick woman had been burned on the mattress on which she lay while her two sons were trying to escape with her. This filial love was rewarded by death to each. Traces of massacre and butchery were more frequent as they neared their destination. The plains around were literally full of Indians, some at no great distance.

They now expected an attack and drew up in battle line, tightening their grasp upon their weapons, with firm resolve to die rather than yield.

They saw rockets ascend from the fort, and had no thought but that they were beacons to guide them there, and not signals of distress. Dr. Williamson and Mr. Hunter [Alexander] went forward, crawling on hands and knees, as by miracle avoiding the skulking Indians and passing the blazing stables, enter the garrison in safety. It was a wonderful exploit, which surprised all within the walls. But the long-desired rest had not come yet.

The exhausted condition of the troops, and the crowded state of the barracks made it inexpedient for more to enter. With disappointment the tidings was received by the hastening party. It was now quite dark, and the glare of burning buildings misled the scalp-seekers who hastened on, further away, in quest of prey. With suspended breath and fluttering hearts they heard them pass, and again, with as much speed and little noise as possible, pushed on. In fording a stream the exhausted teams gave out. They unhitched and let them graze, despite the danger. So tired were all that they sank down on the wet grass to rest, while one only, each in turn, stood guard.

They knew the blood-hounds were upon their track, and that just before daylight was their time for attack, so, as this danger approached, they were again on the move. Four of their number now left. Scarcely were they out of sight, when their friends heard the firing of guns; afterwards the decayed bodies of these men were found where they fell, scarcely a mile from the main party.

On Saturday morning, August 23, after a siege of four days, the Indians despaired of success, ignorant of the condition of the garrison. Leaving a few men to starve the garrison out, they withdrew for another attack on New Ulm. Scarcely five miles away were the mission party, to whom their guns were visible, and distinctly heard. Burning buildings one after another lit the sky, or sent up lurid columns of smoke.

That night another tragic scene was enacted at Norwegian Grove, two miles from which they "encamped" in a deserted house. Weary and worn, they slept securely, while those who fled two hours before were already dead. From this point their dangers lessened until all had been welcomed by friends, who had been mourning them as among the slain.[47]

[47]Stephen R. Riggs briefly describes the flight of the missionaries in his *Mary and I. Forty Years with the Sioux*, Chapter XI. A fellow-refugee was Adrian J. Ebell, who published an illustrated article about his experiences in *Harper's New Monthly Magazine*, June, 1863.

Chapter XVIII

Massacre at Big Stone Lake

ON the banks of Big Stone Lake, far from white settlements, government agents had sent four men to cut hay, build a blacksmith shop and stables, preparatory to establishing an Agency. They had with them for cook John Julien, a lad of sixteen, whose parents lived near the lower Agency and were among the first victims.

The first part of their work done, they were camped on the shores of the lake, cutting logs. On the morning of the 21st of August, unaware of any danger, they were aroused by a loud and repeated war whoop, and quickly surrounded by fifty or sixty Indians, some on foot and some on horse.

Within ten paces of the tent a volley was fired, killing Henry Manderfield instantly. Two others escaped, to be murdered by another party thirty miles away. Anthony Manderfield, brother to the above, plunged into the ravine, on the brow of which their tent stood, was closely followed, and several shots fired upon him. Reaching the lake, he waded along the shore for two miles, followed by three Indians in a canoe. Seeing they were about to lay violent hands upon him, he plunged into the bushes, where he remained concealed till danger passed. He then pushed on with bare and bleeding feet to the foot of the lake;

though passing very near an Indian village, a rain providentially obliterated his footsteps.

At Lac-qui-parle, at the house of a half-breed [John Launche] he saw Mrs. Sophia Huggins, whose husband had been murdered, and Miss Julia La Frambois, captives. He was kindly cared for, his bleeding feet bound up, and his stomach satisfied. But they urged him away with all possible speed, for they knew it was unsafe for him to remain. After four days of almost incessant travelling, with very little food, he arrived at Fort Ridgley, to avenge their treatment of him, and the death of his brother, by joining a cavalry company.[48]

The boy mentioned above was taken prisoner, the details of which we reserve for a separate chapter.

When the "Expedition" passed this point in June after, George Spencer and others went over to see the ruins of his trading house. Here they found the skeletons of two human forms, one of whom George rec-

[48]A fuller account of this massacre at Big Stone Lake, near the western boundary of the State, is given by Bryant and Murch, *A History of the Great Massacre by the Sioux Indians*, pp. 149–153. Major Galbraith had contracted with George Loth for the construction, coal-burning, and hay-cutting at the lake, where at the time four trading posts existed, belonging to Louis Roberts, William H. Forbes, Dailys, Pratt & Co., and Nathan Myrick. The first name of the man who escaped was properly Anton Manderfield. His own narrative, translated from the German, is printed by Bryant and Murch, pp. 379–388. According to Anton, the fourth man in the party was his cousin, Hilliar Manderfield; and the boy hired as cook was John Schmerch, from Beaver Creek. Relative to the latter, see Note 106.

ognized by the shreds of clothing left as the clerk in his employ when the outbreak commenced. The other, was in the employ of Louis Roberts at a trading post two miles away, who lost $80,000 by the Indian raid. They were now by friendly hands buried, where by savage hands they fell.

Chapter XIX

Murder of Amos W. Huggins

SOME thirty years before this great tragedy was enacted, Revs. Riggs and Huggins, then in the vigor and prime of manhood, settled on the banks of Lac-qui-parle,* several hundred miles from civilized life. The salvation of the red man, for whom Christ had died as for themselves, was the impulse of their hearts. In due time a son was given to Mr. Huggins, which the Indians learned to love. After years of toil, these men and women were able to rejoice in perceptible good to the people among whom they lived.

Amos W. Huggins, at the age of sixteen, was sent away to finish the education commenced under the tutelage of his mother. Meantime, a change in missionary operations took place, and this point was left for more urgent fields of labor. Amos returned to his father's house, bringing with him a fair young bride.[49] Government had designated him as its agent, teacher, and superintendent of Indian affairs at Lac-qui-parle. On the very soil where his boyhood was spent, he dwelt among the very people of boyhood's memory. Thus, isolation was not unpleasant.

*The lake that speaks. [H.M.]

[49]The bride, Sophia Josephine Huggins, published a narrative of her experiences in the St. Paul *Press*, February 3–5, 1863 (reprinted, somewhat condensed, in Isaac V. D. Heard, *History of the Sioux War*, pp. 209–228). On this source Mrs. McConkey based the present chapter and several that follow.

Employed as female teacher, Miss Julia La Frambois had long been a valued member of his household. Though a half-breed, she was a young lady of high cultivation and spoke several languages fluently.

Two cherubs blest their happy home, and a more beautiful morning never dawned than the 19th day of August, 1862, Mrs. Huggins' twenty-fourth birthday. Mr. Huggins had been in the field, superintending the work in which the Indians were engaged, and at four o'clock in the afternoon returned home, bringing the oxen they had been using.

Previous to this, two [three] Indians from Red Iron's village came to the house, seemed unusually talkative, asked many questions of Miss Julia about the sewing machine she was using, but excited no suspicion. As soon as Mr. Huggins came up they left the house, and next moment the women heard the report of two guns. Julia rushed out as the Indians rushed in, who in a wild, excited manner exclaimed to Mrs. H.:

"Go out, go out; you shall live—but go out—take nothing with you!"

In the bewilderment of the moment, she scarce understood their meaning, and supposed that their enemies, the Chippewas, were upon them. She was aroused to terrible consciousness by seeing Julia kneeling by the lifeless form of her husband. "O, Josephine! Josephine!" told the awful tale. A ball had entered his back, killing him instantly. Seeing they were really going to shoot her unless she went away, she hastily threw over him a lounge cover on which she was sewing when she ran out; and with bursting heart left him there, without even a last kiss. Julia had preceded her to Mr. De Cota's, a half-breed Chippewa trader with a Sioux wife, who lived near, taking with her little Letta.

When the heroic girl, with their host and hostess, returned to the tragic scene (it was not deemed safe for the wife to go), they found many excited savages gathered around, ready almost to "gnash on him with their teeth," for the crime of being a white man; and others, among whom was the chief of the village, Wa-kan-ma-ni, or Walking Spirit, who denounced the deed, saying, had he been there, he would have died before harm should have come to Mr. Huggins.

Before the sun went down, these friendly hands had buried him without shroud or coffin, while the Sioux pillaged the house and divided among them, for their breakfast, the oxen he had driven from the field. With a brave heart Julia had entered the house, while full of pillagers and murderers, and secured some articles, afterwards of great value to them.

Among these spoils were two pocket Bibles, one of which was the well-thumbed companion of Mr. Huggins. O, what a comfort was this, in the anxious days of captivity which followed—precious for the sake of him who had read and loved its teachings, as also the "hidden manna" of its leaves—the promises which fed her sore heart. Therefore she trusted its teachings, and waited.

Chapter XX

Cause of the War—What is an Indian?

WE append the reply of one, George Spencer, whose opinion is entitled to respect and consideration. His whole statement will be found of thrilling interest:

"Ever since the treaty, which was made in 1851, with the nation of Dakota or Sioux Indians, they have been finding fault, complaining that the government did not strictly comply with the stipulations of the treaty. While some of the causes of these complaints have been imaginary, there can be no doubt but that there have been good grounds for others. In regard to the management of affairs among the lower Sioux, where the recent outbreak originated, I cannot speak knowingly, as I have not resided among them since the treaty went into effect. But among the upper Sioux, the Sissitons in particular, with whom I have been engaged, in trade, for the past two years, there has been some cause for complaint, on their part.

"I have often heard Standing Buffalo, the Sissiton chief, complain about the whites not fulfilling their promises in regard to the location of mills, schools, mechanics, physicians, etc., among his tribe. It is true that the lower bands enjoyed all the advantages to be derived from these sources, but as they were located at a distance of nearly one hundred miles from the villages and fields of the Sissitons, they derived but little, if any, benefit from them. It is too often the case, that the parties who are employed by the government to hold councils, form treaties, etc., with Indian tribes, do not sufficiently understand the character of the parties with whom they are negotiating; and, consequently, although matters may go off smoothly enough at the time, difficulties are liable to arise in the future, the consequences of which may be disastrous.

"As there are other savage tribes, standing in the same relations to the government to-day, that the Sioux occupied, previous to the insurrection, it may be well enough to examine, minutely, one or two points connected with Indian affairs, which, if properly observed, may be the means of preventing a repetition of the cruel blow, by other tribes, which has been so fearfully inflicted by the Sioux. In the first place, let us examine the Indian himself. What is an Indian?

"Simple as this question may seem, yet it is one that, in my opinion, is not thoroughly understood by our officials, and others, who have Indian affairs in charge. In the great chain of nature, the Indian is a connecting link between the wild beast and the human species. In shape he is human, and has the gift of speech, and, to a limited extent, the use of language. In almost all his actions, he seems to be guided by instinct, rather than reason; to say that he possesses *no* intellect, might possibly be saying too much; but if he does, it seems to be so clouded and obscured, that it does not avail him much. Long association with the whites has developed, in some of them, the reasoning faculties, and shown them to to be possessed of some little intelligence. So the same thing may be said of some animals, whose performances seem to be more the result of reason than instinct. The treachery of the Indian is proverbial. Unaccustomed to the comforts and luxuries of a home, there is, in his language, no word which answers to our word home. Accustomed, from infancy, to witness scenes of violence and bloodshed, and, as soon as he can speak, it is impressed upon his mind, that the greatest achievement he is capable of performing, is to dye his hands in the blood of his fellow-creatures, whereby he may become entitled to wear a scalp-feather. He soon learns to take delight in participating in the excitement of the chase, and in following the war path. His passions being subjected to no restraint whatever, his imagination is constantly taxed to invent some new mode of torture, to apply to the victim that may have been unfortunate enough to fall into his hands. The brutish propensities largely predominating, it requires but slight provocation to cause him to turn his murderous weapons against his fellow-beings. Poets may sing, and romancers may write, as much as they will, about the "noble savage," the "dignified and majestic bearing of nature's nobleman," the "generous traits of character" possessed by the "sons of the prairies," etc., but "distance lends enchantment to the view," and after having been, more or less, intimately associated with them, for the last ten years, I have been unable to perceive but a very few of those noble attributes which have been so plentifully ascribed to them. There are some individual exceptions, it is true. As you will find, among our own race, persons, who have been reared under the holy influences of Christianity, possessing the spirit of fiends, so you will find, occasionally, an Indian who is possessed of some feelings of humanity. Skilled to perfection in the peculiar craft pertaining to his calling, and his powers of endurance being almost incredible, when aroused, he becomes the most dangerous of foes.

"When difficulties and misunderstandings arise between civilized nations, they may be amicably adjusted by negotiation, or, that failing, a resort to warfare, conducted on scientific principles, but never losing sight of the great principles of humanity. But not so with a race of savages. Diplomacy is something unknown to them.

"When they feel that they have been wronged, they proceed (actuated solely by a desire for revenge) to wreak their vengeance upon defenceless, helpless women and children. Such being the state of things, how important it is that the government should see that the stipulation of the treaties now existing with those tribes who yet remain friendly, should be strictly and faithfully complied with. Since open hostilities have been commenced by one tribe, it will not require much to induce other tribes to follow their example.

"Another point, which is a very essential one, is the employment of competent interpreters—men who have a thorough knowledge of the two languages. It is my opinion, that more than one-half of the misunderstandings which have arisen between the Indians and the government, may be traced to the fact that the interpreter did not understand, himself, what had been said to him. As a general thing, half-breeds are employed to interpret.

"White men, who are capable of interpreting, cannot afford to accept the position of government interpreter, because the salary is so small that they can make more other ways. To explain what I mean, more fully, we will examine the languages. Ten thousand words will probably more than cover the number of words in the Sioux language, while our language is said to contain over forty thousand words. Now, the half-breed, of course, is raised among the Indians, and acquires his mother tongue perfectly. As he grows up, he becomes associated with the people of the frontier, and from them acquires his knowledge of English, which is not such English as is spoken among the elite. The person who has acquired his education, and has graduated from our high schools, speaks a different language, you might say, from the backwoodsman, who, probably, never saw the inside of a school-house.

"The excess of thirty thousand words in our language over that of the Indian, renders it very easy to say things which cannot be literally interpreted into the Indian tongue. In such cases, you can only convey the idea; that is, if the interpreter has intelligence enough to catch the idea himself. Now, our officials are generally intelligent and educated men. In councils with the Indians, they use the English language in its purity, to which the ear of the poor half-breed is entirely unaccustomed. He hears big sounding words; they are all Greek to him, and, under such circumstances, to convey the proper idea, is next to an impossibility. Under such circumstances, treaties are formed, and, when signed by all parties, the Indian is, half the time, as ignorant of the contents of the document, as a native of Africa. On the other hand, I have known instances where white men, who were wholly unfit for the office, have received and held the responsible position of interpreter for the government; men whose knowledge of the Indian tongue scarcely enabled them to carry on simple every day conversation. They were favorites of those in authority, and therefore received the appointment, the question of competency never being taken into consideration. Under such circumstances, it is the easiest thing in the world for serious misunderstandings to arise between the Indians and the government.

"Now, in regard to the Sioux, they knew that the Federal Government had been carrying on an expensive war for a long time; they believed that almost all our able-bodied men had gone South to take part in the war. The customary time arrived for the payment of their moneys and distribution of goods, and the Indians were assembled to receive them; but the money did not arrive.

"They were put off, with promises that, by such and such time, they should have their money, but were as often disappointed.

"Two months after the customary time for making payments had passed, when their agent volunteered to go into the service of his country, and taking almost every able-bodied man on the reservation with him, he left his post, to be gone, nobody knew how long.[50] The Indians, finding that their agent had thus left them, without giving them any satisfactory explanations, were at once impressed with the idea that the Federal Government had ceased to exist, and that their money had been expended for the purpose of carrying on the war, and that they were left to take care of themselves, as best they could."

When they broke camp at Red Wood and started for Yellow Medicine, Mr. Spencer says:

"A fine large flag, of the Hudson's Bay Company, was flying out to the breeze, from one of the wagons in front, and a few American flags, which had been captured, were raised at different points of the procession.

"It did not occur to me, to inquire how they came by that emblem of British authority, but I supposed it to have been presented to some chief or soldier, many years ago, and it had been preserved until the pres-

[50]The allusion is to Galbraith's recruiting of the Renville Rangers.

ent time. In the early part of the present century, British flags, medals, &c., were freely distributed among all the Indian tribes by the British traders.

*   *   *

"Here much time was spent in counselling. Little Crow was very anxious to move up in a body, and place themselves under the protection of the English, at the Red River settlement, but a majority were against him. In the meantime, the attacks upon New Ulm and Fort Ridgley had been made, but their statements were so conflicting, and I was suffering from my wounds so much, that I took no pains to ascertain the particulars; one thing is certain, however, that they did not lose so many men as the whites have always supposed to have been killed.

"At New Ulm, the Sioux were assisted by some of the Winnebagoes, and the conduct of 'Little Priest,' in that engagement, was very highly spoken of by the Sioux.

" 'Little Priest' is the head chief of the Winnebagoes, and lost two of his warriors in that attack. Messengers were sent from here to the Sissitons, Yanctons, Yanktonais, and to the governor of Selkirk Settlement, to inform them that they (the Mede-wa-kan-tons and Wa-hpe-kwtes) had declared war against the whites, and praying for their assistance. They considered it almost certain, that the western tribes would join them, and they confidently believed that the English would assist them. They say, that many years ago, the English gave them a small piece of artillery, and named it, 'Da-ko-ta-chis-tina,' or 'Little Sioux,' and promised them that, in case any difficulty should arise between the Americans and themselves, they could look to them (the English) for assistance. I could not hear, in any of my conversations with them, anything that caused me to suspect that secessionists had anything to do with it. If the tribes on the Missouri had been tampered with by secessionists (which may have been the case), this outbreak, I think, was no part of the programme.

"While encamped here, 'Standing Buffalo,' the head chief of the Sissitons, came down with about two hundred warriors, and, in a council with Little Crow, demanded the goods that had been taken from the Agency buildings at Yellow Medicine, as his property. This demand Little Crow refused to comply with, saying that as he had done all the fighting he was entitled to the plunder. Standing Buffalo then refused to take any part in the war, and threatened Little Crow or any of his people with death, if they came into his country for protection, in case they were defeated by the whites."

Chapter XXI

Lake Shetak Massacre

LAKE Shetak in Minnesota, ninety miles west of New Ulm, is the headwaters of the Des Moines river in Iowa. Attracted by its loveliness and fertility of soil, some six or eight American families, making a community of some fifty souls, united in a settlement on its banks. Industry was well rewarded, and comfort smiled at their hearthstones. A weekly mail brought them tidings from the outward world, in the strifes of which they had no wish to mingle.

On the memorable twentieth of August, they went about their daily avocations as usual till past midday, little dreaming of the terrible siege raging at Fort Ridgley, or the fate which awaited them. So general was the onslaught from one extreme of the state to the other, it is hard to divest ourselves of the belief of preconcerted action.

Some two months before the outbreak, Mr. Phineas P. [B.] Hurd, formerly of Steuben county, New York, but for three years a resident at Lake Shetak, with one man and a team left home for Dakota Territory, since which time no tidings had come from him. His wife was daily watching for his return; and his own heart too bounded with joy at the anticipated welcome, as the distance decreased between him and home.

The farm was left in charge of a Mr. [John] Voigt, and the tidy, skillful housewife and dairy woman, was evinced by the cheerful aspect within doors, and the golden butter and rich cheese which sent their fragrance from the dairy room. Mrs. Hurd was an industrious woman and early riser; hence, before the sun was up or her children awake, she, with the hired man, was out milking the cows. On the morning of August 20, 1862, they are surprised at the appearance of some twenty Indian horsemen, and more at seeing her husband's horses among them. Suspicion was aroused and they hastened within, to be followed by the whole gang, who at once commenced an indiscriminate plunder. Beds were ripped open and the feathers sent kiting in the air; cheese, for which they have the greatest abhorrence, were pitched into the yard; trunks and drawers were rifled; and a ball was sent to the heart of Mr. Voigt, who fell with Mrs. Hurd's baby in his arms as he was trying to hush its cries.

That was an awful hour; her home desolated, her husband (though her fears were not yet confirmed) a mangled carcass, a few leagues from home; and now driven out with her children, denied even a sunbonnet or shawl, and life granted only on condition of giving no alarm and starting across the prairie for the towns. Under an escort of seven Indians on horseback, with one child toddling by her side and another in her arms, she was hurried through an unfrequented trail for three miles, then bidden to go alone, "to look not behind, nor tarry in all the plains," under penalty of sharing death with all the other settlers.

The August sun was shining with unusual brightness, and the thick matted grass was heavily beaded with dew, which also soon set bleeding the bare feet of the pedestrians. Most piteously cried the little boy Willie, of only three years, to return home, and repeatedly asked where she was going. Alas, she could not tell him. Death by savage hands was behind, and starvation with all its horrors before. The repeated firing of guns convinced her that her neighbors were suffering with herself.

It was some relief when her little boy ceased to complain and manfully trudged along by her side with apparent confidence in his mother's course, and the younger rested in blissful unconsciousness on her bosom.

Now burst upon the wanderers that terrible storm of which mention is elsewhere made—which, sweeping over the prairies and bluffs, obliterated tracks, produced a lull in battle, and saved hundreds of wanderers from bloody death. For three hours the storm reigned; the thunder and lightning were terrific, and the water fell in a blinding deluge, washing out the trail, and covering the lower portions of the prairie. But He who folds the lambs in his bosom, gave her strength to wander on, breakfastless and dinnerless, to a slight, sandy elevation, where, supperless, she laid down her precious charge for the night. Her heart ached that she could not respond to her boy's pleadings for food. Her scant garments drenched to the skin, all that long night, she leaned over her children, her own shivering body protecting them from the wind. Willie slept most of the night, but the baby worried almost constantly; happily its wail reached not the savages' ears.

The second day was a duplicate of the first till toward evening, when she had the additional trial of seeing her little boy become very sick, and his physical powers fast failing him; but the baby still slept and nursed. At night she struck a road. With all her walking, she was but four miles from home, having doubtless wandered in a circle. Her heart sank and a sense of exhaustion came upon her. After two days' constant travel, her journey was just begun.

But cheered that she was no longer lost upon the prairie, she pushed on in the road to New Ulm, till nature demanding rest, she halted for the second night. Willie's sickness increased, and he asked no more for food. In the morning he could no longer walk, but craved water from every spring or pool they passed.

To carry both children was quite impossible for the exhausted mother. She conceals one child in the grass, and taking the other in her arms, passes over the first half mile, when she deposits this and returns for the other. Thus all that day she travels three times over the same path. We read of Spartan mothers and Cornelia's "jewels," but it is left for Minnesota mothers of 1862 to evince to the world the powers of human endurance in the strength of maternal love!

A distant cabin revives her sinking heart and nerves her with the hope of rest and food. On she presses, telling her boy of the relief so near. She enters, no sound breaks upon the silence. She commences her search for food, but not an article could be found. In despair she sank down in exhaustion, to be aroused by the plaintive cry of her boy, demanding food, of which they had now been four days destitute. She thought of the garden, and found some carrots and onions, but her sick child refused them. That night they slept in a cornfield, and she made her supper on raw corn, having no fire to roast it. The following morning with much joy did Mrs. Hurd find the decaying remnant of a ham, not to exceed a pound. Of this she fed her boy, and had the satisfaction of seeing him revive, and his vomiting cease. She was here joined by some refugee neighbors, and they continued together till they reached "Brown's," sixty miles from Shetak, where the inmates had been murdered. There they remained ten days, making themselves at home while awaking to the terrible reality of their fate.[51]

[51]According to Heard, *History of the Sioux War*, p. 99, the settlement at Lake Shetak was attacked "by Lean Bear and eight of his men, and by the bands of White Lodge and Sleepy Eyes." Altogether, about fifteen are thought to have been killed in this neighborhood. Bryant and Murch, *A History of the Great Massacre by the Sioux Indians*, pp. 153–159, gives a general account of what occurred, and also (pp. 343–375)

prints the statements of Mrs. Lavina Eastlick and Mrs. Alomina Hurd. The first reports obtained from these women were printed in the St. Paul *Pioneer and Democrat*, September 10, 1862. Mrs. Hurd's statement, given to the U. S. Commissioners who adjusted the Sioux damage claims, and dated April 28, 1863, is so closely followed by Mrs. McConkey as to indicate that she saw it as printed in the Davenport, Iowa, *Gazette* soon after. In this statement Mrs. Hurd says the first place reached was "Dutch Charley's" 16 miles from Lake Shetak. Subsequently, at Brown's, she fell in with two neighbors, Mrs. Eastlick and Thomas Ireland, both wounded. Compare Heard, pp. 102–110.

Chapter XXII

The General Onslaught

THE note of alarm sounding from the door of Mrs. Hurd, soon extended through all the settlement. The people aroused to their danger and collected in one house for defense; but finding they were insufficient in numbers and means, determined on flight. Women and children were loaded into farm wagons, the men on foot as bodyguards, shaping their course towards New Ulm.

Two miles on, eight or ten Indians suddenly came upon them. Women and children hid in the high grass while the battle raged. Two of the men deserted at the onset. The others stood their ground till all were wounded, and Mr. Eastlick and eleven others killed.

The Indians now called to the women to surrender, pledging life and protection if they did so; if not, threatening them with death as soon as their retreats could be hunted out. Their wounded husbands, hoping they might be ransomed by Government, encouraged the surrender. Without a parting kiss, and scarcely a parting glance, they were driven away from husbands, and children in some instances, with scarcely an idea of what their fate was to be.

The supposed dying husbands watched the receding forms of their families, till lost amid the foliage, and then assisted each other to their feet to escape —all save Mr. Ireland, who was left to die.

Half a mile away, the captives were overtaken by Burton Eastlick, who for the love he bore his mother, had determined to follow, but she entreated him to return for the sake of his fifteen months' old baby brother, ruthlessly torn from her, with the injunction to save him if possible, and carry him as far as he could, or till he reached some settlement. A sacred charge, and how regarded by this boy of twelve years we are yet to see.[52]

Burton obediently turned to retrace his steps, when the sharp crack of muskets made him look back to see his mother and three other women, with several of the children, fall in death. Three bullet wounds in the head, back and knee of Mrs. Eastlick, had not produced the effect designed, and a young monster beat her on the head with the butt of his gun till she was insensible, then with the spared captives they hastened away.

When Mrs. Eastlick revived, darkness had settled upon the earth. Her last recollections were of her friend and neighbor, Mrs. Everett, lying near her quite dead, and her infant vainly endeavoring to draw sustenance from the source to which it had never before appealed in vain, and a little girl crying over them. Now, these children were dead; the Indians had returned and shot them.

[52]The eldest Eastlick child, miscalled Burton by Mrs. Mc-Conkey and other contemporary writers, bore the name Merton; the youngest was named Johnny. An early account of their experiences appeared in the St. Paul *Pioneer and Democrat*, September 3, 1862; but much fuller and more graphic is that by Mrs. Eastlick, cited in the previous note.

To find her husband, Mrs. Eastlick crawled through the dew-matted grass to the battle ground. Cold and stiff she found him, and the little son of six years she left wounded in the feet was with him—he too had ceased to suffer. There she must leave them. She kisses lips and forehead, and turns away in tearless agony, resolved to find her children.

Four miles from the main settlement of Lake Shetak had resided the family of Mr. Aaron Myers. Early in the day he had become convinced that Indians were prowling around. But there was no time to confer with his neighbors, so with a sick wife on a bed in an ox wagon, with four little children, he started for some point of safety.

The wounded men before mentioned had progressed about sixteen miles, and the following day fell in with the Myers party. There was joy in that meeting, though their hearts were full of grief. The heavy, springless wagon in which they found a place relieved their wounded limbs and broken bones; but slowly, very slowly, moved those plodding oxen, and sadly their aching hearts kept time to the dull creaking of the wheels. Their undressed wounds were painful in the extreme, and why or how they lived through these days is not in the human mind to understand. Their only food was flour and water cakes baked in the sun, they fearing to make a fire lest Indians be attracted by the smoke.

On one occasion they took shelter for the night in a house which had been sacked by the Indians. Scarcely ten rods distant was another house where some Indians spent the night in feasting and plunder, but left without making any discovery as to the occupancy of the other.

Approaching New Ulm, Mr. Myers left the team to go into town for assistance. When too near to remedy his error, he saw the Indians had already besieged it, the work of destruction was going on, and their horrid war whoop rung on the air. Happily he eluded pursuit, and though he could not return to his anxious family, he bent his steps for Mankato, twenty-five miles below, where he arrived in safety.

The wagon party, alarmed at his long absence, concluded he would not return, and moved on toward Mankato. Excited, anxious and alarmed at every sight or sound, worn out with suffering, hunger and waking, and constantly watching for Indian "signs," they mistook the encampment of U.S. troops for Sioux teepees. They left their wagon and hid in the swamp, but fortunately had been seen by the soldiers, who hunted them out and brought them into camp, where a safe escort into town was furnished them.[53]

[53]The Ninth Regiment's history, by C. F. Macdonald, in *Minnesota in the Civil and Indian Wars*, vol. 1, p. 417, says that after Company E elected its officers at Fort Snelling, "they were ordered to return to Mankato, where the company was mounted and proceeded to Lake Crystal, only to be called back to protect Mankato from an anticipated raid by the Winnebago Indians. This did not occur, and the company moved back to the vicinity of Lake Crystal. It shortly afterward proceeded to New Ulm, and was the first company to reach that

It was eight days since their wounds were received, to which neither lint nor bandage had been applied. But now broken arms are set, putrid wounds dressed, and the sufferers made as comfortable as the circumstances would allow in a town of only two thousand inhabitants, already crowded with refugees.

------

place. While there a wounded settler came in and reported that two women were wounded and exhausted twenty-five miles from New Ulm. A party was sent out at night and brought them in. One of the company was killed by the Indians on the return march . . ."

CHAPTER XXIII

Outbreak at the North

LIKE a spark of fire in a magazine of powder had been the war spark ignited at Acton, and from the extreme north to the southwestern boundary of Minnesota, the explosion was being felt.

On the 24th of August a party of Sioux crossed the Red river of the north at Breckinridge, where the entire "town" was comprised in a mammoth hotel—took possession of the horses, and slaughtered or drove off the cattle. Their next onslaught was on the "Breckinridge House," strongly barricaded by those who had resolved to defend it or die in the attempt. Doors and windows were smashed in, and no man left to tell the tale. On the following day, a reconnoitering party drew up before the house, and scarcely had their eyes surveyed the destructive work, ere a large force of Indians sprang up, as from the earth. Swift-footed horses, as well as riders, saw the danger, and they reached the fort in safety. A day or two after, another body of men went up to learn the true state of affairs. A woman came forth from the saw mill. She wore but two garments, and these stiff with the blood which for twenty-four hours had flowed from her wounded side, during which time she had not tasted food. Her home was at "Old Crossing," sixteen miles distant, where with her son she kept a "station," and with them lived little Jimmy Scott, her pet grandson, only five years old. The Indians attacked the house before breakfast. Young Scott was killed, and his mother severely wounded. She lay upon the floor while they plundered the house. Then they came round her, kicking and punching her with sticks and guns, stripped off her dress, preparatory to mutilating her body, when the sound of wheels drew their attention without, and they rushed for the farmer's loaded market wagon, she not daring to move a hand to staunch the blood of the wound, lest they return and note its change of position. But she opened her eyes, and saw little Jimmy almost powerless from fright, and whispered him to do the savages' bidding —they *might* let him live.

The farmer had escaped to the woods. They did not pursue; but driving the wagon to the door, emptied the flour from the sacks and drove off taking little Jimmy, who in obedience to his grandmother's injunctions submitted to his fate. Not till the sound of the wheels had died on her ear, and no other sound broke upon the silence, did she again venture to open her eyes. Then she crawled to the door, where lay her murdered son, her youngest born, and faint from the bleeding wound, without bonnet, shawl, or dress, she started. Fifty dollars in silver had been overlooked when the Indians robbed the house, and this she hid in a haystack with the hope of its doing good to some one. All that day she walked and crawled, eating nothing but some savory herbs that grew in her path. As twilight fell, she crawled to the door where she had hoped a friendly admittance. One glance and she knew the fiends had been there. Though she did not know of the three dead bodies within, she turned to the saw mill for shelter, and was found, as described. The ladies at Fort Abercrombie made her as comfortable as their own wardrobes would allow, and with kind care, her wound was in due time healed.[54] A party went down to "Old Crossing" to bury her son, and brought her the money she had hidden. A few days after, others found the body exhumed, with a stake driven through it, into the earth.

The reconnoitering party entered the Breckinridge House, where they found the three dead bodies with chains on their legs, by which they had been dragged from room to room, leaving a bloody trail, as the work of plunder progressed. They had now been several days dead, and were very offensive.

[54]The grandmother whose adventures are thus described is identified in *Minnesota in the Civil and Indian Wars*, vol. 2, pp. 187–188, as a Mrs. Ryan, but a contemporary letter by P. Lamb, Fort Abercrombie, September 22, 1862, printed in the St. Cloud, Minn., *Democrat*, August 2, 1862, gives her name as Mrs. Scott. (For this and other letters from Fort Abercrombie at this time, see *North Dakota Historical Collections*, 1908, vol. 2, part 2, pp. 10–18. The same publication, vol. 2, part 1, pp. 179–185, contains a letter by S. V. Carr, November 16, 1862, with a journal entry for September 22 giving further details of Mrs. Scott's experiences.) Bryant and Murch, *A History of the Great Massacre by the Sioux Indians*, pp. 234, 238, tells of the adventures of 65-year-old Mrs. Scott, and adds details respecting the killing of the three men who holed up in the Breckenridge House, as related in the next paragraph.

On further search, Burbank & Co.'s stage was found in the river, the top cut off, the horses taken, and the driver killed. Articles of minor value were scattered around, and a distributing office had been improvised for the mail, letters, and drafts sent to the four winds. Thus commenced the conflict along the northern line of travel, and so few were the men and arms at Fort Abercrombie that all who were there, and more, were needed for its protection.

Many of the people who were driven from their homes, could not get to the Fort, so made their way to the nearest village. Thrilling tales are told of these adventurers—of their almost miraculous escapes, and providential guidance beyond the reach of savage hands. We remember a man and his wife, with a little boy of four years brought forty miles on their backs, coming into St. Cloud. Never had they a mouthful to eat, and never a loud word was spoken. Once or twice only did the little hero whisper, "*I am hungry.*"

Another man was shot at his own door. His wife drew him in and bolted the door, when he continued to load the gun, which she fired through the window till the Indians, after several had fallen, withdrew. The husband, sure he must die, and feeling that every moment's delay increased her peril, begged his wife to save herself by flight. Reluctantly she did his bidding, and after incredible hardships reached a friendly shelter. A few days later, some white men entered the dwelling, expecting to find a putrid corpse. To their surprise the man was still alive, though he had made repeated attempts to end his agony. In a short time he was re-united with his wife, rejoicing in the failure of the dull butcher knife to perform his bidding.

Chapter XXIV

Siege of Fort Abercrombie

WHEN the northern stampede began, Fort Abercrombie was garrisoned by only forty men in command of Captain Vanderhock,[55] with no protecting walls or even embankments. The danger becoming known, messengers were sent forth to warn the citizens, government and Red River trains known to be on the route, which it was rumored the Indians had gone to intercept, and also to St. Paul for military re-enforcements. The citizens banded with the troops for defense of the post, and soon completed a breastwork, from cord wood, covered with earth on the three most exposed sides.

The list of women and children soon swelled to sixty-two, who, being crowded into the soldiers' quarters, the only bullet-proof building, made a one room community of two hundred and fifty. Here commissary stores were brought, water hauled, and whatever of comforts could be supplied. Eyelids were held open in suspense, and the nerves of the women

[55]John Vander Horck's name appears in most of the contemporary accounts spelled as by Mrs. McConkey. He was born in Germany in 1830, came to the United States in 1852, and after living in Chicago and Galena, moved to St. Paul in 1855. After recruiting Company D of the Fifth Minnesota Volunteers, he was commissioned its captain and ordered to Fort Abercrombie. Later he served in Pennsylvania and Kansas, and after the Civil War settled in Minneapolis. See *North Dakota Historical Collections,* 1908, vol. 2, part 2, p. 10.

set quivering, at the least note of alarm. There was neither eating nor sleeping, only as each gnawed at hard tack when faintness from hunger came over them, and slept on a blanket, which was rolled up for a seat during the day. The men kept guard without, while the women worked at cartridge making, or moulded bullets.

The first show of Indians was on the 28th [30th] of August. A large company of horsemen came in sight of the fort and killed the herdsman, surrounded and drove off nearly three hundred cattle, and many of the horses and mules of the fort, which in defiance of the guns they entered the stables to obtain. A few almost reckless men went forth to dispute their right, actually drove them from the stables, and saved a few of the horses. The Indians fled to the woods, where Capt. V. thought imprudent to follow them, as the fort had poor protection at best. Take away the handful of men, and who would save it, if attacked from another side? The three successive days, the Indians bivouaced in sight of the Fort while they barbecued and feasted.

At early dawn on Sept. 1st [3rd] the actual siege of the fort commenced, and for several hours raged against fearful odds. The loss on our side was comparatively small, one killed and several wounded. Their casualties were unknown, as only two were left on the field; the prairie was strewn with cloths and paper saturated with blood, which indicated more than it proved.

At the fort every soldier and citizen worked with a will in anticipation of a renewed attack, till on the morning of the sixth—just as the sober gray was yielding to rosy tints—the pickets announced the enemy's approach. This band, estimated at from five hundred to one thousand strong, spread the mounted ones ahead in the form of a fan, till three sides of the fort were enclosed. As they dashed on to the attack, their yells were terrific, and their appearance hideous in the extreme. This was so unlike anything the men had ever heard or seen that the first effect was not very cheering; but they rallied behind the breastwork, and though attacked at four points, fought with a coolness and heroism equal to anything we read of in history. Had they met this superior force with other than determined wills, all must have fallen into savage hands, and the buildings reduced to ashes. The fire from the howitzer scattered them like autumn leaves. One shell entered a log building where many of the savages had taken refuge, doing deadly work. The blood on the floor revealed its effect. After three hours' hard fighting, the unequal conflict ceased with a decided repulse to the assailants. Scarcely had their war whoops ceased when a messenger, two weeks away, returned, with the cheering news of re-enforcements near. In forty-four hours, Mr. Hill had made the trip of two hundred and fifty miles to St. Paul, and his demand for troops was responded to; but these could not move with the celerity of fleet horses, nor could each man carry in his haversack sufficient food for his journey.[56]

Though there were no more direct attacks, small scouting parties kept up a harassing fire from the opposite shore, where bushes and weeds concealed them. The dwellings, to which some of the families had returned, were being riddled with balls, and some persons had very narrow escapes. A friend of the writer was guest at the house of Mr. Stone, the sutler. After two weeks' fasting, the women went over, with the hope of being unmolested while they should have a week's rations prepared. A ball whizzed past their heads, and lodged in the casing of the door as they were about to enter; then, like "rain on the roof," fell all around, while the inmates lay upon the floor, almost breathless with fear. Personal ablution or tidy apparel was not to be thought of, and for three weeks the husband of the friend above alluded to removed his boots from his feet only to shake out the fleas.

[56]Bryant and Murch, *A History of the Great Massacre by the Sioux Indians*, pp. 244–245, relates the adventures of Walter P. Hills, "who three times came as a messenger from the fort during the time it was in a state of siege." Accounts of the attack on Fort Abercrombie, more or less under siege from September 3–23, and directly assaulted on September 3 and 6, may be found in *North Dakota Historical Collections*, vol. 2, part 2, pp. 10–19; and for a modern summary, see W. W. Folwell, *A History of Minnesota*, vol. 2, pp. 165–168. Vander Horck estimated that about 800 Indians took part in the onslaught of September 6. Isaac V. D. Heard, *History of the Sioux War*, p. 142, says the attackers were Sissetons and Yanktonais.

Under circumstances like those described, the existence of three immortal beings commenced. Two of these just opened their eyes, drew a few breaths, and then passed on to that eternal state of which this life is but a shadow. In a soldier's bunk, partitioned from the main quarters by canvas, the chill wind whizzing between the logs, laid my friend, Mrs. L., pale, weak and senseless. Bravely had she endured the terrible siege, but the reaction came. The little one soon passed away. Her husband lay on a stretcher in the same little place, for his wound was not healed. All are to leave —the band of women and children whom a common misfortune had bound so closely, and almost made friends of uncongenial spirits. They drew around her bunk for a last leave of one whose manner ever endeared her to all. Yet an All-wise Being had "ordained her unto life," and in due time the anxious hearts of friends were relieved by her presence.

Three weeks they worked, watched, and waited, till, at last, three hundred men are added to the number already there. But eight had died since the siege commenced, but several were helpless from wounds. Small parties sent out to reconnoitre every little while would discover an Indian, his head popping from 'neath a bush, or from amid the weeds, tempting a shot. These parties were several times surprised by superior numbers, when desperate fighting would follow; but the savages were always vanquished. Once our men effected a retreat, though leaving two dead on the ground, and others wounded. One of this party actually died from fright, a few hours after his return. Another gave out, but with encouragement and aid stood upon his feet in time to send a ball to the heart of an Indian who aimed at his comrade, though not in time to prevent a flesh wound in his leg.

The sad presentiment of the parents of a young man in this rencontre, which was distinctly heard at the fort, proved correct. A few days after, a volunteer party went out to find and bury him and another, killed at the same time. The last lay on his face with his skull smashed in and his brains scattered about, eighteen bayonet thrusts in his back, and on one leg a gash nearly to the bone, from the hip to the calf of the leg.

The body of the other, Edgar Wright, had been ripped open to the throat, the heart and liver taken out, the lungs left on the chest, the head cut off, scalped, and stuck in the cavity of the abdomen, with the face toward the feet. The hands were cut off and placed side by side, two feet from the body, but what was indicated by this arrangement was not understood. The victim was a young man of unblemished reputation. They knew him well, and had received frequent hospitality at his hand. This case is not an exception, for they have been most ingenious in cruelty toward those who have most befriended them, and for whom they professed most friendship.

CHAPTER XXV

Indians at Sioux Falls City

WHEREVER the magic wand of civilization had passed, there went the fiends, intent on bloody work. We have seen them in the interior; we have seen them at the extreme north; and now to the very southwestern corner of the State, and even a few miles beyond, in Dakota Territory, we see them watching for a mark to shoot at. Sioux Falls City on the Big Sioux river, had just commenced an existence, and eight families were all its boast. Their nearest neighbors to the east were at Lake Shetak, sixty-five miles distant, and the nearest on the south at Yankton, about the same distance. Fortunately, on the 25th of August, a small force under Lieut. J. A. Bacon was stationed here, else doubtless there would have been a general massacre.

Mr. Joseph B. Amidon, who had emigrated from St. Paul three years before, was, as also his wife, a former resident of Essex county, N. Y., and they were among the "first settlers." He resided on a "claim" one mile from the main settlement, and was with his son at work in the hay field, nearly a half mile from his dwelling. The supper prepared by his waiting wife, remained untouched, for husband and son came not from their toil. The clock struck ten, and unable longer to endure her suspense, she went to the soldiers' camp. With soldierly promptness, they searched without avail the field where, during the day, they had seen the missing ones. Across the road was a cornfield, and there, just as morning dawned, the cold, stiffened bodies were found; a ball had pierced the father's heart, and earth had drank his blood. The soft plowed earth where they lay showed very plainly Willie's severe struggles with death. Three balls had pierced his body, to the effects of which he yielded not easily or soon. They are taken home, where the wife, well nigh paralyzed with shock, prepared to bury her dead.

Scarcely was the dust to dust consigned ere the Indians appeared. A sharp engagement ensued, in which seven Indians were made to "bite the dust."

In rapid succession came the news of the outbreak, and the Governor's order to leave for some point of safety. Government conveyance and military protection would be furnished, but only one hour was allowed to prepare for departure. What an hour was that! But there was no alternative. Savage eyes were even then watching their movements, awaiting the withdrawal of troops for a general conflagration. This sad-hearted cortege was obliged to make a circuit of a thousand miles to reach a point two hundred and fifty miles distant.[57]

[57]A statement by Henry Masters, printed in Bryant and Murch, *A History of the Great Massacre by the Sioux Indians*, pp. 160–161, similarly describes the murder of Joseph B. and M. Amidon on August 25. The account continues: "About forty soldiers were stationed at Sioux Falls, and, on the morning of the 26th, after the finding of the bodies of the Amidons, all but about a dozen of them started out on an expedition in

search of the murderers. Soon after they left, about fifteen Indians, supposed to be Sioux, attacked the camp. As the scouting party returned to camp the savages retreated, were pursued, but eluded our men and escaped." On August 29, under orders from Governor Jayne, Lieutenant Bacon evacuated the town, escorting the settlers to Yankton, where the soldiers remained for some time. "This company of cavalry was the only protection for the whole region of country from Fort Randall to the Big Sioux, a distance of one hundred and thirty miles, a portion of which was well settled, on the Big Sioux, and on the Missouri slope. In one week after the murders at the Falls, one-half of the inhabitants of the Missouri slope had fled to Sioux City, Iowa, six miles below the mouth of Big Sioux." For further details, including official Dakota correspondence, see *South Dakota Historical Collections,* 1916, vol. 8, pp. 101–104.

Chapter XXVI

The Heroic Boy

WE have seen Burton [Merton] Eastlick following the captive party, and returning by the urgent desire of his mother. He had seen his mother shot, and supposed her dead. Beside his dying brother he watched till the angels bore his spirit above, placed the dear little form beside his idolized father, and with a bravery which would have honored men of mature years, took his baby charge and commenced preparations to start, in obedience to his mother's dying wish. Mr. Ireland, who was *left to die*, remonstrated. "He could never carry out the design, and it was better that they die there together." But the boy was resolute and *firm*. "Nothing should deter him—he would carry the baby as long as he could—they *might* be saved."

The spirit of the boy incited Mr. Ireland with new hope. "Why should I die here alone, when such a boy can do so much. I, too, will try and get away." And so he went, bleeding and suffering, every rod gained increasing his desire to gain another. Mr. Ireland's body had been the target for eight balls, three of which had passed through his lungs. His wife and two of his children were killed, and two daughters, Rosanna and Ellen, carried into captivity, compelled to walk the entire distance to the Missouri River, over seven hundred miles.

Can imagination paint the sufferings of Mr. Ireland during his wanderings of fourteen days, weakened by loss of blood and want of food? How painful the progress, how bitter the thoughts of the future, for he knew not that one of his family lived, or *if* alive, but that a fate worse than death was theirs.

Ninety miles thick with dangers lay before him, but Burton faltered not. His arms became *very* tired, but then he placed this precious burden on his back, and the first day made sixteen miles, and thus traveled on, making sixty miles in ten days. His food was raw corn and such as he could find in deserted houses. How carefully he munched the coarse fare, to relieve the baby cravings for its mother! How tenderly he folded him in his arms to shelter him from the chill night— how lovingly soothed his wail, lest the very breeze announce their living to those from whom they fled.

The reader has seen the resolute mother crawl back to her precious dead, and turn from them for a lone, weary march over the prairies. She traveled by night and hid in the grass for several days, till almost exhausted. At the risk of being murdered, she crawled to a cornfield, but her stomach rejected the raw corn. She became deathly sick, obliged to lie by for some time.

The festering, undressed wounds were occasionally bathed by a cool spring, and on she moved, an illustration of human endurance. At a deserted house she killed a chicken, and with her teeth pulled the raw meat from its breast. She continued very sick during the night, but the following morning, tore the remainder of the chicken into strips to be dried in the sun as she went, this, with three ears of raw corn, was all she had to eat during ten days. Oh! the night wanderings!—the listening days when the very silence was painful—the terrible stomach cravings and the bitter heart throbbings for the loved and slain, as also for the living!

From Sioux Falls City in Dakota Territory, to New Ulm, August Garzene, a Frenchman, was employed in carrying the mail. Lake Shetak lay on his route. On his route he meets Mrs. Eastlick, whom he scarcely recognizes, so changed is she. He gives her a seat in his sulky, and at "Dutch Charley's," ere many hours, she folds to her heart her emaciated children, in whom the reader will recognize the *heroic boy* and his baby brother.[58]

There too was Mr. Ireland, with eight balls in his body, whom the boy's courage had saved, together with Mrs. Hurd and her two children. These last had fallen in company several hours before. A glad meeting! A few miles further at "Brown's," they find comfortable quarters, from whence Mr. Ireland is sent ahead to New Ulm for assistance.

Lieutenant Roberts, with twelve men and a team, was dispatched to their relief and reached them about midnight. The following morning at daylight they

---

[58]Without giving his name, Mrs. Eastlick's statement as cited in Note 51 tells at length of the help rendered by the mail carrier, Garzene.

were on their way to join their neighbors at Mankato, who supposed them dead. After fifteen days of intense suffering they enjoyed the luxury of food and rest. [59]

Twelve had fallen at Lake Shetak, Aug 20, 1862. Twelve months and more, through winter's snow and summer's heat, the angels watched their unburied dust. On the 28th Oct., 1863, friends had the mournful satisfaction of consigning the "dust to dust." Each body had retained its own impress so distinctly that there was no difficulty in marking the graves.

[59]Mrs. Eastlick speaks appreciatively of the aid given her at New Ulm by Captain Jerome Dane and Second Lieutenant John R. Roberts; see Bryant and Murch, *A History of the Great Massacre by the Sioux Indians,* pp. 264–265, and compare Note 53 above.

Chapter XXVII

Siege of Hutchinson

THE main body of troops, as we have seen, were marching up the Minnesota Valley, to the centre of hostilities. Detachments were stationed in exposed localities. Some had brisk skirmishes with the foe, and others were left unmolested. Several companies of mounted citizens did efficient service.

Captain Richard Strout with a company of fifty men was stationed at Cedar City, whence all the people had fled. Here they were unexpectedly attacked by one hundred and fifty Indians. They fought like heroes until nearly overpowered by numbers, when they retreated to Hutchinson, a town eighty miles above the capital, and the first beyond the Big Woods.

From Cedar City this savage band moved towards Forest City, making a determined assault but repulsed by the inhabitants, who had fortified the town.

Thwarted, they advanced on Hutchinson, where Capt. Strout and his fifty men, with citizens of town and vicinity, repulsed them. Capt. Strout's dispatch of Sept. 3 says:

"I was attacked to-day by about one hundred and fifty Indians, about half of them mounted. They numbered full double my force, and fought us for two hours and a half. I threw my company into four sections, and in open order, pressed against them, as skirmishers, after which, as they so far outnumbered my force, I made a fierce march against their main body, which was still in front. Our loss, in the engagement, was three killed, and fifteen wounded. A number of the men were very much injured by exhaustion.

"I think I am safe in saying, that the Indians lost, in killed and wounded, two or three times our number.

"We lost most of our rations, utensils, tents, and some arms, from the excitement. Some horses ran away, others got mired, so that we lost nine, in all, from these causes.

"The Indians had excellent guns. They were bright, and carried better than our guns. They were dressed partly in citizen's dress, and many of them rode fine horses. Their ponies would lie down when they dismounted. Sometimes the Indians would rush up to within one hundred yards of my force.[60]"

Near the village of Hutchinson lived a Mr. Adams, who with his wife and child were fleeing to the protection of the town, when he abandoned them to their fate. Finding themselves closely pursued, he threw the child, which he was carrying, and made his escape. She stopped to pick up her child and was captured. Her captor wished to take the child upon his horse, but she clung to it. The Indian became enraged, and shot

[60] Strout's brief dispatch of September 3 was printed in the St. Paul *Press* and the St. Paul *Pioneer and Democrat* two days later.

it. These facts, I have from Mr. George Spencer, who had been a captive three weeks when Mrs. Adams was brought into the Indian camp. During this time he had heard no news from the whites, though many captives had been brought in. He says, "I told my friend (Chaska) that I should like to see the white woman who had just been brought in, when he immediately sent for her.

"I found her to be a very pretty and intelligent little woman, and from her learned the latest news in regard to the preparations which were being made by the whites to punish the Indians.

"In relating to me her history, when she spoke of the murder of her child, her first born and only child, she wept bitterly. Upon seeing which, the Indians inquired the cause. They then directed me to explain to her the reason why her child had been killed: that if she would have let the Indian take it, he would have brought it along safely."

Chapter XXVIII

Battle of Birch Coolie

THE citizens of Minnesota had now begun to realize the horrors of a home war. The murdered dead remain unburied, and their effluvia taints the air at Red Wood and elsewhere. A detachment, composed of one company of cavalry under Capt. Joseph Anderson, and another of infantry under Capt. Hiram P. Grant, in command of Maj. J. R. Brown, were sent out August 31, by Col. Sibley, commissioned with the sad burial of these victims. At night they encamped opposite the Lower Agency. The following morning they find and bury about thirty bodies, in every conceivable state of mutilation, mostly the heroes of Capt. Marsh's company. A detachment, having crossed the river to the Agency, engaged in the same sad and unpleasant duty there. About eighty-five in all were buried that day.

Re-united, they moved on some three miles, to Birch Coolie. There were no traces of Indians having been in the vicinity and precaution was less in their thoughts than personal comfort when their camping ground was selected. Had they apprehended an attack, they would have sought the protection of the timber, not more than two hundred yards away, instead of the smooth prairie, the most unpropitious spot that could have been found for the ordeal which followed. Fortunately, the camp was made in the usual way, with the wagons packed around, and the teams fastened to them. The horses of the mounted men were fastened by strong picket ropes. A guard of thirty men and two non-commissioned officers were detailed, and ten sentinels were on constant duty. Around the campfire the men talked over the sickening scenes of the day till drowsiness settled upon their eyelids, when each sunk into slumbers profound, unmindful of the sentinel's tread.

Sept. 2 was giving notice of dawning morn, and an officer of the guard was completing his round. The sentinel saw, by the waving furrows of the tall grass, that objects were moving along in zigzag lines not far away. Unwilling to give alarm without cause, he recalled the officer and pointed them out. At this moment, came war whoops from all sides, and a raking crossfire poured in upon the sleepers. Most of the guard fell, some killed and others wounded. The tents were riddled with bullets. Many in them were wounded, and others received their death shots, before aware of danger. Not sixty seconds was required for all this, and had the assailants charged into camp, a general slaughter would have followed. The panic and confusion which such events create gave place in an almost incredibly short time to calm, deliberate action. Every wounded man whose hand could clutch a rifle, crawled from his tent, and with those uninjured ranged himself behind the prostrate bodies of horses, wagons, or whatever could answer for a barricade. Some dug trenches with their bayonets, throwing up the earth with their tin cups, while others, loading as they lay, would rise on one knee, fire and fall, to repeat the process. Meanwhile, the hoarse braying of the animals in their dying agonies was mingling with the groans of the wounded and dying men. When the men were thoroughly roused, they deported themselves with coolness and bravery, though they had been scarcely two weeks in the field. Every man was a host. It is but justice to make some allusion to the honored dead who fell here.

Among the first to enlist in the company of "Young Men's Guards," raised in St. Paul for national service, was Benjamin S. Terry. When the burial party went forth from Fort Ridgley Sergeant Terry volunteered to accompany them. His object was to identify his bosom friend, George Spencer, as a stranger could not (for all supposed him dead). No sooner was the alarm given than, rifle in hand, he sprang from the tent, when a ball pierced his side and he fell. Several times after his wound was dressed, he crawled from his tent, and took unerring aim at a grass-hidden foe. He was perfectly aware of his situation, and before the sun went down, had fought his first and last battle with the Indians. He was a member of the First Baptist Church in St. Paul, and of three brothers, was the second who had fallen by savage hands; the first in 1852 while acting as their teacher and missionary, at the north. His body was afterward removed to St. Paul, and more than one eye was dimmed as they saw the friend for whom his own life had been given acting as first bearer at his burial.

Corporal Wm. M. Cobb of St. Paul was a young man of many virtues, the pride of his father's household. He received four bullets at one volley but fought on for an hour, when, exhausted from loss of blood, he walked to the surgeon's tent, where his wounds were dressed. He lived until the next morning. His dying injunction was *"not to give up the camp."*

Sergeant Wm. Irvine for thirty hours lay upon his face without food or drink, discharging his gun as often as he could "sight an Indian." He had just sent a message to Capt. Grant that he had killed three or four, when a ball pierced his head. He died on his way to the fort, after relief had come.

These, with others, were afterward removed to St. Paul, and with suitable honors buried in Oakland Cemetery.

All that day and all night, the battle raged. The little brave band was completely surrounded. Many a one lay soaking with his own blood the soil of the trench he had dug with his bayonet and tin cup. On the morning of the 3d, the crack of the rifle is still heard, and continues to tell upon our men. With savage yells and demoniac war-whoops the work goes on till nearly night.

In Capt. Grant's force were several half-breeds, who had fought valorously. On Wednesday morning the Sioux commander called out in his own language for these to leave the whites, come over to their side, assuring them that only the white blood was sought, and that they were going to charge and put every person to death. This was understood by all the half breeds, and by Maj. Brown, who translated it for Capt. Grant.

But Heaven sent the boom of approaching cannon, and at the same moment an Indian rode up to their commander to say that "two miles of white men" were coming to the relief of the besieged, which was followed by the quick command to "cut them off—annihilate them!"

The pickets around Col. Sibley's camp at Fort Ridgley, fifteen miles distant, heard the firing early on Tuesday morning, and reported the same at headquarters, but the echoes from the woods and reverberations from the bluffs prevented them from determining from whence the sounds proceeded. Convinced that the burial detachment was in imminent peril, *somewhere,* two companies with a few mounted men, with a six pound howitzer, under Col. Samuel McPhail, were ordered to their relief. As by intuition, their march was shaped in the right direction.

The savages hastened to meet and annihilate them, leaving a few men around the camp, which they thought now almost defenseless. Little Crow had proclaimed to his people that Col. Sibley's army was composed of old men and little boys—hence but little to be dreaded. But when they saw the formidable array, with all the paraphernalia of war, they deemed annihilation less sure, and concluded to defer it till the next day, while they demonstrated their prowess by firing from a distance, brandishing their hatchets, waving their blankets and sounding the horrid war whoop.

To the inexperienced eye of our men, the savages seemed greatly magnified in numbers, and they fancied themselves too weak to cut their way to the struggling, suffering band; they bivouaced for the night and returned a messenger for greater re-enforcements. This messenger was the intrepid Sheehan, of Yellow Medicine and Fort Ridgley renown. The Indians tried to cut him off, chased him seven miles, sending more than fifty bullets at him—but his work was not yet done. Col. Sibley with his entire remaining force took up the line of march the same evening, reaching the second detachment about midnight. At early dawn the column was in motion. As the sun rose, the sheen of bright muskets in the hands of distant running Indians was seen all around but quite out of range. They had delayed their attack for rest and food, but now, when they saw this column twice the length of the previous evening, they were powerless with wonder, unable to account for its sudden growth, and declared that "five miles of white men and a big gun were too much for them to fight."

A sufficient number of the enemy had remained at Birch Coolie to keep up a harassing fire. The main body of the Indians continued to brandish their weapons, which flashed back the sun's rays, and louder and more defiant became the continuous war whoop.

Thus was each party deceived with the number and strength of the other. Our force continued to advance in battle line, their fire, however, having but little or no effect on the distant foe, unless to impart an impression of superiority in strength and discipline, and keep them in the distance, till they finally retired.

When first the group of conical tents appeared across the distant ravine, there were doubts whether they were friends or foes. To annihilate them if the latter, to relieve them if the former, the march is quickened. Dead horses form the barricade, but not a sign of life appears. Had all been slaughtered? *Live men* were in the trenches and joyfully aware of the approach of friends, for they could hold out but a few hours longer. The want of water alone would have made them powerless. Had the savage force remained undivided, doubtless all would have been found slain. A strange wild joy reigned in camp. Some clapped their hands and laughed, others danced in delight—some gave praise to God, and others were mute with gratitude.

There was but little time for congratulation. Thirteen lay unburied, and sixty more were suffering from wounds. "The hero of a thousand battles" no more deserves the laurel wreath than the heroes of Birch Coolie. For thirty-six hours, without food or rest, they had held their camp against three hundred savage foes.

Mattresses of prairie grass, placed on the hard wagon bottom, served for ambulances, and at sundown commenced the return march. At midnight, worn out with fighting and marching, they entered Fort Ridgley.

According to reliable sources, the Indian force at Birch Coolie was three hundred and nineteen men, who had come from their encampments at Yellow Medicine with the design of separating in two columns and simultaneously attacking Mankato and St. Peter. The event proved that the detachment started from Fort Ridgley at the right time. Had these savages met with no check, they would have laid those flourishing towns in ashes, and many of the people would have shared the fate of those of New Ulm —and it was their purpose to follow up this success to St. Paul, attack it in the night time and reduce it to ashes.

Those whose graves were made on the battle-ground were not the only victims of the Birch Coolie battle. One after another of the wounded swelled the list of dead, so that in ten days they numbered twenty-three. Robert Gibbons is worthy of special mention, being a humble Christian and prominent member of the Methodist Church in St. Paul. He had given two sons to the national army, and when a sudden home emergency arose, joined a cavalry company to die the soldier's honored death, and when his remains were removed, to receive the soldier's honored burial.[61]

[61]Gibbons' first name is given as Richard in a compilation from the muster rolls printed in *Minnesota in the Civil and*

Mr. J. W. DeCamp had entered the ranks to fight in retaliation of the supposed death of his wife and three children. He fell while fighting, and though he reached the fort alive, did not live to know but his worst fears were true.

Mrs. DeCamp was a companion in captivity with Mr. Spencer, and the utter neglect with which she was treated was almost as unendurable as the surplus of attention to others. She was claimed by no one in particular, and consequently, often went to bed hungry, if indeed so fortunate as to find a blanket bed on which to sleep. Our informant besought the pity of the inhuman brutes and obtained something for her to eat.

One dark rainy night, with no one to guard her, she found little difficulty in seeking the river, where a flotilla of canoes awaited herself and children, together with the family of her rescuer. For three days and nights they floated or paddled down stream in a cold, drizzling rain, with insufficient clothing or food.

On their way, they discovered a woman and five children lurking in the bushes, their clothes and flesh rent with the briers, and much emaciated from long fasting and anxious watching. This was Mrs. Robideaux, who was made as comfortable as circumstances

---

Indian Wars, vol. 2, p. 212. Joseph Warren DeCamp, mentioned in the next paragraph, is also mentioned in Brown's report; see the next chapter. The recollections of his widow, Jannette E. Sykes DeCamp Sweet, are printed in *Minnesota Historical Society Collections,* 1894, vol. 2, pp. 354–380.

would admit. These were all brought safely into port by Lorenzo Laurence, a Christian Indian who jeopardized his life in this and other kindred acts, and with John Otherday, and others, is entitled to the gratitude and protection of white people for all time.

Simon, another Christian Indian, and an old man, rescued Mrs. Newman and three children, and rested not till he had placed them in friendly hands at the Fort. But the hopes poor Mrs. DeCamp entertained of meeting her husband went out when she reached her destination. His grave had been made several days when she reached the Fort.

CHAPTER XXIX

Battle of Birch Coolie—
Official Report of Maj. J. R. Brown,
Commanding Detachment

Fort Ridgley, Sept. 4, 1862.

Col. H. H. Sibley, Commanding Expedition in Sioux Country:

SIR:—In compliance with your order, I left the encampment at this post, on the morning of August 31st, 1862, to visit the different settlements between this post and Beaver River, to search for and bury all persons that could be found murdered, and at the same time, to examine the country about the Lower Sioux Agency and Little Crow's village, to mark all indications of the movement of the Indians, and the course taken by them in their retreat.

Capt. Grant's Company A, 6th Regiment; Capt. Anderson's Company of mounted men, several volunteers from the officers of the expedition, a fatigue party of twenty men, and seventeen teamsters, with their teams, formed the force of the detachment.

On the 31st of August, the detachment moved in a body and encamped on the Minnesota bottom, at the mouth of Birch Coolie and opposite the Lower Sioux Agency, having found and buried sixteen corpses during the day.

On the 1st of September, the detachment marched in a body to the river bank, when the mounted company, with one team and eight of the fatigue party, accompanied me across the river, under the protection of the infantry. After searching around the Agency, and becoming satisfied there were no Indians in the vicinity, Capt. Grant was directed to remain with his company, and twelve of the fatigue party, and sixteen teams, on the east side of the river, to bury what murdered persons could be found at the crossing and at the settlements, as far as Beaver river, and from the Beaver river to return to the upper timber on the Birch Coolie, and encamp.

I proceeded with that portion of the detachment that had crossed the river, to bury the dead about the Agency, and then proceeded to Little Crow's village, and from there I went alone to where the road leading to the Coteau de Prairie diverges from the Yellow Medicine road, to ascertain whether the Indians had gone to the Coteau, or continued up the Minnesota, towards the Yellow Medicine.

The road and the camps about Little Crow's village, indicated that the main body of the Indians had an immense baggage train, which had gone forward about six days previous, and a smaller baggage train coming from the lower part of the reservation, had gone forward two days subsequently, the entire force keeping the Yellow Medicine road.

In all our examinations, no signs could be found about the village, along the road, or at the river crossing, near the village, that any Indians had been in the vicinity for the four days previous. This was the united opinion of Maj. Galbraith, Messrs. Alex. Faribault, Geo. Faribault, and J. J. Frazier (who were among the volunteers), and myself; and, as the Indians, when encamped near their villages, invariably visit them frequently, the general supposition was, that upon learning of the approach of troops, the lower Indians had gone up to join the Yellow Medicine Indians, that they might subsequently act in concert in their defense against the troops, or in their movement west.

Having accomplished the object of my visit to Little Crow's village, I proceeded to the ford, near that village, and re-crossed the Minnesota river, and near sunset, reached the encampment selected by Capt. Grant, near the upper timber of the Birch Coolie, and about three miles from the Lower Agency.

The two divisions of the detachment buried, during this day, fifty-four murdered persons. Capt. Grant found a woman who was still alive, although she had been almost entirely without sustenance for fourteen days, and was severely wounded. She escaped from the massacre at Patterson's Rapids.[62]

This camp was made in the usual way, on the smooth prairie, some two hundred yards from the timber of

[62]The woman thus encountered was Justina Kreiger, whose narrative is printed in Bryant and Murch, *A History of the Great Massacre by the Sioux Indians,* pp. 298–323. She and her husband had settled on the Minnesota River, 11 miles above Beaver Creek, in the spring of 1862.

Birch Coolie, with the wagons packed around the camp, and the team horses fastened to the wagons. The horses belonging to the mounted men were fastened to a stout picket rope, between the tents and wagons, around the south half of the camp—Capt. Anderson's tents being behind his horses, and Capt. Grant's tents being inside the wagons, which formed the north half of the camp.

A guard of thirty men and two non-commissioned officers was detailed and organized—ten sentinels being stationed about thirty yards from the wagons, at intervals, around the camp, with instructions to keep a good lookout, and report any noise or other indications of the approach of Indians.

Nothing was reported from the guard, until half past four o'clock, on the morning of September 2d, when one of the guard called out, "Indians," and almost instantly afterward, a shower of balls fell upon the camp. The firing, for probably a minute, was entirely on the part of the Indians, during which time, many of our men were either killed or wounded; but the mortality among the men, at that time, was, by no means, as severe as might be supposed, owing to the protection afforded by the horses.

Capt. Anderson and his company promptly availed themselves of the protection afforded by the wagons near him, and opened fire upon the Indians.

Capt. Grant's company and the fatigue party promptly seized their arms, and commenced firing; but they, for some minutes, continued to expose themselves, imprudently, and, consequently, were very much cut to pieces. After the entire detachment became settled under the shelter of the wagons and dead horses, but few were killed or wounded, and the close firing on our side soon caused the Indians to withdraw to the shelter of the woods.

After the withdrawal of the Indians, the construction of rifle-pits was commenced in different parts of the camp, which, although the men worked with a will, progressed slowly, owing to the hardness of the soil, and the want of proper tools. Three spades, one pick, bayonets, tin pans, etc., constituted our means for excavation; and yet rifle-pits to the extent of about two hundred feet in length were completed. From the time the first rifle-pit was commenced, but one man was killed and two wounded, although the fire of the Indians was continued until the arrival of re-enforcements.

Although the Indians had great advantages over us in the early part of the engagement, I think that the mortality on our side, fearful as it was, did not exceed that of the Indians, judging by the numbers they carried across the prairie from the timber from which they fired. Our men were cool, and had orders to discharge their pieces only when a prospect of hitting a foe was presented.

About two o'clock, on the 2d of September, the report of a cannon, which we were confident was discharged by friends approaching to our relief, was hailed with joy, and as we were then in a condition to laugh at all the attacks of Indians upon our position, we felt confident that they would be cheated of a victory through starvation or thirst.

As the re-enforcements advanced, the Indians began to withdraw from us, and prepare for operations against the approaching force. We could see and hear the Indians, and learned through them that the force was not large, and they hoped to cut it off. This gave us some uneasiness, because we feared the troops might attempt to cross the Birch Coolie about dark; but we soon learned they were halted, and that the Indians proposed to wait until morning to make an attack upon them. In the morning of Sept. 3d, we again observed the manoeuvers of the Indians, and could plainly hear their lamentations at the discovery that you with your entire force had reached Col. McPhail's camp during the night. From that time, the Indians had no hopes of either capturing us or defeating the re-enforcements. Still they kept up a fire on us until your van reached within two or three hundred yards of us.

The Indian force which attacked our camp, I estimate at from two hundred and fifty to three hundred, all well armed and many mounted on good horses.

Enclosed, you will find Capt. Anderson's report, detailing the force, operations, and casualties of his company. His officers and men (with the exceptions he indicates), acted with the utmost coolness and courage. The captain, although twice severely wounded, continued in active command of his company until your re-enforcements reached our camp. To the prompt movements and energetic action of himself, and his officers and men, the early retreat of the Indians from the prairie, is in a great measure due.

Capt. Grant rendered important service in the construction of the main line of rifle-pits. Lieut. Gillam [Harry J. Gillham], of Capt. Grant's company, with a small party, located themselves on the left of Capt. Anderson early in the fight, and did gallant service. Lieut. Jacob E. Baldwin, of the same company, also acted with cool courage in the different portions of the camp where his duties called him. Lieut. Joseph H. Swan, of the 3d infantry (a volunteer), was in charge of a party near and on the left of Lieut. Gillam, where he and his party did good service. Mr. Alex. Faribault, with his son, J. Frazier, and other volunteers, had position on the north portion of the camp, where good service was done during the continuance of the battle. Major Galbraith and Capt. G. D. Redfield, both volunteers, were wounded early in the morning. Maj. Galbraith received two wounds, but continued to assist in the construction of the rifle pits. Lieut. A. J. Patch, (volunteer) and Sergeant William Pratt, of Capt. Grant's company, also rendered valuable service in the defense of the western rifle-pit.

There were wounded, of the volunteers, in addition to those mentioned above, Daniel Blair and Warren DeCamp, the latter very severely. Mr. J. C. Dickenson, of Henderson, and R. Henderson, of Beaver river, also volunteers, left the camp in company with four others at the first fire, and were probably killed. The body of Mr. Henderson was found a short distance from the camp.

Having received no report from Capt. Grant, I am unable to give the names of the killed and wounded of his company, and the fatigue party attached to it.

There were a few men who behaved badly, mostly, I think, teamsters; but with these exceptions, the entire detachment acted with commendable coolness and courage. Probably the desire of Capt. Grant's company to charge upon the Indians, led to their exposure, and consequently so many deaths and wounds. After they took position behind the wagons, but few casualties occurred.

It is a singular fact, that the woman found by Capt. Grant escaped unhurt, although she lay in a high wagon, exposed to the fire of the Indians, and which had several balls pass through it. The killed and wounded were reported to Van on the 3d instant, by Dr. Jared W. Daniels, who accompanied the detachment. That report I believe to be correct.

Every horse belonging to the detachment was killed, excepting six, which were left at the camp, being wounded and unable to travel.

The tents belonging to the detachment were perfectly riddled, one having one hundred and forty ball holes through it. They are unfit for service.

Very respectfully,

Your obedient servant,

JOSEPH R. BROWN,

Maj. Gen., 3d Division Minnesota Volunteer Mil.,

Com. Detachment.[63]

[63]Brown was not a Major General, or even a Major, his courtesy title, "Major," being one commonly applied to Indian Agents, or former Agents. Although a civilian, Sibley may have placed faith in his greater experience of the Indians as compared with Grant and Anderson, and for all practical purposes placed him in command. (The whole Sioux campaign was a rather irregular affair.) This presumably "official" report by Brown is supplemented by the unquestionably official report by Captain Anderson and the reminiscent accounts by Captain Grant and James J. Egan, printed in *Minnesota in the Civil and Indian Wars,* vol. 2, pp. 212–223. A letter by Anderson to his wife, Fort Ridgley, September 4, 1862, was printed in the St. Paul *Pioneer and Democrat* three days later. At the end of a critical discussion of the affair, W. W. Folwell observes, *A History of Minnesota,* vol. 2, pp. 150–156: "Admirable as was the behavior of the men who made the gallant defense at Birch Coulee, nobody now considers it a victory in any sense. The innate cowardice of the Indians alone saved the whole personnel from massacre. The affair may have had the effect, however, of diverting the Indians from an enterprise which might have resulted in much mischief . . ."

CHAPTER XXX

Wandering Refugees

ALONE in the morass, through tangled bottom-land thickets, crawling in tall prairie grass, and subsisting on hazel-nuts for eight days, a mother wandered with her child. Her scant house covering was poor protection from the chill night air, and the dew-beaded grass added to the discomfiture of her ramblings. No Indian trail, even, marked the course to tread; but her eye marked the course of the stars, and her heart sought guidance of Him who "stayeth the rough wind in the day of the east wind." The infant nestled in her bosom had ever been fretful and loud crying. Often she detected the savage foe prowling upon her path. Then she would kneel and pray for deliverance, and that the angels would keep quiet the babe, that its wail reveal not her lurking place — so would the danger pass.

This woman, Mrs. Almira Harrington of Leavenworth, Brown county, had a severe bullet wound in the back. The same ball had killed a man near her and severed a finger from the hand of her infant.

The first night of encampment by the New Ulm cortege on their mournful route to Mankato, she was crawling through the grass towards the encampment when discovered by a picket. He snapped two caps at her before he discovered she was a white woman. But for their defect he would have shot her. This mistake occurred from her hailing him in the Sioux language —he mistaking her for one of the tribe. Her story is thrilling and affecting and given with no ordinary intelligence. Her escape and rescue may be regarded almost a miracle.

The escape of Mrs. Caruthers of Beaver Creek is hardly less remarkable. Two Indians claimed her, both determined to make her *his squaw*. The contest became fierce, each unwilling to yield his right. In the heat of the quarrel one of their squaws, fearful of being supplanted in the affections of her lord, spirited Mrs. Caruthers and her two children off to a cornfield, from whence she made her escape.

After two days and nights with little rest, she reached the Minnesota river, where she found a canoe and tried to paddle herself over. Her frail craft playing funny antics, she laid down "the paddle," and floating on with the drift-wood five or six miles, was providentially thrown on shore near the Fort. She rapped for entrance, with one child in her arms and another on her back.[64]

[64]The narrative of Helen Carrothers (as the name is there given), printed in Bryant and Murch, *A History of the Great Massacre by the Sioux Indians,* pp. 283–297, differs in some respects from Mrs. McConkey's account. According to this narrative, a squaw told her that four Indians wanted to claim her, and when no decision could be reached, Little Crow as umpire decided to kill her. The squaw was ordered to take her into a cornfield, where some Indians would dispose of her. Another Indian came into the field and said she was not going to be killed (which suggests that Little Crow had simply adopted a tactical expedient). A chance offered for her to

An amusing incident occurred with a young lady captive at the Lower Agency. The house of the Episcopal clergyman, Mr. Hinman, had been pillaged, and his clerical robes desecrated to savage use. With the red man, as with many white men, the dress makes the man—hence their increased pomp and stately bearing when new blankets are distributed. No doubt he had looked in some time at the open door when the good man had been ministering at the altar, with an envious eye for his priestly robe. Now it was *his*, he had got it, and he would wear it—he would even honor his fair captive with the escort of his dignified self in pontifical robes. He stalked around, imagining himself the admired of fair eyes, when a witty thought struck him. Turning to Miss ————, he asked if she "belonged to his church?" The ludicrousness of the scene produced an *audible*

escape with her children, and she reached the Minnesota River next day. She was unable to cross with the children, the water being up to her chin, but on the seventh day she found "a board box, pointed at one end and square at the other, nearly filled with water." This, bailed out with a teacup, was her "canoe." On the far shore she took the road to Fort Ridgley, fearful that Little Crow had killed everyone there, and eventually fell in with a German refugee who carried her young daughter while she herself carried her son. "When within half a mile of the fort, Lieutenant Culver and Warren DeCamp came out to meet me, Mr. DeCamp supposing me to be his own wife, until he came within twenty feet of me. We stopped where I met the men from the fort, until some clothing could be brought for me." Wrapped in a blanket, she made her joyous entry into Fort Ridgley, having been out eight days, carrying the two children all the way, except about half a mile.

smile, at which the poor fool was so elated, attributing it to his witticism alone, that he arose in rapture, and for the moment forgot all but himself. The opportunity was seized for escape.[65]

A young man lay all that Monday in concealment. He then moved on till, finding himself nearly surrounded, he crept away in the grass. Here he remained till a heavy rain came on, when he felt he had little to fear. From a high bluff he has surveyed the scene, and no signs of Indian for miles around. Down the hill he rushes but at the base is brought to a halt. One hundred and fifty warriors at least are huddled in the tall grass, not ten feet from him. The noise of the rain prevented detection, and their backs were toward him, blankets drawn over their heads, and heads under their arms. Quick he drops to the ground and commences a worming ascent—hunger and weariness creeping upon him. Another day and night he rests, when again he resorts to the *creeping* process, and finally succeeds in reaching a standing where erect locomotion is comparatively safe.

[65]Another version of this incident is given by Lieutenant-Governor Ignatius Donnelly in a letter to Governor Ramsey, Fort Ridgley, August 29, 1862, printed in the St. Paul *Pioneer and Democrat* four days later: "Rev. Mr. Hinman an Episcopalian Missionary at one of the Agencies escaped to the Fort. Shortly afterwards, and in the midst of all the horrors of the massacre, a woman trying to escape met an Indian strutting around in Mr. Hinman's long, ministerial coat. The savage grinned and asked her if 'she belonged to his church.' The force of the fellow's wit seemed to have so mollified him that he allowed her to escape and she reached the Fort in safety."

Chapter XXXI

The Maniac

WHEN Captains Richard H. Chittenden and Anson Northrup, under Col. McPhail, passed up the Minnesota Valley to raise the siege of Fort Ridgley, they were joined by Charles Nelson, a Swede whose home at Norwegian Grove Settlement was burned the day previous. He had seen the tomahawk cleave the head of his wife. His two little sons he last saw running for the corn, the Indians in close pursuit. He, with bleeding feet, walked twenty-five miles to Henderson, where he met the troops, and supposing himself the only survivor of his family, joined to avenge their fall.

Passing the spot, so late his happy home, he seemed stupefied with grief, and closing the gate of his garden, inquired "When it would be safe to return." *His reason was gone!* This incident incited the following lines a few days after, while Captain Chittenden was seated under the Falls of Minne-ha-ha, which our nation's poet has immortalized in his wondrous (?) song of Hiawatha:

> Minne-ha-ha, laughing water,
>   Cease thy laughing now for aye,
> Savage hands are red with slaughter
>   Of the innocent to-day.
>
> Ill accords thy sportive humor
>   With their last despairing wail;
> While thou'rt dancing in the sunbeam,
>   Mangled corpses strew the vale.

Change thy note, gay Minne-ha-ha;
  Let some sadder strain prevail—
Listen, while a maniac wanderer
  Sighs to thee his woeful tale:

"Give me back my Lela's tresses,
  Let me kiss them once again!
She who blest me with caresses,
  Lies unburied on the plain!

"See yon smoke; there was my dwelling;
  That is all I have of home!
Hark! I hear their fiendish yelling,
  As I houseless, childless roam!

"Have they killed my Hans and Otto?
  Did they find them in the corn?
Go and tell that savage monster,
  Not to slay my youngest born.

"Yonder is my new-bought reaper,
  Standing 'mid the ripened grain,
E'en my cow asks why I leave her
  Wand'ring unmilked o'er the plain!

"Soldier, bury here my Lela;
  Place me also 'neath the sod;
Long we lived and wrought together—
  Let me die with her—O God!

"Faithful Fido, you they've left me;
  Can you tell me, Fido, why
God at once has thus bereft me?
  All I ask is here to die.

"O, my daughter Jenny, darling!
  Worse than death is Jenny's fate!"

*   *   *

Nelson, as our troops were leaving,
  Turned and shut his garden gate.

Chapter XXXII

Tales of Suffering

BEFORE the protracted engagement of Birch Coolie, Capt. Grant found a woman and four children in the swamp, who, for three weeks had subsisted on nuts and wild plums. They had seen no fire, found no covering while rains had beat and fierce winds blowed, their tattered garments hardly sufficient for covering, and the chill night air piercing to their very vitals. During this time she had given premature birth to an infant which her own hands had buried. Exhaustion and constant fear made her a half wild woman, and she endeavored to elude her rescuers by crawling deeper into the morass. For some time she could not be made to understand that they were friends.

She had seen her husband and two children butchered, and her own back was the receptacle of seventeen buck-shot, not removed till after she was brought to St. Paul. Three were lodged in the bone, and none had entered the vitals, it having been a side shot. By superhuman effort, she and her two remaining children eluded her pursuers, and to her own were added two others, of a slain neighbor. Day and night, these four little ones clung to her, begging for food and shivering with cold. She had not expected ever again to see a white person, believing herself the only one living in all that region.

During the memorable thirty-six hours of Birch Coolie, this poor woman, with the children, was lying quietly, as if fear and suffering had paralyzed the senses, in a wagon, protected only by a tent canvas. Several balls passed through the wagon box. Gradually she came to realize the change in her condition, and appreciate the comparative comfort and kindness she received.[66]

Soon after the war whoop had rung through the State, the citizens of Saint Paul were startled by the bringing hither of two shockingly mutilated children, the first exhibition we had seen of savage barbarity. Four children were alone in the house, two of whom were killed outright, and the other two left, one of eleven years, with fourteen frightful tomahawk gashes about the breast, arms and head — the other, a mere baby, had three severe cuts on the head and face. No human skill could save them.

The mother, with four other persons, was out of the house when the attack was made. Those with her were killed, and she barely escaped. The father, after a day's absence, returns to find his mangled children lying upon the floor, and all in silence save the groans of the two in whom life yet lingered. How his soul yearned for the presence of her who doubled his joys and divided his sorrows; nor was he long to endure

[66]Mrs. Kreiger's narrative, as cited in Note 62, makes it clear that she was alone in the post-massacre adventures described, only reunited with some of her surviving children after reaching Fort Ridgley; and clearly there was no miscarriage as described.

the suspense. She crawled from concealment, when night made it safe. But there is no time for tears or even the burial of their dead — they must fly with the mangled living.

A detachment of soldiers sent up the Big Cottonwood for the purpose buried nine bodies, all terribly decomposed.

One man, evidently surprised at his meal, had fallen forward on the table. A woman was lying across a wagon-rack, near the body of a man, doubtless her husband, with his head cut off and several bullet-holes in his body. A child was found nailed through its hands and feet to a tree. Another literally skinned! O, the horrors of savage butchery!

The first process of torture is usually to strip off clothes, and the varied and cruel modes would seem incredible, were they not authenticated beyond dispute; but we withhold the most sickening pictures. The most horrid features of this Indian war will never be written.

A wife and several small children were butchered before the eyes of the husband and father, he being detained for the purpose. Hastening the advent of her infant, they threw it around her neck as she was bound to the tree, and to the husband said, "there, you go to St. Paul and tell them we are going to serve all the women there the same."

On the 27th of October, two months after quiet had been restored, and troops were encamped at Yellow Medicine, two emaciated figures were brought into camp. They were Mrs. Boetler and her child, three years old, who had wandered since the outbreak, not having seen a human being. There is no power in language to convey what she suffered, never seeing fire, and living mainly on raw potatoes, till from extreme weakness she could not speak above a whisper. She made her escape with three children, two of whom died from starvation. With her own hands she dug their graves in the sand and heaped them up with leaves. The little girl who lived was as weak and emaciated as herself, but with good nursing physical vigor returned.[67]

The foraging party which brought Mrs. Boetler into camp buried forty-seven bodies, and left seventeen unburied. There is little doubt but hundreds have been left unfound, while houseless wanderers roamed here and there, till the last shred of clothing gone, and cold weather upon them, they lay down to die.

[67]Justina Boelter's narrative is printed in Bryant and Murch, *A History of the Great Massacre by the Sioux Indians,* pp. 324-335. She escaped the massacre with two children, not three. The eldest died of starvation after five weeks in hiding, but Mrs. Boelter was too weak either to bury the child or to leave the vicinity. She subsisted on grape vines and a few potatoes until found by the troops. Mrs. McConkey's account is based on a brief story in the St. Peter *Tribune,* November 4, 1862, quoted in Bryant and Murch, p. 335.

Chapter XXXIII

The Athenaeum

SO vigorous were the efforts of our troops that ere one month had passed fears were subdued, and alarms ceased, save in night-mare dreams.

Minnesotians had never anticipated that her fairest portions would be drenched with blood, or that the most remote frontiersman needed any stronger protection than his own powerful arm. The Indians, we all thought, would never dare molest a settler. Too late have they awakened to the need of strong frontier defenses—a cordon of military posts extending from the Red river of the North to the Red river of the South.

The *direct* loss by savage hands was not much less than that occasioned by the panic and flight. Many of the dead found on our prairies were the victims of starvation, after having fled the actual danger.

Scarcely a town but gave shelter to the homeless; citizens opened their dwellings to give comfort and solace to the stricken ones. Societies were formed for their relief, food and clothing provided without stint, and for many weeks large donations from eastern cities, in money and goods, were daily received by the committees, and distributed to each "as they had need." The thanks of Minnesotians are due, and given, for the prompt relief of these suffering thousands.

Take one example. The vast German Athenaeum of St. Paul was given up to refugees. Benevolent hearts were devoted to their needs. Of that one-roomed community, more than one half were children. Arrivals and departures were of daily occurrence, and some days five hundred persons were there to be fed, and many clothed. Sleeping arrangements had to be provided, and, as the weather was becoming colder, there was a large demand for bed coverings.

Many spoke only a foreign tongue. A striking characteristic of all was the seeming extreme age — lines of grief and care. Nor is it strange. Most had been reduced from competence to penury. One day, and O! how changed! Farms are dreary wastes, the stock driven off or roam over the prairies, houses and barns pillaged or a heap of smouldering ruins, and the family ranks invaded by ghastly death.

Here at the Athenaeum is one family, whose home, just without the village of New Ulm, was the admiration of all. Their carriage and elegant matched horses were conspicuous during the besieging of that town; for their buildings had all been burned, and their valuables seized. Their broad acres were now one desolate waste, over which the cattle roamed uncared for, and several thousands in money and promissory notes were burned with the house. But the family circle was unbroken.

One little child, with violet eyes, of deep meaning, the only living member of its family, is being nursed by a self-constituted foster-mother. This woman was fleeing from those whose war-whoop was ringing in her ears, when she fell prostrate. Regaining her feet, she cast her eyes backward for the cause of her downfall. The fall, rise, and seizure of the child was but the work of an instant, and she soon eluded pursuit. Then she first looks upon the child. Its mother, whom she knew to have been killed, was a dear friend. The story being told, this darling baby elicited no little interest, and many of our best citizens desired to adopt him. But the foster-mother said "nay," its grand-parents were its rightful claimants.

Another, with an eye of more than ordinary intelligence, lady-like deportment, had opened her house to the men who so nobly fought in defense of New Ulm, till the excitement of the conflict obliged her to take her couch. Thus helpless she lay while the bullets whizzed and rattled upon the walls. At last, necessity forced firing the dwelling for better range of the foe. Hurried by her husband, she caught an ordinary dress, which was just thrown on, slipped her stockingless feet into slippers and ran out the front door as the savages entered the rear. Her bright boy of ten years and her husband were saved, so she bore in silence the loss of all else.

Here is another; her husband died in her arms from a wound, a few hours after the battle. Her aged mother and herself try in vain to hush the plaintive cry of the children in their arms, both mere infants, but recently "so rosy and fat," now so squalid and pale. The garments they wore had become mere shreds, their place supplied by those of coarser texture than ever worn before. Her home a heap of ashes, she sobs, "all would be nothing if he were only here." Though scarcely thirty, she looked like an aged grandmother of her own children, so terrible is such sudden grief.

As soon as possible, all who desired it were furnished homes, either from private bounty or public resources.

Chapter XXXIV

The Captive's Experience as Further Related by Himself

"WE remained at Little Crow's village five days, during which time all the Indians who had their villages below that place, moved up to our encampment, and in those five days the country for miles around was visited by the warriors, who dealt death and destruction to every person or thing within their reach. A great many female prisoners were brought in every day. I [George Spencer] was the only white man ever taken and spared.

"There were three or four Canadians who had resided among the Indians a great many years, who had married Indian women and had children grown, who re-married with them; but they were not considered as prisoners, as they were allowed to retain their teams and other property. One of these men is said to have made his escape to the whites, but returned to his Indian family again after a few days.

"The attacks on New Ulm and Fort Ridgley were made while we were at this village, and after being convinced that they could not reduce the Fort, they made preparations for a move.

"In a short time the lodges were all struck, and their entire camp was in motion. A great many wagons were broken down on the journey in consequence of their being so heavily loaded. They supposed, of course, that a white man's wagon could carry all that could be piled on to it.

"As I was too badly hurt to walk, my friend got me a place to ride in a small one horse wagon, while he walked along by my side. The train of horses, wagons, etc., I should judge was about three miles long. After crossing the Red Wood river we had proceeded about three miles, when the body of a white man was pointed out to me, lying near the side of the road, upon his face. I got out to look at it, but it was so much swollen I could not have recognized it. But upon the shirt collar I read the name of 'Geo. H. Gleason.' He had then been dead about a week. Poor fellow, he had not a personal enemy among the whole tribe, but was universally beloved by all, both whites and Indians, but those savage fiends had sworn to spare none, not even women nor helpless children.

"About three o'clock of the second day's march we arrived at Yellow Medicine, where a large encampment in shape of a circle was formed, with the 'Ti-zo-ti,' or Soldier's lodge in the centre.

"I would here add that this Soldier's lodge, being composed of the bravest and wisest, governs the tribe. Their word is law, and from their decision there is no appeal. To it the chief must submit in silence.

"Here the Mission houses, the Agency buildings, and the house of Other Day were fired, also some other houses belonging to the farmer Indians.

"We remained here about two weeks, during which time the battle with Capt. Strout's company was fought and the battle of Birch Coolie. Here, also, Gen. Sibley succeeded in opening correspondence with Little Crow. It was here, also, that Mrs. Adams was brought in a captive, some particulars of which will be found elsewhere."

From this point two messengers were dispatched north, south, and west, as spoken of elsewhere, and from here he sent word to his friends that he was still alive.

Chapter XXXV

Efforts to Regain the Prisoners

UNTIL after the battle of Birch Coolie, the Sioux had no doubt of final success. But a reaction comes. The whites have not all gone South, and those that remained had given demonstrations of their fighting qualities. Little Crow feels his influence on the wane, and is often obliged to hide himself at night to escape his dissatisfied soldiers; in the morning he convenes a council and all are ready to do his bidding, after he has feasted them to their full content.

Colonel Sibley had left a note attached to a stake on the Birch Coolie battle ground, as follows:

"If Little Crow has any proposition to make to me, let him send a half-breed to me, and he shall be protected in and out of my camp.

H. H. SIBLEY,
Col. Commanding Military Expedition.

The note was found and given to their male captive to be read to them. Little Crow desired him to pen the reply he would dictate, but his arm, broken by the bullet, was not yet well. He declined, but sent by the flag of truce a message to his friends "that he was alive." The following is Little Crow's letter:

"Yellow Medicine, Sept. 7, 1862.
"DEAR SIR:—For what reason we have commenced this war, I will tell you. It is on account of Major Galbraith, we made a treaty with the Government a beg for what

little we do get and then can't get it till our children are dieing with hunger. It was with the traders that commence. Mr. A. J. Myrick told the Indians they would eat grass or their own dung, then Mr. Forbes told the lower Sioux that were not men then Robert he was making with his friends how to defraud us of our money, if the young braves have push the white man, I have done this myself; So I want you to let the Governor Ramsey know this. I have a great many prisoners women and children it aint all our fault the Winnebagoes was in the engagement, two of them was killed. I want you to give me answer by bearer all at present.

Yours truly,

his

LITTLE × CROW,

mark."

The following day the truce bearers returned with the reply:

"LITTLE CROW:—You have murdered many of our people without any sufficient cause. Return me the prisoners, under a flag of truce, and I will talk to you like a man.

H. H. SIBLEY,
Col. Commanding Military Expedition."

The above was not in accordance with the warrior Chieftain's ideas, and the prisoners were still "held in durance vile."[68]

[68]This correspondence is also printed in Heard, *History of the Sioux War,* pp. 147-148, with grammar and spelling somewhat improved. Sibley wrote his wife on September 8, telling of the exchange of letters. "The half breed bearers of the flag of truce, both of whom I know, say that the mixed bloods, with their families, are not permitted to leave the Camp, and are

The soldiers, the people and the press became impatient for the expedition to proceed. Col. Sibley was charged with negligence and a desire to favor the Indians. Still he kept his own counsels, unmoved by calumny. He knew his men were undisciplined recruits, but never an army composed of better material. Halls of science, business houses and churches had contributed to the list. They must not be sacrificed, and to rush unprepared upon the enemy was madness. Besides, he knew the Indians well—he knew, too, what would probably be the fate of the prisoners, should he be precipitate. Had the attack on them been made before they deserted their camp, it was their design to tomahawk every captive. This was not considered by his impatient slanderers, whose tongues were afterwards silenced, when they saw the wisdom of his plans and his courage in braving censure.[69]

---

virtually prisoners, as most of them are believed to sympathise with the whites. They assure me that the Indians are determined to give us battle, at or near the Yellow Medicine, and are sanguine of success. I sincerely hope they will not change their programme." (Sibley Papers, Minnesota Historical Society).

[69]Sibley wrote his wife on September 10: "We are still awaiting the result of my message to Little Crow, demanding the delivery of the white captives, and I expect a flag of truce today. This question embarrasses me very much, for if I should make an advance movement, two or three hundred white women, and children, might be murdered in cold blood. I must use what craft I possess, to get these poor creatures out of the possession of the red devils, and then pursue the latter with fire and sword. I am also in want of cartridges,

hard bread, and clothing for the soldiers, which I hope will be forthcoming very soon." Next day, having received dispatches from below, he wrote: "Since the affair of Birch Cooley in which our men were attacked, and lost so many in killed, and wounded, the howlers in St. Paul seem to be checked in their onslaughts, as they find that the job we have undertaken, is far from being an insignificant one, and that my policy is the only one, to save the settlements" (Sibley Papers, Minnesota Historical Society).

Chapter XXXVI

Correspondence Between Col. Sibley and Little Crow

IT was hoped that the checks given the Sioux would cause the cessation of hostilities and the delivery of the captives. But always, in their mode of warfare, danger is nigh when least expected. Fair, open field fight is avoided.[70] Small squads prowl through the country on fleet stolen horses striking where they can.

Coursing down the Minnesota valley, we find them in Blue Earth county on the 12th September, committing depredations and murders where comparative security was felt, and no supposition of an Indian within fifty miles. Four men, after taking their families to a place of safety, had returned to secure their crops, as many others had done, and were murdered within one mile of a military company stationed there for the protection of the neighborhood.

On the 12th of Sept. another communication from Little Crow was received at the "head-quarters." The bearer of the dispatch had a secret for Col. Sibley's ear—*a dissatisfaction had arisen in camp,* confirmed by a private letter secretly brought, and it was evident that the war party among the Indians had determined

[70]So might have said the British column, sniped at from any available cover, on its retreat from Concord and Lexington in April, 1775.

BRIG. GEN. HENRY H. SIBLEY

on a desperate stand. We give below Little Crow's
second letter to Gen. Sibley:

"Red Iron Village, or
Way-au-akan.

"To Hon. H. H. Sibley:

"we have in ma-wa-kan-ton band one hundred and
fifty-five presoners—not included the Sisitons and war-
peton presoners, then we are waiting for the Sisiton what
we are going to do with the prisoners they are coming
down—they are at Lake quiparle now, the words that I
want to the governel il want to here from him also, and
I want to know from you as a friend what way that il can
make peace for my people—in regard to presoners they
fair with our children or our self just as well as us.

"Your truly friend,
"LITTLE CROW."

We append the answer.

"Head-quarters Military Expedition,⎱
Sept. 12, 1862.   ⎰

"To Little Crow, Sioux Chief:

"I have received your letter to-day. You have not done
as I wished in giving up the prisoners taken by your people. It would be better for you to do so. I told you I had
sent your former letter to Gov. Ramsey, but I have not
yet had time to receive a reply. You have allowed your
young men to commit some murders since you wrote
your first letter. This is not the way to make peace.

H. H. SIBLEY,
Col. Com. Mil. Expedition."[71]

[71]There are slight textual differences in these letters as
printed in Heard, *History of the Sioux War,* pp. 148-149.
Heard has Sibley speak of "nine" murders committed since
the first letter, and at the end of Little Crow's letter adds,

The following is the *private* letter received at the same time as the other.

"Way-awa-kan, Sept. 10, '62.
"Col. H. H. Sibley, Fort Ridgley:

"Dear Sir:—You know that Little Crow has been opposed to me in everything that our people have had to do with the whites. He has been opposed to everything in the form of civilization and christianity. I have always been in favor of, and of late years have done everything of the kind that has been offered to us by the Government and other good white people—he has now got himself into trouble that we know he can never get himself out of, and he is trying to involve those in the murder of the poor whites that have been settled in the border; but I have been kept back with threats that I should be killed if I did anything to help the whites. But if you will now appoint some place for me to meet you, myself

---

"per A. J. Campbell." This source relates that at the same time the letter was received from Little Crow, "Mr. Robertson, one of the messengers from that chief, brought privately and in a clandestine manner" the note from "Wabasha and Taopee, one of the Farmer Indians." Thomas A. Robertson, who carried this note, said in later reminiscences that the letter signed by Wabasha and Taopee was actually written by himself, at the dictation of Good Thunder, a Christian Indian. See W. W. Folwell, *A History of Minnesota,* vol. 2, p. 173. Sibley wrote his wife on September 13: "I have nearly perfected my arrangements, and intend to move on the 15th with between fifteen and sixteen hundred men. I have another communication from Little Crow, and the bearers of the flag of truce state that there is a party in his camp who are opposed to the war, and deny any participation in the murders and other outrages. Little Crow evidently begins to quake. His camp is only about sixty miles from here, and I expect to reach, and fight him, within a week."

and the few friends that I have will get all the prisoners that we can, and with our families go to whatever place you will appoint for us to meet.

"I would say further, that the mouth of the Red Wood, Candiohi on the north side of the Minnesota, or the head of the Cottonwood river—one of these three places, I think, would be a good place to meet.

"Return the messenger as quick as possible, we have not much time to spare.

"Your true friend,
"WABASHA,
"TAOPEE."

Col. Sibley returned answer as follows:

"Head-quarters Mil. Expedition,
Sept. 12, 1862.

"*To Wabasha and Taopee:*

"I have received your private message. I have come up here with a large force to punish the murderers of my people. It was not my purpose to injure any innocent person. If you and others who have not been concerned in the murders and expeditions, will gather yourselves, with all the prisoners, on the prairie in full sight of my troops, and when the white flag is displayed by you, a white flag will be hoisted in my camp, and then you can come forward and place yourselves under my protection. My troops will be all mounted in two days' time, and in three days from this day I expect to march. There must be no attempt to approach my column or my camp, except in open day, and with a flag of truce conspicuously displayed. I shall be glad to receive all true friends of the whites with as many prisoners as they can bring, and I am powerful enough to crush all who attempt to oppose my march, and to punish those who have washed their hands in innocent blood.

"I sign myself the friend of all who were friends of your great American Father.

"H. H. SIBLEY,
"Col. Com. Mil. Expedition."

As soon as the Expedition was provided with "bread and bullets for ten days in advance," the Col. issued his marching orders, and on the 18th of September crossed the Minnesota river opposite the Fort, nearly two thousand strong, and in mud and rain pushed on for the climax.

On their route the main body found and buried the body of Philander Prescott, an esteemed Christian who for more than thirty years had been employed as interpreter, one of the first victims of savage wrath. His history is full of interest. When a young man he had found his way into the Sioux country, where he adopted the habits, customs and costume of the tribe. He had married a squaw who bore him several children, who were growing up in ignorance. Thus he lived and thus he might have died, had not the Holy Spirit revived the religious impressions of childhood. The man could not leave his wife and children in heathen darkness, and therefore came to the frontier and engaged as Interpreter, first at Fort Snelling and later at the new Agencies. His family everywhere commanded respect. When the trouble commenced, his wife hid him in an oven, where he remained till danger seemed over. Then he started for the Fort, shuddering at the tokens of savage wrath which met his eye. But the savage hounds were upon his track, and his soul basks in the light of eternal day.[72]

[72]Philander Prescott's "Autobiography and Reminiscences," dated at Minnehaha, Minn., February 18, 1861, is printed in *Minnesota Historical Collections*, 1894, vol. 6, pp. 475-491. He had come to Minnesota in the spring of 1820, then in his twentieth year.

Chapter XXXVII

Battle of Wood Lake

COL. Sibley's force was camped on Wood Lake, three miles below the Yellow Medicine Agency. Thus far had they come unmolested but frequently mangled and decaying bodies met the eye. Wherever encampments had been, the ground was strewn with empty trunks, boxes, barrels, fruit and oyster cans, and various other indications of spoils.

A scouting party, among whom was Other-Day, was sent forward on the 21st Sept. They hitched their horses for reconnoissance of the deserted Indian houses. A horse galloped up riderless, and Other-Day hastened out just in time to see an Indian riding off his own horse at full speed. His fire was without effect.

Where he was murdered was found the body of George Gleason, one of the victims of the first day's massacre. There was little else than a dried skeleton. His skull was broken in, and all his clothes gone, save his drawers and shirt. Some gold buttons with his initials, which the savages had overlooked, were the means of identity. Around him were fragments of dispatches he was carrying to the Lower Agency, and other papers. With sad hearts they heaped earth over the remains of their friend. When all terror had fled that region, he was removed by Masonic friends to Shakopee, where the rites of Christian burial were given him.[73]

A daring warrior came to the opposite shore the night previous to battle and counted the tents of Col. Sibley's camp. Seeing but forty-eight, he estimated a force of only three hundred men. *Their* number was seven hundred and eighty, so they felt safe in risking a battle. The "braves" overruled a night attack, reminding their chief of his boast that he could whip the white men. Say they, "let's show them by open day-light that we *can* do it." Crow's plan was to attack with a small force in front, sufficient to draw them from the ravine. At a signal ambushed Indians were to seize the baggage wagons and shoot the drivers. So confident was he of success that their women were brought down to the opposite side of the river to carry off the spoils, while the men should do the butchering and *make a clean sweep* of the camp.

Early on the morning of the 23d a foraging party

[73]A correspondent wrote from Camp Sibley, October 25, 1862, to the St. Paul *Pioneer,* November 4, 1862: "During the day (while marching from Camp Relief) we passed poor Gleason's grave. He lies close to the road, on the left hand side coming down—20 miles from Yellow Medicine. We buried him on our upward march; he was then nearly wasted away to a skeleton: a large stone was imbedded in his skull.

"Some of his clothes were still on him, and on his shirt the Indians had left his gold sleeve buttons. I knew them in a moment, having often seen him wear them. One of the boys took them away to send them to his relatives . . . . Gay, jocund, genial fellow, the very soul of mirth and humor, he will long, long, be remembered among the victims of the murderous savages . . . . "

was surprised, and conveyed the alarm to camp while it was breakfasting. The Renville Rangers, under Lieutenant James Gorman, were sent to their support. In a few moments the surrounding bluffs were covered with Indians, on horse and foot, trying to circumvent the camp. The Third Regiment followed in support of the Rangers, who pushed on a mile in advance, were nearly surrounded, and barely effected a retreat. The artillery kept the opposite shore of the lake clear. Two companies of the Sixth had a skirmish on the left, and the Seventh Regiment, under Lieut. Col. William R. Marshall, made a gallant charge into a ravine on the right, and drove the enemy from shelter there. This charge is pronounced by all one of the most valiant and successful ever made. When we reflect that it was by an undisciplined regiment, not two months from the quiet of home life, and most of them in their first fight, we marvel that the Col. Marshall had not been left in ghastly death instead of leading his men out of that ravine, gloriously victorious.

Other-Day proved himself true as steel, and of great courage. He rushed in amongst the Indians; and several times being mistaken for an enemy, was fired at by our men. After he had shot three Indians, he was led triumphantly into camp with two captured ponies, which more than squared up the loss of his own horse.

During the fight, Little Crow was seen in the distance riding a black horse with a spy glass in his hand, to see how the war was waging. It was a complete repulse to the Sioux, from this time thoroughly convinced that the despised whites were more than a match for them.

Had the cavalry force been sufficient, the whole band might have been destroyed or made prisoners. They being nearly naked, with no incumbrance but their guns and powder flasks, soon outdistanced the infantry. But the back bone of the outbreak was broken—the power of Little Crow vanished, and they sought safety by flight.

The aspect of affairs, as Col. Sibley moved up the Minnesota valley, was extremely threatening, and the difficulties under which he labored of no ordinary nature. Had he yielded to the almost unanimous desire of the people to advance before being fully prepared, and his command been defeated or even repulsed, there would have been a general uprising of all the savages on our border, embracing not only the Dakota bands but the Chippewas and Winnebagoes also, which would have resulted in a repetition upon a larger scale of the murders and outrages committed by the lower bands of Dakotas. The peril to the whole State of a premature movement was constantly present to his mind, and controlled every action throughout. The obstinately contested but successful battle of Wood Lake broke the power of the savage, demoralized the hostile bands, and relieved the entire frontier.[74]

[74]Sibley's official account of the Battle of Wood Lake comprises the next chapter. He had been prevented from advancing toward this climactic scene of the Sioux campaign of 1862 by heavy rain, but on September 17 wrote his wife: "It has

cleared off at last, and tomorrow, we shall cross to the south side of the Minnesota River, and go in search of my *friend* Little Crow, with whom I have kept up a correspondence, and now have a 'crow to pick.' The rascal avows himself the leader in the recent raids upon the whites, but I learn from the bearers of the flag of truce, that many of the savages are opposed to him, and disavow any participation in the outrages. They want to play 'good Indian,' but they must separate from the 'unclean thing,' or share the same fate. Unfortunately, the horsemen not being regularly enlisted, have to the number of two or three hundred, skedaddled in view of dangerous service, leaving me with only twenty-five or thirty of the description of force. If I had a few hundreds of trained cavalry, I could bring the whole matter to a speedy conclusion; as it is, the Indians instead of fighting as they now threaten, may escape from the infantry, and lead us a weary chase in the wide prairie."

After the battle, he wrote again on September 23, dating his letter Wood Lake, 45 miles above Ridgley: "Here we are, far in the enemy's country, and I suppose you are much troubled on my account. Thanks to a kind Providence, I have passed through a sharp battle today without injury, although the balls flew thick around us. About 300 Indians attacked us this morning, and after a desperate fight of two hours, we whipped them handsomely, killed twenty-five or thirty of their warriors, and wounded a large number, with a loss on our side of four men killed outright, and thirty-five or forty wounded, more or less seriously. We have inflicted so severe a blow upon the red devils, that they will not dare to make another stand. They sent in a flag of truce by a half-breed, offering to surrender, if I would promise them immunity from punishment, and would allow them to carry off their dead, both of which conditions were peremptorily refused."

Sibley's letters to his wife are quoted here, as yielding the most insight into his private feelings. A file of his official letters sent, September 12-October 21, 1862, is in the National Archives, Records of the War Department, U. S. Army Commands, Department of the North-West. In the same archive are letters to and from Pope's departmental headquarters in St. Paul, beginning September 16, 1862.

Chapter XXXVIII

Col. Sibley's Dispatch to Gov. Ramsey

Wood Lake, near Yellow Medicine,
September 23, 1862.

To His Excellency, Gov. Ramsey:[75]

Sir: I left the camp at Fort Ridgley on the 12th inst., with my command, and reached this point early in the afternoon of the 22d. There have been small parties of Indians each day in plain sight, evidently acting as scouts for the main body. This morning I had determined to cross the Yellow Medicine river, about three miles distant, and there await the arrival of Capt. Henry C. Rogers' company, of the Seventh Regiment, which was ordered by me from New Ulm, to join me by a forced march, the presence of the company there being unnecessary by the arrival there of another company, a few days previous.

About seven o'clock this morning, the camp was attacked by about three hundred Indians, who suddenly made their appearance and dashed down toward us, whooping and yelling in their usual style, and firing with great rapidity.

The Renville Guards, under Lieutenant James Gorman, were sent by me to check them, and Major A. E. Welch, of the Third Regiment, was instantly in

[75]This text is officially printed (with slight variations in the wording) in *Minnesota in the Civil and Indian Wars,* vol. 2, pp. 240-242.

line with his command, with his skirmishers in the advance, by whom the savages were gallantly met, and after a conflict of a serious nature, repulsed.

Meanwhile another portion of the Indian force passed down a ravine on the right, with a view to outflank the Third regiment, and I ordered Lieut. Colonel William R. Marshall, with five companies of the Seventh Regiment and who was ably seconded by Major George Bradley, to advance to its support, with one six-pounder under the command of Capt. Mark Hendricks, and I also ordered two companies of the Sixth Regiment to re-enforce him.

Lieut. Col. Marshall advanced at a double-quick, amidst a shower of balls from the enemy, which fortunately, did little damage to his command; and after a few volleys, he led his men to a charge, and cleared the ravine of the savages.

Major Robert N. McLaren, with Capt. Horace B. Wilson's company, took position on the extreme left of the camp, where he kept at bay a party of the enemy who were endeavoring to gain the rear of the camp, and finally drove them back.

The battle raged for about two hours, the six-pounder and mountain-howitzer being used with great effect, when the Indians—repulsed at all points with great loss,—retired with great precipitation.

I regret to state that many casualties occurred on our side. The gallant Major Welch was badly wounded in the leg, and Capt. Wilson, of the Sixth Regiment, was severely bruised by a nearly spent ball in the shoulder. Four of our men were killed, and between thirty and forty wounded, most of them, I am rejoiced, to say, not severely.

The loss of the enemy, according to the statement of a half-breed, named Jos. Campbell, who visited the camp under a flag of truce, was thirty killed and a large number wounded. We found and buried fourteen of the bodies, and as the habit of the Indians is to carry off the bodies of their slain, it is not probable that the sum told by Campbell was exaggerated.

The severe chastisement inflicted upon them has so far subdued their ardor that they sent a flag of truce into the camp to express the sentiment of the Wahpetons, composing a part of the attacking force, and to state that they were not strong enough to fight us, and desired peace, with permission to take away their dead and wounded. I replied that when the prisoners were delivered up, it would be time enough to talk of peace, and that I would not grant them permission either to take their dead or wounded.

I am assured by Campbell that there is serious depression in the Indian camp—many having been opposed to the war, but driven into the field by the more violent. He further stated that eight hundred Indians were assembled at the Yellow Medicine, within two miles of the camp, but that the greater part took no part in the fight. The intention of Little Crow was to attack us last night, but he was overruled by others, who told him if he was a brave man, he ought to fight the white man by daylight. I am fully prepared against night attack, should it be attempted, although I think the lesson received by them to-day, will make them very cautious for the future.

I have already adverted to the courage and skill of Lieut. Col. Marshall, and Majors Welch and Bradley, to which I beg leave to add those of the officers and men under their respective commands. Lieut. Col. John T. Averill and Major McLaren were equally prompt in their movements in preparing the Sixth Regiment for action, and were both under fire for some time. Capts. Hiram P. Grant and Carlyle Bromley shared the dangers of the field with Lieut. Col. Marshall's command, while Capt. Wilson, with his command, rendered efficient service. The other companies of the Sixth Regiment were not engaged, having been held in position to defend the rear of the camp, but it was difficult to restrain their ardor, so anxious were officers and men to share with their comrades the perils of the field. To Lieut. Col. Fowler, my A.A.A.G., I have been greatly indebted for aid in all my movements — his military knowledge and ability being invaluable to me, and his assistance in to-day's affair particularly so. To Major William H. Forbes, Messrs. Patch, Greig, and McLeod, of my staff, who carried my orders, I must also acknowledge myself under obligations for their activity and zeal, while to Major J. R. Brown, also of my staff, though suffering from illness, it would be injustice not to state that he aided me materially by his exertions and advice. The medical staff of the several regiments were cool and expert in rendering their professional aid to the wounded. Assistant Surgeon Seigneuret, attached to my staff, is to be commended for his skill and diligence.

I am very much in want of bread rations, six-pounder ammunition, and shells for the howitzer, and unless soon supplied, I shall be compelled to fall back, which, under present circumstances, would be a calamity, as it would afford time for the escape of the Indians with their captives. I hope a large body of cavalry is, before this, on their way to join us. If I had been provided with five hundred of this description of force to-day, I venture the assertion that I could have killed the greater part of the Indians, and brought the campaign to a successful close.

Rev. Mr. Stephen R. Riggs, chaplain of the expedition, so well known for his knowledge of the character and language of the Indians, has been of great service to me since he joined my command.

I enclose the official report of Lieut. Col. Marshall. I omitted to mention Lieut. Gorman and his corps of Renville Rangers. They have been extremely useful to me by their courage and skill as skirmishers. Captain Hendricks and his artillerists won deserved praise to-day, and Capt. J. R. Sterrett, with his small but gallant corps of cavalry, twenty-seven in number, did good service also.

I send reports of the several Surgeons, embracing lists of the killed and wounded.

Very respectfully, your ob't serv't,

H. H. SIBLEY,
Col. Commanding.

Chapter XXXIX

The Chippewas

WHILE these barbarities were being enacted in the west and southwest, "tidings out of the north" troubled the Capital. Indeed, all the surrounding counties are astir, for rumor says the Chippewas have joined hands with their hated enemies the Sioux, and henceforth they will do battle together for the extermination of the whites — that Agent Walker has wronged them, and they will have redress. All this is not without foundation, and ere the excitement has reached its acme, Agent Walker shoots himself, some say under the excitement of an insane mind, and more uncharitable ones from fear of his doings being fathomed.[76]

At this juncture Hole-in-the-day, the head Chief, issued a proclamation that he would not be responsible for the conduct of his people after ten days, and desired all white settlers to leave the country. The Sioux raid had already depopulated many of the fairest portions of the upper country, and now the

[76]For a critical discussion of the "Chippewa Disturbance of 1862," see W.W. Folwell, *A History of Minnesota,* vol. 2, pp. 374-382. An interesting personal account, written in 1887, is George W. Sweet, "Incidents of the Threatened Outbreak of Hole-in-the-Day and other Ojibways at Time of Sioux Massacre of 1862," *Minnesota Historical Collections,* 1894, vol. 6, pp. 401-408. The Chippewa Agent, Lucius C. Walker, shot himself on August 22, 1862.

few remaining on the Chippewa reservation fled to Fort Ripley or Abercrombie for protection even then crowded with refugees.

A messenger came from Hole-in-the-day to Commissioner Dole, asking him to come with Judge Cooper and make a treaty. These, with Senator Wilkinson and Paymaster Thompson, went at once. It was said that Hole-in-the-day had assured his people that we had all we could manage with our brethren the South, and if they pleased to combine with the Sioux, their power would not be resisted. There surely was cause for alarm—alarm for the safety of the State, alarm for the fleeing inhabitant.

In due time, with a strong armed force, the embassy seat themselves in council, at once surrounded by a still stronger force of Chippewas, to their minds bidding defiance to all treaty efforts. Two or three days were consumed, each retaining its military force on the ground, and refusing to be first to withdraw. A messenger was dispatched to Gov. Ramsey to make all haste to the council. He, with two or three others, was soon under way, and met Commissioner Dole, who considered himself fortunate in having escaped with his life. He deemed it hazardous in the extreme, going without a military escort. Therein was the trouble, but the Commissioner comprehended it not.

After an absence of three days from the Capital, the second corps of commissioners returned from conference with the Chippewas. On the 15th Sept. all difficulties were declared settled, and they shook hands, in a better state of mind than had existed for years. The public mind was relieved. Nearly every Chief of the nation appended his signature to a treaty of perpetual friendship, made and signed at Crow Wing, Sept. 15, 1862, in presence of the several bands. Hostile demonstrations now cease, and all return in quiet to their rude village homes.[77]

Not months had passed since the painted savage in our streets, or any number of them, was no cause for alarm. Children followed them from street to street, and old men and maidens were eager to wit-

---

[77]This treaty, to say nothing of the attendant negotiations, was a curious affair altogether. The Minnesota legislature met in special session on September 9, and being excited over both the Sioux uprising and public disquiet over the attitude of the Chippewas, the two houses appointed a commission to act with the Commissioner of Indian Affairs, and asked the governor to accompany it to the troubled area. The commission consisted of Senator Henry M. Rice, David Cooper, one of the first territorial judges, the Chippewa missionary, Reverend Frederick Ayer, and Edwin C. Hatch. The commissioners and the governor left St. Paul on the 13th, met Commissioner of Indian Affairs William P. Dole at Anoka at 2 A.M. on the 14th, learned from him of the failure to effect a reconciliation with the disaffected Chippewas, went on to Crow Wing, and over the objections of Special Indian Agent Ashley C. Morrill, negotiated a treaty on September 15. The legislature afterward memorialized the President to carry out the stipulations of this treaty, though not made under Federal sanction. Folwell remarks: "It is hardly needful to say that, advised by the incensed Chippewa agent and his superior, the commissioner President Lincoln did not trouble himself about the extraordinary, not to say superfluous, negotiation. It may have had a temporary soothing effect upon the disappointed Chippewa and upon the distracted settlers along the upper Mississippi."

ness the celebrated begging or scalp dance. To the ungratified eye, it was a coveted scene, and even those to whom it was no novelty never lost the opportunity. But how vast a change a little time worketh. A red skin becomes a rare sight, and thought of but in connection with rapine and murder. Women turn pale, children scream, and men involuntarily elevate the hand to the cranium, as if to hold fast their scalp, for some forty Indians appear in front of the Capitol on the morning of Sept. 22, demanding an interview with the Governor. The practiced eye could see they were not Sioux, whose bloody knives were still unsheathed; hence the alarm soon subsided.

This delegation represented twenty-one bands, each accompanied by its Chief, tendering the service of the Chippewa nation to Gen. Pope, who was in command of the Department of the North-West, having its head quarters in St. Paul, in fighting the Sioux.[78] After trailing the "stars and stripes" through the streets for an hour or two, while the people looked

[78]The outraged demand of Governor Ramsey, telegraphed to Washington on September 6, 1862, that the Federal authorities arouse themselves to the seriousness of the Sioux uprising, brought belated action that same day, the creation of the new Military Department of the North West, with Major General John Pope assigned to the command. No one need suppose that for Pope the assignment represented an improvement in his military fortunes, however flowery the phraseology of the order; he had commanded the Union army defeated at Second Manassas a week earlier. Pope reached St. Paul, so as to begin sending Sibley instructions, on September 17.

on, preliminaries for a formal reception and "talk," on the following morning, was made.

The time being made known to them, they were seated on the ground, their feet underneath them in the usual manner, awaiting the *best bow* of the Governor. He welcomed them to the city, forgave past indiscretions of young men in taking property of the whites, which he was sure they all now regretted, and was happy that the Chippewas had never shed the blood of the white man, as their bad brothers the Sioux had done. He said that Gen. Pope, the great war chief who had lately come to fight these bad Indians, was not ready now, but would send word when he wanted them. He regretted that they were not here an hour earlier, as they then could have witnessed the deliberations of the great council of the State.* He wished them a happy journey home, promised them a good supper that night, and a ride on the fire wagon† to St. Anthony.

The above speech was responded to with the usual grunts and "ho, hos." The Chief, Berry Hunter, assured the Governor that the words he spoke "went right into his ears, and they were good, and though he was an old man, he had not lost his reason. That they had come down to show their white brothers they felt very friendly, and never desired to have any other feeling toward them."

*An extra session of the Legislature had just adjourned. [H.M.]
†Cars. [H.M.]

Big Dog, another Chief, desiring to display his oratorical powers, as also his warrior prowess, said "his hands were very red—he had painted them on purpose, so that when he came to imbrue them in the blood of the Sioux, they would show no stain."

After some more unimportant speeches, the council broke up in seeming satisfaction, doubtless as much from the promised feast, as any other cause, to which they did ample justice. And the following morning opened their eyes in wondering pleasure, as they swiftly rode over the prairie, but dodging in alarm at the shrill notes of the engine whistle.

Chapter XL

The Captive's Peril

PERHAPS it was the *power* of the whites and the fear of merited punishment, or the influence of Chaska, whom his white friend had impressed with the evil of their doings, which made dissatisfaction apparent in the Indian camp. "The leaven" was surely "hid in the meal," working with its own hidden effect for the formation of a friendly camp. Believing this to be the case, Little Crow and his adherents daily threatened the life of the captive, Spencer. Chaska was the "head soldier" of his chief when the work began, relied on to carry out his plans of ruin and death, but against the whites he would not "move so much as one of his fingers." Threats were made, hard quarrels resulted from his pacific course and the disposition to be made of the "white man." Armed men almost daily rode to the door of the lodge demanding "the white man to be brought out." And this when he was too weak to stand alone, supported by the strong arm of his red friend, with the guns aimed at his heart. Then Chaska would aim his double-shooter: "*Shoot if you like; kill him if you will; but two of you will come out of your saddles if you do.*" They knew his spirit, and did not care to risk a *test* of his steel so the danger would pass, to be repeated in a few hours. Their tent had a large hole dug in the center, where he was concealed when danger was near.

"For the most part of the time, for ten days previous to the arrival of our forces, I was kept concealed, in consequence of numerous threats made, and an order issued by Little Crow that Ta-o-pi, my friend, and myself, should be put to death.

"The friendly Indians, however, guarded me faithfully, notwithstanding I was considered by many as the cause of placing their lives in danger. The night before the battle of Wood Lake, I was disguised and sent to a lodge in a different part of the camp, in consequence of two or three armed Indians who had been discovered lurking round the lodge in which I usually staid, evidently with the intention of trying to get a shot at me.

"Another time a squaw came in and whispered something to my friend, who instantly seized his gun, and bade me put on my blanket and follow him. As I followed, he hurriedly told me that Little Crow and two others were prowling around, and intended to fire into the lodge where I was. I was taken to a neighboring lodge and placed in the hole already dug, and carefully concealed, where I passed a long and sleepless night, with a guard of ten or twelve Indians around on the outside. These and similar occurrences happened so frequently, that I at length became indifferent, and did not care how soon death might come.

"My bodily sufferings were very great, but nothing when compared with my mental anxiety. Being threatened with death so often, sometimes I almost prayed that some of their attempts to kill me might prove successful. I thought that death would be a relief to me.

"Being constantly with my friend, I received the best of treatment from him and his wife. But the female captives were, with very few exceptions, subjected to the most horrible treatment. In some cases, a woman would be taken out into the woods, and her person violated by six, seven, and as many as ten or twelve of these fiends at one time. There was, I believe, but one captive killed; that was a boy, who had in some way offended his captor, who deliberately shot him dead.

"With the exception of being almost devoured by fleas and other vermin, which always infest the Indian lodge, my situation was as comfortable as it could be under the circumstances. Before leaving the Indian camp, my friend restored to me my ring, pin, watch, money, clothes, and, in fact, every thing I had about my person when I was taken.

"I oftentimes contemplated making my escape, or at least attempting it; but my wounds were not sufficiently healed to allow me to undertake it. I am satisfied that, had I been perfectly well, I could very easily have stolen a pony and gun, and knowing the country well, I should not have had much difficulty in escaping.

"The battle of Wood Lake was fought, and the Indians were thoroughly convinced that the whites were more than they could successfully contend against, and sought safety in flight."

CHAPTER XLI

The Friendly Camp

THE day of redemption was drawing nigh; hearts were to be relieved, bitter anxiety, and the sufferings of the captives in the Indian lodges to end. Of the formation of the friendly camp Mr. Spencer gives the following particulars:

"While yet at Red Iron's village, Ta-o-pi, Ma-za-ku-ta, Wa-kin-yan-wash-te, my friend, in accordance with the instructions received secretly from Gen. Sibley, attempted to form the friendly camp, or in other words, to form a separate encampment from the main camp, and to get as many of the captives as they possibly could into their possession, and remain firm, and when the whites came up, to deliver themselves and the captives up to Col. Sibley.

"Several attempts were made to establish this camp, but no sooner would the lodges be set up, than hundreds of armed Indians from Little Crow's camp would come over and push down the lodges and force them back into the main encampment. Some few friendly Indians made their escape, taking captives with them, and succeeded in getting into Fort Ridgley.

"White Lodge left us at this place with his entire band, taking away with him about fifteen captives. They went over toward the Missouri river. One day, when most of the warriors were absent, a party of about twenty-five lodges made another attempt to camp by themselves. They were this time successful. They pitched their lodges in a small hollow, and determined to intrench themselves and fight rather than to again be forced back with Little Crow's party. They accordingly dug large square holes in the centre of the lodges, in which to place the women and children in case of an attack; so that the little camp was in quite a defensible condition. After it was thus fortified, several other Indians who had not the courage to join in at first, came in, and in a few days our camp numbered about one hundred and twenty-five lodges, and fighting men enough to hold it against all the warriors that the opposite party could bring against it.

"Standing Buffalo, the Sissiton Chief, and Wa-a-na-tan, the chief of the Cut Heads, came down while we were at this place and held council with Little Crow, and determined not to take any part in the war against the whites.

"A great deal of credit has been given to Wa-ba-sha, a well known chief, for assisting in the formation of the friendly camp. But I can see no just cause why he should have the credit of doing an action which justly belongs to others. After the battle of Wood Lake had been fought, and upon the return of the Indians; hastily holding a council, Crow and his followers determined to flee to the plains. Wa-ba-sha started off with them, and returned and joined the friendly camp only the day before our forces came in sight. His conduct was most cowardly all through the whole trouble.

"Our camp remained firm, and two days after we had the most welcome news that the 'Long Trader' (the name by which Gen. Sibley is known among the Indians), with his troops, was in sight.

"It was to me a glorious sight. I had been in captivity forty days, and during most of that time my life had been in imminent danger almost every hour. When I rolled myself in my blanket to take a little rest, I knew not whether I should awake in this world or the next. I was now about to be released, and take my friends by the hand. Could it be a reality, or was it only a pleasant dream, such as I had often had, to be again dispelled by sounds of the well known warwhoop, which would warn me to betake myself to my place of concealment? The gleaming of the bright bayonets in the sun, the sound of the ear-piercing fife, and the rattling drums, were sufficient to convince me that it was not a dream, but that I was saved.

"Too much praise cannot be awarded to Colonel Sibley, whose thorough knowledge of Indian character has so successfully enabled him to accomplish the objects of the expedition.

"The rescue of his unfortunate countrymen, who were held as captives, by a savage foe, was ever uppermost in his thoughts, and though others may censure him for not coming up to their expectations, we, who have been rescued, will ever hold the name of Henry H. Sibley dear in our hearts."

Chapter XLII

Camp Release

TWO hundred and twenty captives had been aided into the friendly camp, and now hearts beat with exultant hope. To what brutal indignities had they been obliged to submit! Wives, mothers, young ladies, and young girls, almost children, had met the same fate.

The fairest, most cultivated, and most attractive of the women was Miss Mattie Williams of Painesville, Ohio, who at the time of the outbreak was residing with an uncle seven miles up the Yellow Medicine river. Each sought safety in whatever direction seemed best. Mr. and Mrs. [Joseph and Valencia] Reynolds, the uncle and aunt of Miss Mattie, were nearing a place of safety when a party of armed Indians were seen making toward them. The reeking, jaded horse, just ready to fall, could not be urged out of a walk, and the first thought was to abandon the buggy. But he, being a large man, was dissuaded by his wife, who suggested the strategy of playing Indian. By the time they had their blankets adjusted in the most approved Indian style, the savages were sufficiently near to suppose them of their own people, and so made off in another direction. Miss Williams, with a German servant girl, was in an open buggy with a Mr. Patwell [Francis Patoile], and they had begun to feel safe, when set on by a gang of these worse than blood hounds. The man was killed, the German girl wounded, so that from the wound and other brutal treatment she died in four days. Miss W. was hit by a spent ball in the shoulder, but its pain was forgotten in the terrible anguish that followed in the forty days' captivity. Occasionally she would find the fragment of a book or some coarse needle work, with which to kill time, else it was all given to bitter reflections on her lot. O! how my heart yearned toward her, as she modestly alluded to the indignities, the brutal treatment which may not be penned.

Forty nervous, anxious days, forty restless, sleepless nights, suffering from cold and leaking tents though never from hunger, forty days clad in Indian costume, suffering in every way that savage passion could devise! But the hour of release drew near. A giant mind with strong will had every energy bent to this one object. She wrapped her blanket around her on the night of the 25th September, for the last time in that Indian camp.

How her heart beat, lest the hope be thwarted! Nor was she alone in her night vigils. Only the infants slept as if fear, care or pain had never visited the earth. Were those weary days, those anxious nights indeed to end? At dawn on the 26th the camp was astir, and preparations went forward for the reception of their distinguished guests. Personal decoration was the absorbing theme of the "Master of Ceremonies." Paint of every hue was in active demand, together with eagle's feathers, beads, and wampum, and white flags were displayed all through their village.

At noon a flag of truce, consisting of a stolen bed sheet tied to the end of a pole, went forth to meet the approaching "Expedition." Great indeed was the captives' joy on the sound of the martial music, and at the sight of the bright gleaming bayonets! The Indians, squaws and pappooses, were arranged around the camp for the reception of their guests, or in awe at the imposing display. Col. Sibley marched his column partly around their encampment and into camp near the river. Some of the men whose families were held captives were allowed to go to them, and O! the joy of such meetings! In due time Col. Sibley and staff went over to take formal possession of the camp. Around him crowded those from whom the blood-stains were scarcely washed, with every protestation of friendship and the constant declaration of "me good Ingian."

Col. Sibley assured them that the innocent had nothing to fear, while the guilty would meet the punishment their deeds merited. He now demanded surrender of all the prisoners. The preliminaries concluded, the waiting, trembling captives were delivered up to him who had spent anxious days and sleepless nights devising this object. He says: "I conducted the poor captives to my camp, where I had prepared tents for their accommodation. There were some instances of stolidity among them, but for the most part, the poor creatures, relieved of the horrible suspense in which they had been kept, and some of the young women freed from the loathsome attentions to which they have been subjected by their brutal captors, were fairly overwhelmed with joy." This camp took the name of "Camp Release."

Another, speaking of the profound joy which made them speechless, says: "We brought them into camp and did all we could to make them comfortable, for every heart was moved at the recital of what they had suffered."

Many were so overwhelmed they could have fallen to the ground, doing reverence to their rescuer. One of his officers said, "Col. Sibley, *I would sooner have the glory of your achievement to-day, than the proudest victory ever won in battle.*" There was no reply, but his manhood was stirred, and his eye was far more emphatic than words could have been. He had accomplished this great good to more than two hundred helpless beings. What mattered to him the reproach of envy, or the clamorous tongue bidding him rush on, which would have brought death to every captive. He had the triumph resulting from fearless discharge of duty, and to his own quarters took the only adult male captive, caring for him as a "father careth for a son whom he loveth."[79]

[79]A number of the captives freed at this time set down their recollections afterward, including Nancy McClure and Mary Schwandt, whose reminiscences are printed in *Minnesota Historical Collections*, 1894, vol. 6, pp. 439-474. Another such narrative, by Mrs. N. D. White, appears in the same series, 1901, vol. 9, pp. 395-426. Sibley wrote his wife from "Camp

Release" on September 27, 1862: "You will rejoice to learn, that after having beaten the savages so soundly, I moved up with my command to this spot, where is located the large camp of Indians and half breeds, and to my in-expressible satisfaction, found most of the female captives, and a few children safe therein. I went into the encampment, with a few of my officers, leaving a guard of a couple of hundred soldiers on the outside, and after a brief speech demanded the immediate surrender to me of all the white prisoners. They were brought into the circle, to the number of between a hundred, and a hundred and fifty, and a pitiable sight they presented. The poor creatures cried for joy, at their deliverance from the loathsome bondage, in which they had been kept for weeks, suffering meantime nameless outrages at the hands of their brutal captors. Most of them were young, and there were a score or more of fine, lady-like appearance, notwithstanding the ragged clothes they wore. They all clustered close around our little group, as if they feared that attempts would be made to keep them in custody. I re-assured them on that score, and when all were collected, they were placed in charge of the guard, and conducted to my own camp near by, where tents, and other accommodations, had been provided for their reception. One rather handsome woman among them, had become so infatuated with the red skin who had taken her for a wife, that, although her white husband was still living at some point below, and had been in search of her, she declared that were it not for her children, she would not leave her dusky paramour. There is also a Mrs. Adams, whose six months child was killed when she was captured, who is exceedingly pretty, and has a complexion as white as snow. She says she was let alone and protected by a really friendly Indian, who treated her like a sister. There is one young lady, very respectable and of fine personal appearance, a Miss [Mattie] Williams, who has been very much abused; indeed, I think all of the younger ones have been. I shall send all of these people down to St. Paul tomorrow in wagons."

The woman represented as having been enamored of a redskin was Sarah F. Wakefield, who in her *Six Weeks in the Sioux Tepees* relates that her savior, Chaska, had in fact behaved most honorably during her captivity, so that she openly defended him when he was arrested for the murder of George Gleason. She defended him so warmly as to make matters difficult for both of them. "They soon at the camp began to say that I was in love; that I was his wife; that I preferred living with him to my husband, and all such horrid, abominable reports." She goes on to criticize the rather hypocritical conduct of some of her sister captives.

Chapter XLIII

Indian Prisoners

AFTER proper attention to the rescued, the next "order" in the military programme was the erection of a jail in the centre of Camp Release. Some were detailed to cut the logs, others to haul them in, and others to throw them up and bolt their corners; and before nightfall the huge pen was ready for occupants. These were brought in by Col. William Crooks with an adequate armed force. Those free from suspicion were unmolested. The prisoners were put in chains, and a strong guard set around the jail. A military commission, composed of Col. Crooks, Lieut. Col. William R. Marshall, and Capts. Hiram P. Grant, Hiram S. Bailey, and Lieut. Rollin C. Olin, to which two or three others were afterwards added, was convened for the trial.[80]

[80]Isaac V. D. Heard, before becoming a historian of the Sioux War, had been a St. Paul lawyer who enlisted in Captain Joseph Anderson's company as a private. He performed most of Lieutenant Olin's duties as Judge Advocate, so that he describes himself as recorder of the commission. His *History*, pp. 251-271, interestingly pictures the "trials of the prisoners." It is now clear that many of the Indians surrendered with the expectation that they would be treated as prisoners of war; but punishment of the captives was required by what Stephen Riggs described at the time as "a terrible necessity—the demand of public justice." The proceedings had much the character of drumhead court-martial, and it can scarcely be said that the Indians had benefit of counsel. See W. W. Folwell, *A History of Minnesota*, vol. 2, pp. 190-211.

No more formidable Calendar was ever brought before human tribunal. Four hundred and twenty-five men arraigned for criminal trial! Every precaution was taken that no injustice should be shown, and all testimony was required to be written down, in case of any questioning of their innocence. Those who plead "guilty" to charges had their cases soon disposed of. The equivocation of the guilty who were allowed to testify, was often, to say the least, very amusing, and their statements devoid of all reason. Many would admit they fired in battle, but insisted it was at random, and nobody was hurt! A plea supposed to be valid by the one who rendered it, was that the horse he stole was a very *little* one, and that the oxen he took were for the gratification of his wife.

A man in the prime of life declared that his gray hairs should attest *his* innocence, and some young men, that their hearts were too weak to face fire. Another batch would insist that when the battle raged, they were lying flat on their faces, writhing in physical tortures, such as in babyhood would have been relieved by a dose of catnip tea.

A small army of culprits vowed they had crept under a wonderfully capacious stone (which nobody ever saw there), during the battle at Fort Ridgley, and did not emerge till all was quiet. A still larger number averred that an unsocial spirit kept them from fighting, and then again that they were in the rear of the several battles feasting on roast beef and green corn. One had his tender sympathies so wrought upon to see his kin killing the whites, that he lay down to sleep and did not wake till the battle was over.

Cut-Nose, whose bloody deeds are before recorded, was condemned, and a companion in crime for having butchered nineteen persons. Both made most solemn protestations of "me good Indian," with strongest avowals of friendship for their accusers, proving very conclusively that many in the friendly camp were as black in crime as any who went at large.

All ages, from boys of fifteen to infirm old men, were represented. One said, he "was fifty a great many years ago, when he quit counting."

The party engaged in the captivity of Mattie Williams and the murder of Mr. Patwell [Patoile] were doomed to the punishment their deeds merited. A very old man was identified by two boys, one of more than usual intelligence. Their families had escaped from the vicinity of Beaver Creek, and arrived almost within hailing distance of the fort when met by the Indians, who told them if they would return to their homes and give them their teams, they should not be injured. But when nearly home, the Indians fired into the party, killing several, then took the uninjured women and children prisoners. The stolid old wretch was made to confront the witnesses, who identified him as having taken unerring aim at more than one of the party. "I saw that man shoot my mother," burst forth from one of the boys; and "I saw him," said the other, "shoot a man who had kneeled down to pray." Another was recognized by Mrs. Alexander Hunter as having shot her husband and taken her into captivity.

Several of the Renville Rangers who had deserted were brought before this tribunal. They had been in all the battles, and fought with a daring equal to the fiercest of the full bloods. Particular attention was drawn to a young Hercules, about eighteen, bright, intelligent, and competent for a vast amount of evil. He declared he was outside the fort when the Indians surrounded it, and was thus unintentionally thrown into their ranks, that his hands were as free from blood as his heart from guile. The evidence, however, proved him to have taken the first scalp at Wood Lake, from an old grey-headed man and former comrade, and to have received one of the two belts of wampum promised by Little Crow as a reward for killing the first white man. One amused the Court by asserting that he was the sole cause of the war. He was an old sore-eyed man of lymphatic temperament, and had been living, he said, near New Ulm. The benevolent whites had supported him, and their kindness incited the jealousy of the other Indians—hence the war.

Thus might we multiply instances of strange fabrications and flimsy falsehoods. But enough has been given to show their duplicity and guilt. Three weeks of unremitting labor was given to this business ere Camp Release was broken up, and still it remained unfinished. The troops were ordered "below," and the Court adjourned to the Lower Agency, where the work of death had commenced. Surely no more appropriate place could have been found.

While at Camp Release Col. Sibley was very justly promoted to "Brigadier General of Volunteers," and the same was confirmed by the U. S. Senate, one year after.[81]

[81]Sibley was appointed brigadier general of volunteers by President Lincoln a week after the Battle of Wood Lake, but the Senate rejected the appointment, politics having some part in this. Although reconsideration was voted, no effective action came before that session of Congress closed. A renewed appointment, dated March 20, 1863, was finally confirmed on April 7, 1864.

Chapter XLIV

Captivity of
Mrs. Sophia Josephine Huggins

DRIVEN away from her husband, as seen in a former chapter, it was natural that Mrs. Huggins should look for protection to the one who had evinced a kindly spirit toward her. Believing they would be more safe with the Chief than elsewhere, she with Julia and her children went to his house the same evening.

As they passed through the village, many squaws came out with a show of grief, in the usual way of laying the hand over the mouth, groaning, &c. The men loafed at their tent doors, smoked their pipes and said nothing, pretending not to see them. They were kindly received by the Chief's wife and other members of the lodge, her mother, and their son Naho-ton-mana, a lad of fifteen. A buffalo robe was spread for them at the further end of the lodge, and this "seat of honor" was reserved for her so long as she remained a member of the family. On one of her own pillows, at night she rested her throbbing head, and many other articles from her own house were around her, reminders of the day's experience.

That was a dreadful night. Men went and came to consult their Chief, and loud talking was heard all over the village. Only the children slept, as if in their own little crib at home, with a loving father near. So stunning had been the events of the previous evening that all seemed more hallucination than reality.

The choicest cut from her husband's oxen was set before them for breakfast, but when she thought that he slept his last sleep, she wept but could not eat.

News of their captivity having reached the ears of Mr. John Lagree, on the opposite side of the river some distance away, he came with proffers of a home promising greater security. Walking Spirit left them to their own choice. Their route lay through Lame Bear's village, where they saw Indian children dressed in their own children's clothes — her husband's writing desk and their own chairs, besides evidences that they were not the only sufferers. This was on Wednesday the 20th August, the day of first attack on Fort Ridgley, about eighty miles away.

The hearts of these women were sad in the extreme, and their anxiety none the less from ignorance of the extent of the trouble, and the fact that Lagree and a Frenchman who staid with him, were in turn watching without, or sleeping with a loaded gun at their side. On Thursday dreadful tidings came from the seat of war. All the Missionaries and Government officials, it was said, were killed, and so for more than one long week *everybody* believed. And now Mrs. Huggins must be robbed of her only earthly comforter and counsellor. Julia's brother, hearing of her fate, had come disguised to take her to his home at Yellow Medicine. It would not be safe for the mother and children to go with them, and therefore she must abide her time of release. That night Mr. Anton Manderfield, who had escaped from Big Stone Lake, came in. The women bound up his bleeding feet, and for the time forgot their own sorrows in efforts to relieve his sufferings. He bore the first tidings of their fate to white friends below, who from that time were busy devising plans for her release. On Friday morning Julia bade her companion in captivity adieu, and in Indian costume went forth by the side of her brother, on their perilous journey.

An invitation was received from De Cota to return and make her permanent abode with him at Walking Spirit's village. So after the sad leave-taking of Julia, attended by Lagree, she and her children set out on horseback. As they trotted on through the woods, she imagined every tree hid a lurking foe, for she had become very nervous from continued excitement and suspense. At Lame Bear's village, Lagree, who was a Chippewa half-breed, seeing many Sioux about feared to go further so getting an Indian woman to "pack" Letta, she took little Charlie in her own arms, sick and weak though she was from having eaten nothing that day. Presently an old squaw came running after her, signifying a desire to relieve her of the burden. So she put him on her back pappoose fashion with which the little fellow seemed content.

A little out of the village four hideously painted warriors were lounging by the roadside; but she hid herself behind the women as best she could and passed unmolested. Again, in passing through a piece of woods, she was desired to go ahead, trembling with fear, while the women manifested alarm, the cause of which she could not understand.

Now came another sore trial. Faint, sick, tired and hungry, she came to the door where she expected a friendly welcome. Mr. De Cota, her recent neighbor, silently smoked his pipe without the door of his lodge deigning her never a look, while his squaw wife, coldly though not unkindly, motioned her on to the chief's house. Her heart sank within her. What would be her next step, if coldly received at Walking Spirit's? The old chief was away, but his wife brought water and food, and arranged for her to rest, almost tenderly looking after her comfort.

We are glad that we have comparatively small record of women being aiders and abettors of the transactions which brought such dismay to our frontier. As a general thing they have "fed the hungry and clothed the naked" when in their power to do so.

It is but justice to De Cota to say that he was loyal to the whites, and would have received Mrs. Huggins according to his invitation, had his courage been adequate. Things around him looked stormy and his Sioux wife could not save his scalp, should any act of his excite their displeasure. Not long after, he took his wife and went to his own people, and for several months thereafter was in government employ, carrying the mail through the trackless region from Pembina to Fort Randall.

Chapter XLV

Mrs. Huggins in Care of Walking Spirit

THE old chief was from home, trying to quell
the war-spirit of the young braves, and did
not return till Mrs. Huggins had been several days
in his lodge. The usual gutteral salute—"ho-ho-
ho," sounded very pleasant as he extended his hard
brawny hand, by which she understood she was welcome. This increased her confidence, which he seeing, made still greater efforts, that she should not
feel it misplaced. The language of his actions was
very kind, though she understood little of his spoken
vernacular. In this assurance she says her "poor,
weary, anxious heart felt comforted. This old man
was my friend and protector, I could here find something like rest, quiet and security."

For six weeks she remained a member of the chief's
family, more a distinguished guest than a captive. We
rejoice that there are some alleviating features in the
wretched Dakota character—something to evince
them not hopelessly "the children of wrath." Under
like influence, with the same privileges as the white
race through generations past, the results would be
equal. For ages the Indian has known naught but
his present life, and from infancy has been taught that
his highest achievement was to take the scalp of an
enemy. Hence their glory in the number of scalp-
feathers they are entitled to wear.

Not from Walking Spirit and his family alone was this captive the recipient of favors. All the women seemed to outvie each other in this regard, and addressed her in the language of kindness and respect. They would say, "white woman feel sad; I want to shake hands with her." Their style of living began to tell seriously on little Charlie's health; then the women sent milk for him, and would come and take him out for the air. For days they lived only on potatoes and corn, then occasionally beef or dog meat, and once in a while they had coffee and sugar. Those well provided with food for the day often sent for her "to come and eat" with them. She had learned to make a virtue of necessity, and a cheerful conformity to the society in which she lived conciliated her into favor. Once she was sent for at bed time, to "come and eat." Though not hungry, she went. A piece of nice carpet was spread for her to sit on, and a white towel for her plate, which was one of her own, and one of her own dishes to drink from, the bill of fare consisting of potatoes, rice, dried apples and cold water. She says sometimes when she thought of the dirty dishes her food was on, the dirty kettles it was cooked in, and the dirty hands which prepared it, her stomach rebelled. But she tried to make the best of what she had. She well appreciated the kindness which sent one of the women to Yellow Medicine to bring up flour and other articles for her use, and one frosty morning another came cautiously behind her and threw a warm shawl over her shoulders;

though part of the booty, we credit the kindly spirit which evoked the act.

One of her great perplexities was the means of ablution, which Mrs. Walking Spirit remedied by obtaining a half powder keg. She had no convenience for washing clothes than an old iron heater, which had been used for a dog dish. This she made subserve her purpose. Once or twice she was privileged with a tub and washboard, which had been her own property. She was thankful to get clean clothes, though they went unironed.

All this time, not one of the young men of the village was allowed to speak to her, and there was a commendable pride, "in keeping her very carefully." No work was ever demanded, or expected of her; yet occupation lightened the burden of grief, so she would assist her hostess in sewing, cooking, and even at times brought water from the brook. Many of her own articles of dress were returned to her, and she was permitted to wear her own costume; but it was hard to see her children's clothes, of which they were in need, worn by Indian children, and very painful to see the clothes of her murdered husband on those, if not his actual murderers, who had "consented unto his death."

The children became great favorites, petted and caressed, and afraid of no one, and this partiality came near causing her the severest pang she had known. The chief's wife had a brother who lived far to the north and had no children, and whom she had induced to think could get Mrs. Huggins to give him her little girl. The proposition was made through a French interpreter. Her decided "no" gave no little offense, especially to the old woman, the man's mother. He was very angry. The chief would not suffer the child to be taken without her consent; but the offense was never forgiven, nor could she feel the same confidence in the offended party as before. The fondness of the old woman for the children changed to indifference or hate, and she was ever afterward very cross to them. This, Mrs. H. allowed to pass unnoticed; yet she lived in constant fear of their being taken, and would never trust them alone in her care. She now watched them closely when they were packed around the village by the squaws, and at night folded them in her arms, while she dreamed of waking to find them gone.

Mrs. H. lost the days of the week, and afterward learned that several Mondays had been kept by her as the holy Sabbath day. O, how the Christian woman longed to be where she could worship God, with "none to molest or make afraid." But the time for her removal from the red-heated furnace had not yet come.

Chapter XLVI

The Alarms

THERE was a mighty host of "Northerners" coming through the village. They had many carts. Some of the warriors were on foot and some on horse. The village was in great alarm.

Mrs. Huggins was hurried out to look at them, in the distance, and then to a tent with orders to suffer no noise from the children. The caravan halted just past her tent. Their tumult so excited the children that they cried to go out, and it was some time before they were frightened into silence. There were at least six men to a woman in the crowd. The excitement was intense. Men, women and children were running about as if frightened out of their wits, which the woman could see through a hole in the tent. But unwelcome as were these visitors, they must be fed. This was the only hope of a pacific turn in affairs. The young warriors galloped around, firing off guns, and making other demonstrations of prowess. Then rang forth the stentorian voice of a chief. With a high head, proud look and stately tread, he stalked back and forth as he delivered himself of the eloquent speech burning in his soul. For several hours our heroine lay in her concealment, when all was again quiet.

Now came a time when the village was deserted, and Mrs. Huggins was alone with the nameless old woman. From night till morning, and from morning till night, she trembled with fear and closely hugged her children lest in an unexpected moment they be torn from her.

A week or two after the advent of the "Northerners," a detachment of the band returned. Walking Spirit invited them to his lodge for a feast, more to conciliate peace than from friendship. He guaranteed protection to his captive, and directed her to sit behind him at the door, doubtless for quick egress in case of trouble, while his guests would fill the lodge. With two loaded guns beside him, they sat down to the feast, no other woman being allowed inside, only to bring the food, which was fried bread and coffee, to the door. Several of the guests were attentive to the children, feeding and allowing them to drink from their cups. After considerable speechifying and parade, the crowd dispersed, much to her relief.

One day the chief handed her a nice looking letter, written in Dakota language. She was unable to read it for him, but waited with anxious forebodings the imparting of its contents, and yet with faint hopes for herself and children. The contents were such as to make the friendly chief declare himself "very angry," so angry that he threw the letter into the fire. Good Day, its author, had proposed to buy the captive for a wife.

On another day she was told to stay very closely indoors, that a "bad man was in the village, and would kill her." She was alone with the children, engrossed with her sewing, when of a sudden the blanket door was thrown up and a fierce looking, hideously painted young man, with drawn sword, stood before her. A child from a neighboring lodge followed him in, eyeing first one and then the other with a look of terror. With great self-command, after the first moment of surprise, she bent to her sewing, trembling so violently she could scarcely hold her needle. He went away, without speaking. Then she drew a long breath and thanked God that she and her children were alive. A moment after, the chief, panting and blowing, sprang through the opening. Hers was no feigned joy as she said, "You frighten me, coming in such haste."

"You frighten *me*," he replied, as he sat down. "I was afraid you would be killed before I got here."

Some women came in, and told her about the angry man. His wife had run away, and therefore had he come to the chief's house. Thus was she in constant alarm—her nervous system agitated with the most harrowing fear, and was often hid from threatening dangers.

News from below became more and more exciting, and finally the battle of Wood Lake determined the Indians on flight. "To go or not to go" was optional with the captive. She could not go alone to her friends below, nor could Walking Spirit go with her as he had hoped, as all the region was filled with the fleeing foe. So she committed herself to Providence.

All was now bustle. Corn and potatoes were to be gathered for the journey, or buried. Some pounded corn from the cob, others parched it or bagged it up, and others were packing household goods. Our heroine made herself as useful as she could. She assisted to put up five sacks of corn and potatoes.

All being in readiness to depart, the story was circulated that the white prisoners were killed, and that retributive justice would soon fall upon the Indians. Walking Spirit would have remained, but discrimination between the friendly and unfriendly Indians, he thought, would not be made. The innocent was liable to suffer with the guilty.

Hosts of Sioux were daily arriving from below, with whom many of the villagers "fell in," swelling each arrival to quite a caravan.

CHAPTER XLVII

Leaving for the Plains

THE chief's family were the last to go. Mrs. Huggins had not yet made her decision known. She was perplexed, if not in despair. When the question to *go* or *stay* was again submitted, her answer, "I will go," pleased her protector, and prompted a renewal of "faithful care." To her and her children was accorded the privilege of riding on top of the load, while Mrs. Walking Spirit on foot led the old horse which dragged the load on poles—her mother carried a large pack, and his son led the colt, while he himself drove the oxen. The cow, by especial request of her hostess, was led by Mrs. Huggins.

I see them filing across prairies; through dark ravines; up beetling bluffs and in the forest shade. To lighten the load, in the ascent of hills and through mud-holes, our heroine, often with a child on her hip, and fast hold of the rope attached to the cow's horns, waded ankle deep in mud, then sat down in the shade of some ancient tree, panting for breath.

At night their tent was pitched in a beautiful valley, and when the horses were "staked" and other matters properly attended to, as in well regulated families, they drew around a sumptuous board "groaning" with skunk meat and potatoes.

The sublime silence of the night was a luxury to the soul of Mrs. Huggins. It was sweet to reflect on the constant care of Him whose presence fills the universe. Early next morning, before the family had breakfasted, an excited horseman rode up with tidings which brought all to their feet, followed by hasty arrangements to go. The greatest haste continued till the middle of the afternoon, they meanwhile eating nothing, and with only a little parched corn for the children, who became tired, sick and fretful. For four days they continued the same haste, the little boy growing weaker and weaker. It was hard to see him droop thus, with no means to relieve him, and to feel that this precious comfort might be taken from her. Then there was the fear of starvation, or that Walking Spirit might be overpowered by Little Crow or some of the Northerners, and she taken from him. While her only employment was *to think,* it is not strange that with all her firm and steadfast faith she was perplexed. Then again, buoyant hope would cheer her heart, for she knew that friends were earnestly praying for her safety and release, and she believed that when the divine end was accomplished, the severe discipline would cease. In the presence of danger she ever relied on the judgment of others, to "lie down and cover up," without inquiring as to the why or wherefore—trusting the promise "He shall cover thee with his feathers, and under his wing shalt thou trust."

Chapter XLVIII

Release and Return

THE reader has seen the main body of troops at
Camp Release, from whence, on the day following their arrival, General Sibley dispatched four of
the most trustworthy half-breeds and Indians with
instructions to follow the Indians, and bring back
Mrs. Huggins and children.

The fourth and last night, Mrs. Huggins was made
to understand that many bad Indians were in the very
large encampment. They had many cattle, horses and
wagons, and she counted eighty yoke of oxen, and
knew that all were trophies of their raid upon the
whites. Hope well nigh died, for in the midst of the
great darkness, how could she think of deliverance
as near? The following morning, a message brought
to the chief produced a movement on the part of his
family. The white lady was not made to understand
the reason; she dare not hope it augured any good,
and the suspense threw her into a feverish anxiety.
When at noon they camped, the family bustled
about in preparation for visitors—thus much she
knew.

While wondering and waiting her heart gave a
sudden bound, for the familiar faces of rescuers were
before her. Letters from General Sibley to Walking
Spirit and herself were read, and he declared at once
his intention of returning with her to Camp Release.

Such was the joy of her heart that sleep came not that night.

While Mrs. Walking Spirit got breakfast, Mrs. Huggins repaired the wardrobe of her husband, that he might appear as respectable as possible. When she finished, she returned the thread and scissors to his wife, who pressed her to retain the latter as a memento of her love.

We will note at this point the release of two little German girls and a half-breed boy, who were in the main encampment. One of the girls was very beautiful, whose mother was at Camp Release when she arrived there, and after clasping her in wild joy, she looked to Mr. Riggs, and asked, "Where is the other?" He *could not tell her.*

The first night they camped at Big Stone Lake. Lame Bear and some of his people extended the hospitalities of their camp. Joy and its reaction, after all she had passed through, had nearly prostrated Mrs. Huggins. With a thankful heart she sank upon the comfortable bed made for her, and awoke refreshed.

Approaching Camp Release, when a few miles out, they passed twelve warriors, savagely painted, smoking on the grass. Murder flashed from their eyes, and there was cause for alarm, though some of the men halted to shake hands and smoke with them. But as they drove rapidly away, a close watch was kept. That night the camp was in sight of Lac-qui-parle. They resorted to Sioux stratagem, leaving their wagons and camping some distance from the road. There was little sleep; every ear was alert for sounds of a wily foe, and they suffered much from cold, as autumn frosts had come, and the night winds were very chill.

They halted the following morning for Mrs. Huggins to visit the grave of her husband, around which they drove stakes to protect it from careless intruders. They allowed her time to linger over every familiar spot. How desolate all appeared—and with heart even more desolate she turned away, for her children's sake nerving her soul to battle a little longer with life.

Eight miles further, they entered Camp Release, which is to be memorable for all time in the history of Minnesota. The reaction of a system wrought up so long to the highest tension had come; but with kind care and sympathy, she and little Charlie rallied wonderfully during the two weeks in which the trials of guilty Indians progressed, before being sent down to the anxious hearts awaiting her.

CHAPTER XLIX

Removal to Camp Sibley

ON the 23d of October the condemned and un-condemned prisoners, chained two and two, were loaded into wagons, twelve or fifteen in each, and under a military escort started for Camp Sibley.[82] Here the trial was resumed in a log house formerly owned and occupied by a half-breed named LaBatte, for unromantic kitchen purposes. The main building, separate from this, had been deeply stained with the blood of the owner. From the ashes of his dwelling the soldiers drew forth his charred remains. A few steps away was the store of Nathan Myrick, where Lynde, the first victim, DeVill [G. W. Divoll] and Andrew Myrick were killed. We wonder that fair and impartial trials were given—we wonder at the stay-ing hand which prevented their execution *en masse*—and we wonder at the patience of the commission in the long, tedious trial!

But this heavy criminal calendar was at last cleared. Of the men arraigned, three hundred and three were sentenced to be hung, twenty to imprisonment. They were removed to Mankato, where an immense jail had been prepared, to await execution.

---

[82]Camp Sibley was established at the lower (Redwood) agency. Camp Release, from which the prisoners were this day brought down, was on the Minnesota River opposite the mouth of the Chippewa.

As the train of guarded prisoners neared New Ulm, the citizens who had returned to their homes came out pell mell, the women leading, assailing them with axes, stones and clubs in retaliation for murdered husbands and children. Even at the point of the bayonet the infuriated mass rushed into the midst of the soldiers. In several instances the guns were turned aside, or the axe warded off as the fatal blow was about to descend. One woman actually cleft the jaw of an Indian with a hatchet, and another fractured a skull so that the victim died in a few days. Some eight or ten were badly wounded before the assailants could be driven off. We regret to have this act to record. Still we will not too harshly condemn. They had suffered much, were still smarting under the terrible blow, and a half frenzy seized them when they saw the authors of their misery.[83] Doubtless, more serious

[83]Concerning this removal to the newly established Camp Lincoln, a mile and a half from Mankato, Sibley wrote his wife on November 12: "In passing the town of New Ulm, the wagons containing each ten prisoners, flanked by a strong force of mounted men, was set upon by a crowd of men, women, and children, who showered brickbats, and other missiles upon the shackled wretches, seriously injuring some fifteen of the latter, and some of the guards. The assailants were finally driven back by a bayonet charge and fifteen or twenty men who were among them, were arrested, and made to march on foot, twelve miles to the spot, where we encamped for the night, where after being reprimanded for the insult to the U. S. flag committed by them, and their female associates, they were released, and compelled to walk back the entire distance to New Ulm. I did not dare to fire, for fear of killing women and children. The Dutch she devils!—They were as fierce as tigresses" (Sibley Papers, Minnesota Historical Society).

would have been the results had they foreseen that in fixing the day for execution, the Chief Executive would be moved with pity, and order the punishment of all but thirty-nine suspended.

This fact becoming known, some two hundred men armed with hatchets, knives, and other death-dealing implements, on the 8th of December forced their way through the guard at Camp Lincoln, near Mankato, with the intention of dealing to the murderers the merit of their crimes. Col. Miller,[84] prompt and resolute, had them surrounded before they could effect anything, but released them on a pledge to abstain from further violence. Gov. Ramsey issued a proclamation urging the citizens not to throw away the good name Minnesota had hitherto sustained by rash acts of lawlessness. "Our people have had just cause to complain of the tardiness of executive action in the premises, but they ought to find some reason for forbearance in the absorbing cares which weigh upon the President. If he should decline to punish them, the case will then come clearly within the jurisdiction of the civil authorities."

[84]Stephen Miller, a Pennsylvanian who settled in Minnesota in 1858, was appointed Lieutenant-Colonel of the First Minnesota Infantry in April, 1861, and demonstrated his courage and ability at Bull Run and other battles. In August, 1862, he was named Colonel of the new Seventh Regiment, succeeded Sibley in command at Mankato on November 17, and oversaw the execution of the Sioux prisoners the following month. In January, 1864, he became Governor of Minnesota. Miller died in 1881. The incident described occurred December 4, 1862. Governor Ramsey's proclamation was issued two days later.

CHAPTER L

Removal of the "Good Indians" to Fort Snelling

THE army of "good Indians," some eighteen hundred men, women, children and half-breeds, on the 7th of November took up their line of march for Fort Snelling under escort of Lieut. Col. Marshall's command, a train four miles in length.

The "winter quarters" was an immense pen in which their teepees were set according to latest approved city surveys—with streets, alleys and public square. Around and without, armed soldiers paraded day and night for six months, and the Government outlay for their support was little less than $2,000 per month; while the hundreds of women and children whom their tribe had made widows and orphans, were mainly dependent on their own exertions, or a sympathizing public. Visitors daily thronged the enclosure with "passes" from the post commander. When admitted, a filthy sight met the eye. The streets were the receptacles of all the offal of the lodges, where barefooted women and children splashed around in the filthy slush, as much at home as my reader on a velvet carpet.

Here we saw old Betsey, whom we knew before the State was a State, or the Territory had a name, and without whom its history would be incomplete, so identified is she with frontier life and pioneer experience. Her ugly old phiz is seen in every photograph gallery in the land, and recognized by every street urchin. Everywhere she has warm friends, and it is her boast that none of her family have taken part against the whites. Even she was pattering around barefooted, as lithe as a girl of sixteen. We bade her good-bye, supposing it the last time, and she actually kissed our hand at parting. But when the encampment was broken up to go to the new "hunting grounds," by the earnest desire of her farmer son Ta-o-pee, old Betsey was permitted to remain with him, so we may have another parting kiss.

It will be recollected that Ta-o-pee was very active in the formation of the friendly camp, and made the first move for the release of the prisoners. Wabashaw, too, was there. These had kept aloof from crime, using every means to subdue the rage of their red brothers. When an answer came from their letter to Col. Sibley, the utmost caution was requisite to conceal the fact. Great excitement that night prevailed in their camp, on account of the letter Little Crow had received, the contents of which, when interpreted by Spencer, was proclaimed by Little Crow in thunder tones to the clamorous throng which crowded around his tent. Ta-o-pee had a secret for the white man's ear. Excitement ran high, and the tent was full till the small hours of morning—Ta-o-pee, with anxiety hidden beneath a calm exterior, frequently coming in and going out again. At three o'clock, all was quiet; now was the time. They knew that evil, design-

ing ones were prowling around; so, throwing a blanket over their heads, that the light might not be seen,
they lighted a candle, and in a soft whisper, read the
important missive, the first hope-inspiring note.

Chaska, too, came with the train. While in various
ways making himself useful to our people, he was
charged, as having taken life before he rescued his
friend, for which charge he was a long time under
guard awaiting trial. He was honorably acquitted,
and engaged as scout to the expedition the following
spring. Having renounced his birthright, he was to
all intents and purposes a *white man,* doing his duty,
whatever and wherever it might be.

CHAPTER LI

Protest of Senator Wilkinson
and Others

WITH the groans of the wounded still deadening our ears, and while the shrieks of the already dead, still reverberate from bluff to bluff, sympathy for the "poor, wronged red man" is being roused in some parts of our nation. We love the EAST, its people and its lofty principles, but we ignore their argument of the Indians' wrongs.

In discussing the "*good Indians,*" we confess to a desire to see them turned loose on Boston common, as Congress was memorialized to do by several thousand citizens of Minnesota. Had the tragic scenes, of which we have given but a faint outline, been concentrated in any Eastern city, had their streets been drenched with blood, had fire and ravishment come to *their* homes, we know the New England heart well enough to say that quite as little leniency would have been desired for the perpetrators as by us.

We think the protest against Presidential clemency, from Senator Wilkinson and Representatives Aldrich and Windham, worthy of record, and here reproduce it.[85]

[85]This protest by Morton S. Wilkinson, William Windom, and Cyrus Aldrich, with a memorial from citizens of St. Paul, was printed in 37th Congress, 3rd Session, *Senate Executive Document* 7 [Serial 1149], "Indian Barbarities in Minnesota."

"*To the President of the United States:*

"SIR:—We have learned, indirectly, that you intend to pardon or reprieve a large majority of the Indians in Minnesota, who have been formally condemned for their participation in the brutal massacre of our people, in the months of August and September last. If this be your purpose, as representatives from that State, we beg leave, most respectfully, to protest against it, and we do so, for the following reasons:

"These Indians were condemned, most of them, upon the testimony of women, whom they had carried into captivity, after having murdered their fathers, husbands and brothers, and who were treated, by these Indians, with a brutality never known before, in this country, nor equaled in the practice of the most barbarous nations. There were nearly ninety captives, who were wives and daughters of our neighbors and friends. (This does not include the children.) They were intelligent and virtuous women—some of them were wives and mothers—others were young and interesting girls.

"These savages, to whom you propose to extend your Executive clemency, when the whole country was quiet, and the farmers were busily engaged in gathering their crops, arose with fearful violence, and travelling from one farm to another, indiscriminately murdered all the men, boys and little children they came to, and although they sometimes spared the lives of the mothers and daughters, they did so only to take them into captivity, which was infinitely worse than death.

"Mr. President, let us relate to you some facts with which we fear you have not heretofore been made acquainted.

"These Indians, whom (as we understand), you propose to pardon and set free, have murdered, in cold blood, nearly or quite one thousand of our people, ravaged our frontier for more than one hundred and fifty miles north and south, burned the houses of the settlers, and driven from their homes more than ten thousand of our people. They seized and carried into captivity more than one hundred women and girls, and in nearly every instance treated them with the most fiendish brutality.

"To show you, sir, the enormity of these outrages, we beg leave to state a few facts, which are well known to our people, but delicacy forbids that we should mention the names of the parties to whom we refer.

"In one instance, some ten or twelve of these Indians visited the house of a worthy farmer, who at the time was engaged with his sons stacking wheat. They stealthily approached the place where the honest farmer was at work, and seizing the opportunity, shot the father and two sons at the stack. They then went to the house, killed two little children in the presence of their mother, who was quite ill of consumption, and then took the sick mother and a beautiful little daughter, thirteen years of age, into captivity. But this is not all, nor is it the most appalling feature of this awful tragedy. Its horror is yet to be revealed. After removing these unhappy prisoners to a lodge some two miles away, these fiends incarnate, after placing a guard over the weary and exhausted mother, took her little one outside the lodge, removed all her clothes, and fastened her back on the ground. Then they commenced their work of brutality on this young girl. One by one they violated her person, unmoved by her cries, and unchecked by the evident signs of approaching dissolution. This work was continued until the Heavenly Father relieved her from suffering. They left her dead upon the ground. This outrage was committed within a few feet of the sick and dying mother.

"There is another instance of a girl eighteen years of age. We knew her well before and at the time of her capture. She was as refined and beautiful a girl as we had in the State. None had more or better friends; no one was more worthy of them than she. She was taken captive by these Indians, her arms were tied behind her and she was tied fast to the ground and ravished by some eight or ten of these convicts before the cords were unloosed from her limbs. The girl, fortunately, lived to testify against the wretches who had thus violated her. Without being more specific, we will state that nearly all the women who were captured were violated in this way.

"Again there was a little boy brought to St. Paul (whose father and mother had been murdered), whose life was spared as a witness of the horrid nature of this massacre. His right eye was cut completely out, it had fallen from its socket and perished on his cheek. His two little sisters, aged respectively six and four years, were also saved, but in an awfully mutilated condition. Their tender arms had been mangled with the savages' knives, and otherwise fearfully wounded and left on the ground for dead.

"Mr. President, there was no justification or pretext even for these brutalities. We state what we know, when we say that the Sioux Agent, Mr. Galbraith, has labored faithfully and efficiently for the welfare of these Indians. The Government, as you know, has built a house and opened a farm for every one of these Indians who would reside upon and cultivate it. Missionaries have labored zealously among them for their spiritual welfare. There has been paid to them yearly the interest upon $2,000,000. Farming implements have been purchased, and farmers have been employed by the Government to improve and cultivate their lands.

"These Indians have been called by some, prisoners of war. There was no war about it. It was a wholesale *robbery, rape and murder.* These Indians were not at war with their murdered victims.

"The people of Minnesota, Mr. President, have stood firm by you and your administration. They have given both it and you their cordial support. They have not violated *law.* They have borne these sufferings with a patience such as but few people ever exhibited under such extreme trial. These Indians are now at their mercy; but our people have not risen up to slaughter them, because they believed that their President would deal with them justly.

"We are told, Mr. President, that a committee from Pennsylvania, whose families are living happily in their pleasant homes in that State, have called upon you and petitioned you to pardon the Indians. We have a high respect for the religious sentiment of your petitioners; but we submit that is a bad taste, indeed, that it is entirely unbecoming them to interfere in matters with which they are so little acquainted, and which relate entirely to the security of our own people.

"We *protest against the pardon* of these Indians, because, if it is done, the Indians will become more insolent and cruel than they ever were before, believing, as they certainly will believe, that their great father at Washington either justifies their acts or is afraid to punish them for their crimes.

"*We protest against it*, because if the President does not permit these executions to take place under the forms of law, the outraged people of Minnesota will dispose of these wretches without law. These two people cannot live together.

"We do not wish to see mob law inaugurated in Minnesota, as it certainly will be, if you force the people to it. We tremble at the approach of such a condition of things in our STATE.

"You can give us peace, or you can give us lawless violence. We pray you, sir, in view of all that we have suffered, and of the danger that still awaits us, *let the law be executed—let justice be done our people.*"

Chapter LII

Cause of the Dakota Uprising

WE have scarcely hinted at the *cause* of the strange and sudden uprising of this powerful tribe. Mr. Spencer said to the writer that had he been less a sufferer while a wounded captive, had not his life been daily threatened so that he had little hope of living; in short, had he foreseen what he now sees, he might have probed the whole matter. He heard nothing to confirm the view we present, or by which he would feel justified in declaring it to be an offshoot of the rebellion.

However deep and long they slumber beneath the rubbish of sloth or fear, the fires of discontent, of envy and hate, are ever burning in the savage heart. Sooner or later they will burst forth, when peace treaties are forgotten, the buried tomahawk exhumed, and woe to the victim over whose head the scalping-knife is flourished. In every normal savage heart exists a principle of reckless hate towards the whites, which may be stimulated by real or imaginary wrongs. Like a spark in a magazine of powder, the ignition is as sudden, the results as terrible. That the great Sioux raid of '62 was somewhere premeditated, plans intelligently matured and admirably arranged for secrecy, is beyond a doubt.

We have seen squads of daring warriors all over the counties of the north, west, and southwest, striking a simultaneous blow, desolating an area of four hundred miles, filling the woods and marshes with panic-stricken women and children, bestrewing the prairies with corpses of men, and desolating the fields. The reaper lying dead in his swath, sickle in hand; cattle roaming at large, and bellowing in inquiry; the swollen bodies of others mingling their nauseous affluvia with the headless bodies of men; hogs rooting in the long ringlets, or feeding on the fair cheek of beauty, and dogs going mad from the same—in short, the tide of desolation sweeping over all.

Some hidden leaven has been at work. Investigation shows conclusively that Secessia had sent her emissaries not only to the Dakotas, but all other tribes of the northwest—fostering a spirit of unrest, magnifying mole-hill grievances into mountain realities, inciting the barbarous war-spirit, and infusing a death-dealing fury. A savage menace to the frontier might mean that the northwestern troops, noted for their valor, would be recalled from the national field to subdue a savage foe. Hence they prated of wrongs, and encouraged a hope of a re-possession of garden Minnesota. The task was no difficult one, the subtlety of rebellion taught, for all the fighting powers were engaged with a southern foe.[86]

[86]Not so "conclusive" in the light of a fuller record is the showing that "Secessia" had anything to do with the Sioux uprising, however plausible the idea may have seemed while the Union was convulsed by civil war. The newspapers of 1862 were filled with speculations on the subject—one example is

It has been conclusively proven that runners, after the great rebellion began, were going back and forth among the various tribes, and particularly to effect their object with the Minominees.

In one of their grand councils, convened in Wisconsin, it was stated on the authority of a head chief that all the western tribes were going to join the South, and that there would be a general uprising among the Indians in the summer, 1862.

There is no doubt but the Chippewas did seriously contemplate an alliance with the Sioux, but discountenanced by the foresight of some of their number, it was nipped in the bud by the wise policy of Gov. Ramsey.

A Lieut. Colonel in Ashby's rebel cavalry wrote from Virginia, under date of Aug. 20, 1862, to his brother-in-law of Columbus, Wisconsin, advising him to haste to the Confederate lines for safety. But if he failed in this, to seek an asylum in Illinois, giving as a reason for the warning "a general uprising of all the Indian tribes in the north-west, about the first of September." The Divine hand held in check all but the wrathful Sioux, and Little Crow dared to attempt what some of the nations of Europe dare not risk.

What fearful guilt rests upon the plotters—the

a letter of September 9 by Senator H. M. Rice: "The Sioux Indians were induced by rebels and traitors to make war upon our people. Last year they sent emissaries among them, as well as among the Chippewas, which was no secret" (St. Paul *Pioneer and Democrat,* September 16, 1862).

proxy desolaters of the fair land and domestic peace, for that secession is the root and base of the widespread ruin, the evidence admits scarce a doubt. The magnitude of the desolation can be somewhat comprehended by the figures on which we rely.

It will be recollected that 30,000 persons were actual sufferers, in flight, loss of property, and loss of life. Two thousand, nine hundred and forty persons claimed redress from Government for the loss of their earthly all. The total amount of claims for losses sustained is $2,600,000. For the disbursement of these claims, the annuities (forever forfeited) are appropriated, an arrangement just and equitable.

May God yet make the wrath of these Sioux praise him, and so overrule these events as to result in both individual and national good. [87]

[87]The Sioux who had no part in the violence attendant on the outbreak, who were simply caught up in the current of events (like settlers who fled homes not actually attacked), must have had another viewpoint on the justness of these proceedings; and the Christian Sioux might have felt that God was not giving as much attention to their welfare as moralists like Mrs. McConkey were disposed to think. W. W. Folwell, *A History of Minnesota,* vol. 2, pp. 247-248, discusses the work of this commission set up in 1863, which allowed $1,370,374 to 2,635 claimants, and adds: "A tradition has survived that the commission in distributing this Indian money was becomingly generous and that attorneys for claimants on shares were well compensated." Folwell also observes that in the St. Paul press at the time, comparatively little was said about the abrogation of treaties and the relief of sufferers, the people of Minnesota evidently being much more concerned about removal of Indians from the State.

Chapter LIII

Preparations for the Execution of the Condemned Indians

AS soon as the President's order postponing the day from the 19th to the 26th Dec. was received, the military authorities at Mankato commenced preparations for the execution. The gallows, twenty-four feet square, arranged to afford room for hanging ten on each side, was erected on the levee, opposite the "winter quarters" of the condemned. The people felt that justice was being defrauded, and that the gallows might have been of more extended capacity had the President been less squeamish.

On Monday the 22d of December, the condemned prisoners were separated from the "suspended" ones and removed to a strong stone building, where every precaution was taken to secure their safe keeping from violence by excited, misguided, but injured men.

On the afternoon of the same day, Col. Stephen Miller, the officer in command, through his interpreter, Rev. Mr. Riggs, announced to the prisoners the decision of their "Great Father" at Washington:

"Tell these thirty-nine * condemned men, that the commanding officer of this place has called to speak to them upon a very serious subject, this afternoon.

*The death sentence of one was afterward suspended. [H.M.]

256

"Their Great Father at Washington, after carefully reading what the witnesses testified in their several trials, has come to the conclusion, that they have each been guilty of wantonly and wickedly murdering his white children. And for this reason, he has directed that each be hanged by the neck until they are dead, on next Friday. That order will be carried into effect on that day, at ten o'clock in the forenoon.[88]

"That good ministers are here, both Catholic and Protestant, from amongst whom each one can select a spiritual adviser, who will be permitted to commune with them constantly, during the four days that they are to live.

"That I will now cause to be read the letter from their Great Father at Washington, first in English, and then in their own language." (The President's order was now read.)

"Say to them now, that they have so sinned against their fellow men, that there is no hope for clemency, except in the mercy of God, through the merits of the blessed Redeemer; and that I earnestly exhort

[88]President Lincoln's letter to Sibley, December 6, 1862, ordering the execution of thirty-nine of those originally condemned, is the most prized single manuscript in the collections of the Minnesota Historical Society, where it has been preserved since 1868. It is reproduced in facsimile in *Minnesota History*, Summer, 1952, vol. 33, pp. 77-79. The executions were to have been carried out on December 19, but were necessarily postponed for one week. One of the thirty-nine, as Mrs. McConkey notes later, was reprieved and eventually pardoned, so that thirty-eight altogether were hanged.

them to apply to that as their only remaining source of comfort and consolation."

The prisoners received their sentence very coolly, some smoking their pipes composedly during the address. One, when the time for execution was designated, quietly knocked the ashes from his pipe, and re-filled it; while another slowly rubbed a handful of kinnekinnick, preparatory to a good smoke.

The preference of clergymen being signified, the Colonel and spectators withdrew.

During the four days before the sentence was executed, nearly all made confession of their guilt to their spiritual advisers, but felt it "a shame" for them to suffer the penalty of their crimes while others, equally as guilty, went unhung. Their confessions, made to and written out by Rev. Mr. Riggs, were generally done in a cool, truthful manner, and these were checked by the others, and told that they were all dead men, and that there was no reason why they should depart from the truth. They dictated letters to their families or friends, expressing the hope that they would join them in the world of the Good Spirit.

On Tuesday evening they extemporized a dance, with a wild Indian song. It was feared this was a prelude to something else, so their chains were thereafter fastened to the floor. Mr. Riggs says it was probably their death song they sang. Those who had friends in the main prison were allowed to receive a visit from them, and then they parted. These partings, with the messages conveyed to wives and children, were sad and affecting, and many tears were shed. Good counsel was invariably sent to their children, and in many cases they were exhorted to a life of Christianity and good feeling toward the whites.

Several of the prisoners were completely overcome so that they were obliged to suspend conversation. Others laughed and joked, unconcerned as if they had been sitting around a camp fire smoking their pipes. One said he was old, and could not have hoped to live long; that he was dying innocent of white man's blood, and that he had every hope of going "direct to the abode of the Great Spirit, where he would be always happy."

Another said, "Yes, tell our friends that we are being removed from this world over the same path they must shortly travel. We go first, but many of our friends will follow us in a very short time. I expect to go direct to the abode of the Great Spirit, and to be happy when I get there; but we are told that the road is long and the distance great, therefore, as I am slow in all my movements, it will probably take me a long time to reach the end of my journey, and I should not be surprised if some of the young active men we will leave behind us, will pass me on the road before I reach my destination."

In shaking hands with Red Iron and another Indian, this man said, "Friends, last summer you were opposed to us. You were living in continual apprehension of an attack from those who were determined to exterminate the whites. You and your fami-

lies were subject to many insults, taunts and threats.
Still you stood firm in your friendship for the whites,
and continually counselled the Indians to abandon
their raid against them. Your course was condemned
at the time, but now we see your wisdom. You were
right when you said the whites could not be exterminated, and the attempt indicated folly. You and your
families were prisoners, and the lives of all in danger.
To-day you are at liberty, assisting in feeding and
guarding us, and we shall die in two days because
we did not follow your advice."

The night before the execution, Col. Miller received
an order from the President postponing the execution of Ta-ti-mi-ma, the Sioux name for David Faribault, a half-breed, and a former pupil of the writer.
He was convicted for murder, and the capture of
women and children; but there were strong doubts
of his guilt of murder, and this belief was daily
strengthened by new evidence.*

The last night allotted them on earth, they smoked
and chatted, or slept as usual, and seemed scarcely
to reflect on the doom awaiting them. "As we gazed
on them," says one who visited the prison that night,
"the recollections of how short a time since they had
been engaged in the diabolical work of murdering
indiscriminately both old and young, sparing neither
sex nor condition, sent a thrill of horror through our
veins. Now they are perfectly harmless and look as
innocent as children. They smile at your entrance

*He has since been pardoned. [H.M.]

and hold out their hands to be shaken, which appear to be yet gory with the blood of babes. Oh! treachery, thy name is Dakota!" The Catholic priest spent the entire night with them, endeavoring to impress upon them their condition, and before morning his efforts were rewarded by the privilege of baptising several, who also partook of the communion of that church before leaving the world. They wished their friends to know how cheerfully they met their fate.[89]

[89]Nothing in American history compares with this mass execution at Mankato on December 26, 1862. Pictorial representations of the event were published at the time, and even a quarter of a century later, in the form of large colored lithographs. It is clear to us now, as it was clear to very few at the time, that there were grave defects in the proceedings; and on the whole, the behavior of the condemned men compels admiration. One of those who died on the scaffold was the Chaska who had been the benefactor of Sarah F. Wakefield. In her *Six Weeks in the Sioux Tepees* she writes: "I was in Red Wing when the President sent on the list of those who were to be executed. I noticed the name of Chaskadon, but knew it was not Chaska's number, and that he was not guilty of the crime that Chaskadon was to be punished for.

"Sunday after the execution, when the papers were brought in, I noticed my name immediately, and I then saw that a mistake had been made. The Indian named Chaskadon, that the President ordered to be hanged, killed a pregnant woman and cut out her child, and they hung Chaska who was only convicted of being present when Mr. Gleason was killed.

"After passing eight weeks in Red Wing, I returned to St. Paul. I then saw Rev. S. R. Riggs . . . who was present at the time Chaska was hung, and he said he was really hanged by mistake, as his name was on the list that were recommended to mercy. In a letter I received from him, he explained the matter in this way:

"Mrs. Wakefield—*Dear Madam:*—In regard to the mistake

by which Chaska was hung instead of another, I doubt whether I can satisfactorily explain it. We all felt a solemn responsibility, and a fear that some mistake should occur. We had forgotten that he was condemned under the name of We-chan-bpe-wash-tay-do-pe. We knew he was called Chaska in the prison, and had forgotten that any other except Robert Hopkins, who lived by Dr. Williamson, was so called. We never thought of the third one; so when the name Chaska was called in the prison on that fatal morning, your protector answered to it and walked out. I do not think any one was really to blame. We all regretted the mistake very much, &c."

In her bitterness Mrs. Wakefield commented: "I will never believe that all in authority at Mankato had forgotten what Chaska was condemned for, and I am sure, in my own mind, it was done intentionally." Many years later Riggs wrote in *Mary and I. Forty Years with the Sioux,* p. 211, that mistakes were made, as there were three or four *Chaskays* and two or three *Washechoons,* and despite extraordinary care, reliance mainly placed upon Joseph R. Brown, who better than any other man knew all the condemned: "after it was all over, when we came to compare their own stories and confessions, made a day or two before their death, with the papers of condemnation, the conviction was forced upon us that two mistakes had occurred."

CHAPTER LIV

The Execution

THE spiritual advisers of the condemned Indians were all with them on the morning of the 26th December, now listened to with marked attention. They had painted their faces, as if for the begging dance, and frequently their small pocket mirror was brought before the face, to see if they retained the proper modicum of paint. They shook hands with the officers, bidding each a cheerful goodbye, as if going on an ordinary journey. Then they chanted their monotonous but very exciting death song.

The irons being knocked off, one by one, their arms were pinioned with small cords and the wrists fastened in front, leaving the hands free. Songs and conversation gave a cheerful appearance to the scene, while they moved around shaking hands with each other, the soldiers and reporters bidding the frequent "goodbye." This over, they arranged themselves in a row and again sang the death song, after which they sat down for a last smoke.

Father Ravoux,[90] the Catholic priest, now addressed them, and then knelt in prayer, some re-

[90]Father Augustin Ravoux published his own account of these events in *Reminiscences, Memoirs and Lectures* (St. Paul, 1890), pp. 72-81. In his autobiography Riggs says that the prisoners were given liberty to select such spiritual counsel as they desired, but they were advised not to select him, because he was acting as government interpreter. At the time, almost

sponding, while they were even affected to tears. Long white caps, made from cloth which had formed part of the spoils taken from murdered traders, were placed upon their heads, leaving their painted faces still visible. Their repugnance to this was very evident. Shame covered their faces, and they were humiliated by it, as chains and cords could not do. The singing ceased, and there was little smoking or talking now. The three half-breeds seemed most affected, and their countenances were pitiable to behold.

Crouched on the floor, they awaited their doom till precisely ten o'clock, when they were marched in procession through a file of soldiers to the scaffold, crowding and jostling each other to get ahead, as a lot of hungry boarders rush to the dinner table in a

the only champion the Sioux had was Henry Benjamin Whipple, who had come to Minnesota three years before as missionary bishop of the Protestant Episcopal Church. In his *A History of Minnesota,* vol. 2, pp. 208-209, W. W. Folwell says: "So far as known, he was the only public man who had the courage to face the whirlwind of popular denunciation of all Indians and of the Dakotas in particular. To punish the guilty would avail little if the traditional Indian policy was to be left unreformed. In some quarters the bishop came in for denunciation almost as spiteful and unsparing as that directed against the Sioux themselves, but he never retracted a syllable nor budged an inch." Some of his contemporary communications may be found in the St. Paul *Press,* December 4, 1862, and in the St. Paul *Pioneer,* December 3 and 17, 1862. His vigorous "Appeal for the Red Man" is reprinted as an appendix in Isaac V. D. Heard, *History of the Sioux War.* In *Lights and Shadows of a Long Episcopate* (New York, 1899), pp. 122-141, the Bishop views these times in unrepentant retrospect.

hotel. At the scaffold they were delivered to the officer of the day, Capt. Burt.

As they commenced their ascent to the gallows, the air was made hideous by their death song. It was a moment of intense suspense—every breath in that immense throng seemed suspended, when one of the baser sort improvised an exhibition of his contempt of death and the lookers on, in the most vile and indecent manner, accompanied by foul impromptu song, insulting to the spectators, and such only as the vilest could conceive or execute—a mockery to the triumph of that justice whose sword was suspended over his guilty head. One young fellow smoked a cigar after the cap was drawn over his face, managing to keep his mouth uncovered. Another smoked a pipe till the noose was adjusted over his neck.

The general aspect of the scene was intensely solemn, though many little incidents under other circumstances would have been ludicrous. Thirty-eight men awaiting the moment when one blow would launch them into eternity! Did civilized world ever look upon the like before? All who looked approved the sentence, and would, had it been ten times as large.

The silence was intense—then came three slow, measured and distinct beats on the drum by the signal officer, Major J. R. Brown, when each of the condemned clasped hands with his neighbor, which remained in firm grasp till taken down, and then the rope was cut by William J. Duly, who with his family were among the Lake Shetak sufferers.

One loud cheer went up as the platform fell, and then all relapsed into silent gaze at the thirty-seven bodies dangling in the air. One rope had broken, and the body was upon the ground. This incident created horror in the vast assemblage and complete satisfaction to the morbid curiosity which led them to be eye witnesses. Though there was no sign of life, the body was again suspended. There seemed to be little suffering—the necks of nearly all were dislocated by the fall, and in twenty minutes life was declared extinct.

The bodies were placed in four army wagons, and with Company K, under Lieutenant Colonel Marshall of the Seventh, for a burial party, were deposited in one grave, prepared on the sand bar nearly in front of the town.

The other condemned Indians were chained in their quarters, that they might not witness the execution. When the death song of their associates fell upon their ears, they crouched down with their blankets over their heads, seeming to feel all the horrors of their situation. All day they were much dejected.

The disposition of the military force, amounting to 1,419 men, as also the entire arrangements for the execution, were most perfect. Great credit is due Col. Miller for carrying out his well directed plans, and for preserving the quiet, order and discipline which distinguished the day.

Chapter LV

The Condemned

DURING the winter, those whose death sentence had been postponed continued to receive spiritual advice. Those who from daily intercourse were best prepared to judge, felt that the Spirit of God came into that jail of guilty ones, for whom Christ died, with mighty and convincing power—that darkened understandings were opened to receive the truth, and hearts stained and blackened by crime were regenerated by His blood. Others hardened themselves against the truth, and would have none of "the reproofs of the Spirit."

One hundred and fifty became earnest scholars and learned to read the Bible and Hymn Book, in which they took great delight, and often held religious service among themselves. Whether these were true converts to the Christian faith we leave it for a religious world to judge, and the day of final account to decide. But they were never in so favorable circumstances for *thought* and for the mind to receive lasting impressions. Their roving life has been the greatest drawback with which the Missionary has to contend. They would not stop to *think*. Now they had no other employ, and the time for instructing them was well improved by those who had long sought their souls' good. If "Christ died for the chief of sinners" surely he died for them, and great sinners, with enlightened consciences, have been pardoned.

During the winter, several deaths occurred in the jail, so that when those whose sentence was suspended were removed to Davenport, Iowa, they numbered but two hundred and sixty-three men, with whom went sixteen women for cooks and laundresses. The quarters there provided for them was an immense prison pen of boards, inclosing four large shanties.

A decided improvement is noticed by those who visited them there, and before they left the State. Instead of dozing and idling away their time, as was their wont, they were often seen reading, writing or solving the first lessons on the slate. Habits of industry, too, were formed; may be because compelled to do so, but cheerfully they set about cleaning camp, digging wells, or whatever work assigned them. Thus a transforming power has been at work, and though those who visited them and looked for the first time upon an Indian went away disgusted, a decided change for the better had taken place.

CHAPTER LVI

The Winnebagoes Declare War
with the Sioux

AN Indian, a savage, untamed, unchristianized Indian, be he Sioux, Chippewa or Winnebago, *is an Indian,* wherever you find him. They delight in cruel deeds, and are ready to join any tribe in war against a weaker party.

At the commencement of the outbreak, the Winnebagoes, not as a tribe or band but many individuals, distinguished themselves for bravery and daring, entering as vigorously into the battles as the aggressors themselves. But the Sioux are driven away, and now war is declared upon them by the Winnebagoes, more to curry favor with the victorious whites than for any other cause, probably hoping the removal of their families deferred. Certain it is that some other motive than friendship for the whites has instigated so small a tribe to take up arms against their Sioux neighbors, with whom they have heretofore been on friendly terms.

The Sioux left behind are hunted out, and no opportunity for a good shot allowed to pass unimproved. Instances occurred where as brutal, barbarous treatment was given the Sioux as they were ever guilty of towards the whites. The bodies of their victims would be mutilated, hearts torn out, large knives run through their centre, and then hung upon poles.

A scalp dance was even improvised in the streets of Mankato, in which all the warriors, squaws and chil-

dren joined. One young Winnebago brave paraded
the main street with the tongue of a Sioux warrior
recently murdered, apparently torn from his mouth
and swollen very thick, stopping, as occasion occurred, to gratify the curiosity of passers-by.

The Indian whose tongue had given such offense
had a wife of their tribe, with whom he had lived
during the winter, among her own people. Hearing
of the murder of two of his own people, his Sioux
blood was aroused, and he declared his intention of
imparting the information to the tribe; only his wife
knew of his design when he left, but he was overtaken
and murdered before he left the reservation.

But not of long continuance were the troubles with
these two tribes. One fled beyond the reach of harm.
The return of spring brought a change. The Winnebagoes no longer held their Reservation in the very
Eden of the Minnesota Valley. Far up the Missouri
river, their home is now where they could "worry and
devour each other," were it not for the watchful eye
of Government.[91]

[91]The Winnebagoes, a Siouan people, had a reservation ten
miles south of Mankato, in Blue Earth County. A few of them
seem to have participated in the attack on Fort Ridgley. A
chief, Little Priest, and eleven tribesmen were examined at
Camp Lincoln by a military court, having been arrested on
October 12, 1862, by order of General Pope. They had been
present at the Lower Agency at the time of the outbreaks, but
were discharged, "to the great disappointment and dissatisfaction of the people of the State." See Bryant and
Murch, *A History of the Great Massacre by the Sioux Indians,*
p. 460. In 1863 some 2,000 Winnebagoes were removed to a
new Missouri River reservation.

Chapter LVII

An Alarm

DURING the winter of 1862–3, comparative quiet prevailed. Military forces were stationed all along the frontier, to prevent further incursions. Marauding savages lurked in the Big Woods, and as often as opportunity offered, murdered, stole horses, and committed various depredations in the more distant settlements.

As winter advanced into spring, they became still more daring, and horse thieving more general. Little Crow had sent thieving parties all over the State, and things again assumed an alarming aspect.

Col. Miller, at Mankato, was awakened one morning to act upon the following alarming dispatch:

Medalia, April 17, 1863.

Col. Stephen Miller:

DEAR SIR:—This morning, at two o'clock, two men from a detached post, on the south bend of the Watonwan, reported here, with the information that the settlement was attacked yesterday morning, by a large party of Indians, estimated by the Lieutenant in command, at not less than fifty. We have but one man killed and three wounded, and one boy, ten years of age, was killed. The Indians have taken all the horses they could get hold of—one belonging to Government. Lieutenant Hardy writes, that he thinks the Indians will renew the attack this morning. I shall start re-enforcements at four o'clock, and send for the wounded. We will need a surgeon to attend to the wounded, also a force of cavalry, with which to pursue the Indians.

Your ob't servant,
T. G. HALL,
Capt. Co. E, 7th Reg't Volunteers.

The settlement attacked was distant, southwest of Medalia, about twenty miles, and from Mankato forty-eight miles. A detachment of twenty-one men from Company E of the Seventh Regiment under Lieut. Hardy was engaged in building a stockade, which was unfinished when the attack was made—at dawn on the 16th of April.[92]

As soon as the alarm was given, messengers were sent to collect the settlers in the stockade, and the force was deployed to cover their flight. One woman, Mrs. Targerson, was wounded in the thigh before she left her house, where one man was killed, and another severely wounded with arrows. The wounded man grappled with the foremost Indian, broke two arrows, grasped his gun, and fired at them, when they fled. Mrs T.'s wounds retarded her, so that the Indians soon overtook her, when they beat her over the head in a most cruel manner with the butts of their guns. This act was seen by some soldiers, when the Indians

[92]Lewis Hardy, whose name appears in some records as "Hardy Lewis," was then an officer of the Third Regiment, afterward of the Seventh. He was killed at Tupelo, Mississippi, July 15, 1864. The stockade he occupied on the south branch of the Watonwan River during the winter was known as Fort Union. See Bryant and Murch, *A History of the Great Massacre by the Sioux Indians,* pp. 486-489.

fled. She reached the stockade, without further molestation.

The Indians appeared to be well armed, but had no horses except what they stole in that neighborhood. They drove off cattle belonging to the settlement.

One company of cavalry and two of infantry, under Lieut. Col. Marshall, reached Medalia the same night, the following morning meeting the wounded, in charge of Lieut. Hardy.

Upon receipt of the same intelligence at Fort Ridgley, Lieut. Col. Pfender [William Pfaender] started a cavalry company of fifty well armed men to unite with Col. Marshall's command. This swelled the cavalry to one hundred, which with several teams, forage and ammunition, started on Sunday morning, the 19th of April, in pursuit of the Indians. The infantry companies were left at Medalia and the stockade, to guard against another attack.

The companies in charge of Col. Marshall scoured the country as far as Lake Shetak, and though often finding traces of where they had camped a day or two previous, returned to head-quarters without having seen an Indian.

Chapter LVIII

Removal of the "Good Indians"

DURING the session of Congress in the winter of
1863, a new reservation was appropriated in the
vicinity of Fort Randall in Dakota Territory, instead
of Boston Common, for the guiltless ones taken in
charge at Camp Release, in September, 1862.[93]

All winter, we had seen their uninviting camp, the
curling smoke from their tepees, and their filthy or
gaily painted faces peeping from 'neath the folds of
their blankets, on the flat at Fort Snelling, where the
waters of the Minnesota and Mississippi meet.

Just before their departure, a cargo of several hundred contrabands was landed near the same spot. It
was a novel sight as each party gazed at the other in
seeming wonder. The blacks had thought no mortals

[93]Mrs. McConkey might better have said that Congress, by
its act of February 16, 1863, bereft the Sioux of a home by
abrogating all treaties. Another act of March 3 provided for
the removal of all Indians then in the custody of the Federal
government, to some place beyond the boundaries of any
State. The President thought best to settle them on the
Missouri, within a hundred miles of Fort Randall, where
presumably they would be secure from white intrusion. In
May, Clark W. Thompson, Superintendent of Indian Affairs
for the Northern Superintendency, announced choice of a
reservation about 80 miles above Fort Randall. Here the
Santee Sioux deported from Minnesota eked out a miserable
existence for the next three years, adjacent to the Winnebagoes,
until a better reservation was found near the mouth of the
Niobrara River.

as degraded as themselves, but found themselves out-done. The Indians had thought themselves the black-est of the human race, but now looked upon those of a deeper dye. And so they looked, and gazed, and talked, the few days they were neighbors.

But the steamer has "rounded to," to convey from our sight those government pets. Lodges are struck and packed with all their worldly goods, and with a strap round the forehead, slung over the backs of the squaws, as they move into their moving quar-ters.

In military order the bands were marched on board, the celebrated chief Wabashaw taking the lead, and counted to see that none were missing. They were followed by the bands of Good Road, Wacouta, Pass-ing Hail, and Red Legs. The greater portion were women and children. Many of the trustworthy Indians remained for scouts in Gen. Sibley's expedition, their families encamped on the prairie in rear of the fort, provided for at public expense, and guarded day and night by armed men. In this company of some fifteen or twenty tepees were some quite intelligent and cul-tivated women. Though most retained their native costume, some wore dresses and crinoline. One was pointed out to us as a teacher, acting in that capacity to the juveniles of the encampment. Industry in the domestic department prevailed, and we were struck with the improvement in personal cleanliness.

To their shame be it said, when the boat having the "good Indians" on board landed at St. Paul, a crowd of soldiers, led by one who had been wounded at Birch Coolie, commenced throwing stones and other missiles into the Indians on the boat, impossible for them to avoid, as they were so closely packed on the boiler deck. Several squaws were hit upon the head and severely injured. A threat by the commanding officer to charge bayonets on the offending crowd soon dispersed them. Such a gross outrage was strongly condemned by all good citizens. These were not the murderers, hence no apology for such an act.[94]

While the boat "lay to," many of the Indians were engaged in prayer and singing, in which last exercise they took great delight, but whether with devout hearts it is not ours to say.

From Hannibal, Missouri, these Indians were taken by cars to St. Joseph, and embarked on the Missouri for their new Reservation.

The new Winnebago Reservation is contiguous, divided only by a small creek. Here, under the supervision of Col. Thompson, the Agent, they began to thrive, even in a desolated region with scarcely a sign of cultivation.

"The Colonel's improvements," says one who writes so early as July 15, "are certainly a striking

[94] The deportees were loaded aboard the steamboat *Davenport* on May 4, even before the site of their new reservation had been designated. Altogether, 770 Indians were thus started on their way to the Missouri River. Another 540 Sioux were embarked the following day in the *Northerner*. See W. W. Folwell, *A History of Minnesota,* vol. 2, pp. 258-259.

and cheering sight. In the foreground was a small camp of soldiers; to the right, a steam saw-mill, in full operation; to the left, a large, two story frame house, in course of erection; while temporary buildings and tents were scattered around, occupied by the workmen; and prominent in the centre, a temporary breastwork, constructed of supplies, brought for the workmen and for the Indians, in the centre of which stood a temporary building, used as an office and kitchen, the latter department presided over by 'Bill,' a darkey from St. Louis.

"The Colonel was pushing on the work, superintending everything himself. Buildings are rising as if by magic, and by autumn, if nothing untoward transpires, a model Agency will be nearly completed. It is laid out four hundred feet square, to be enclosed by a stockade fifteen feet high, inside of which all the buildings, of both Agencies, will be located. It will be more impregnable to Indian attacks than any I have ever seen.

"He is also making preparations for the erection of fifty houses for the Indians, to be finished before winter. For the short time the work has been in progress (only about six weeks), it is astonishing that so much could be accomplished, and no one but a western man would believe it, if *told* the amount of work that has been done. Several of the buildings are finished and occupied. The saw mill is turning out lumber and shingles daily. The Indians are killing both deer and buffalo only a few miles away."

A company of captive Sioux from White Lodge's band were confined at Fort Randall; with them was a man sent there by Col. Thompson for cutting and abusing his wife, who afterward hung herself. He made his way to the Agency, was informed on by an Indian, and sent back to prison. Two weeks later he was given over to the Indians, as the offense was against one of their own people. A council resulted in a decision for death, the uncle of his injured wife appointed executioner. The prisoner went forth to the execution, of which he was informed on the way. He evinced no alarm. His hands were left unbound, and in the brief interim between arrival at the ground and the fatal shot he bounded upon his executioner and stabbed him thrice. Throwing away his knife, he expressed a readiness to die, and calmly waited till the son of the man he had stabbed was sent for to shoot him, according to the custom that the nearest kin must avenge the death. The boy came, but had not the courage to do the deed. An Indian from the crowd volunteered to do it for him.

Chapter LIX
Horse Stealing

AS the season advanced, horse stealing became the order of the day, or rather the business of the night. *Imaginary* Indians were often seen, *real* ones occasionally, perhaps as they were mounting the favorite horse of the owner and leading another, to gallop off so rapidly that a shot would be without effect.

On the night of the 7th of June a span of horses was stolen from a stable near Silver Creek, in Wright county. The following morning a party started to track the thieves. The trail led through many difficult windings in marsh and timber, giving assurance that Indians were the thieves. All day they wandered, when at nightfall they saw the objects of their pursuit not forty rods in front. Where was their courage now? In less time than I am writing it, their horses' heads were wheeled; not so soon, however, but they heard the sharp crack of a cap. Indians and horses were left in the rear at a quick pace. The pursued skedaddled with quite as much haste as the pursuers, leaving two packs of useful articles on the ground, and many other things scattered around which nothing but fright would have prevented their taking.

Emboldened by success, this gang of stealing, murdering desperadoes were encroaching further and further into the settlements, threatening to overrun the State.

A young man was found murdered in Pine county, under circumstances to incite suspicion against another, with whom he was in company. It was supposed he had made for parts unknown; and as the former was robbed of all valuables, that he had appropriated it to his own use.

The body of the murdered man bore evidence of severe treatment with both club and knife. After evidence developed that Indians were his murderers, and that the suspected one escaped only to share a like fate. Everywhere blood drenched the soil.

On the 14th of May a man was killed near New Ulm, and four horses with which he was plowing made off with; and this where one or two companies of troops were stationed. An order embodying a bounty of twenty-five dollars, afterward increased to two hundred, was issued by the Adjutant General for every Sioux scalp, and other high inducements offered volunteers to scour the Big Woods, search out the lion in his lair and lay the trophy at the feet of the Historical Society—a relic of the unparalleled tragedies to which our State has been subjected.[95]

[95] The Minnesota Historical Society has long since ceased to make collections of this kind, but the allusion shows how intimately this Society—founded so early as 1849—has always been associated with Minnesota's frontier era. W. W. Folwell, *A History of Minnesota,* vol. 2, p. 289, found as the only resulting records: "July 6, bounty for scalp, $25.00; August 7, bounty for killing one Sioux warrior, $75.00; August 31, tanning an Indian scalp, $5.00; October 9, bounty for killing one Sioux warrior, $25.00. These were paid out of the adjutant general's contingent fund."

Chapter LX

Murder of the Dustin Family

HENNEPIN county, west of the Mississippi and
north of the Minnesota rivers, is one of the
best populated in the State. Nearly every quarter
section is occupied and *improved* by industrious
farmers.

Minneapolis, the seat of this county, is located on
the west side of the Falls of St. Anthony, having a
population of five or six thousand. Within six miles
of this place the Indians came, bold in execution of
evil designs, yet cat-like in manner. When their presence excited no alarm, when a score of Indians was
seen to every white man, many a time has the writer
been startled from a reverie by a slight rustle at her
side, or a heavy breathing, to find herself in the presence of a stalwart Indian. Once, on Third street in
St. Paul, though grass-grown *then*, a sound somewhat
like a high pressure steam engine on a Mississippi
sand bar in low water came to my ear, distant only
the thickness of my bonnet. Half turning my head, I
encountered a monster Indian with gaily painted face,
delighted with my embarrassment, or his wit thus
to exhibit himself for approval, though "never a word
he spoke," but with the usual grunt passed on.

Eight miles from Minneapolis a farmer with his son
was at work in the field when seven Indians came in
view. As soon as they saw they were discovered, they

fled to the bushes. The farmer hastened to collect his neighbors, of whom twelve or fifteen returned to the spot, and followed them round Madison Lake, two miles nearer town, when they lost the trail.

On Monday the 29th of June, the day before this skulking party was seen, in a sparsely populated region a few miles away, Mr. Amos Dustin and his family of five was passing over the prairie in an open lumber box wagon. When found on Wednesday following, Mr. Dustin was in the front of the wagon— dead. An arrow was sticking in his body, and a deep tomahawk wound was in his breast. His left hand had been cut off and carried away by the Indians.

Beneath his seat crouched a little girl of six years; her hair matted, her garments saturated, her face covered, and her shoes literally filled with the blood which had trickled from the mangled body of her father. She was the only uninjured member of the family; she said that "the Indians looked very sharply at her, and supposed they would kill her too," but not a hand was laid upon her.

The mother, and another child twelve years old, were alive when found, but mortally wounded. For two days and nights they had lain thus beside the dead, unable to procure sustenance or assistance.

The mother of Mr. Dustin lay with her head hanging over the wagon, her long silvery hair matted with blood waving in the wind. An arrow in her body had done the work of death. The horses of course were gone, conveying the perpetrators from the scene.[96]

More vigorous measures for *home* defense were at once taken. Seventy stand of arms were issued to Hennepin county. No means were spared by State and military authorities to prevent future outrages.

[96]The Dustin murders are also described in Isaac V. D. Heard, *History of the Sioux War,* pp. 302-304, an account deriving like that of Mrs. McConkey from one in the St. Paul *Press,* and at greater length in W. W. Folwell, *A History of Minnesota,* vol. 2, pp. 442-443.

Chapter LXI

Little Crow's Whereabouts

WHERE now was the Commander-in-Chief of the mighty Sioux, whose parties were doing so much evil in the land? He had not idled away the winter. Wherever he might find a British subject, hither he went, setting forth his grievances and begging his alliance in driving off the Americans. At Fort Garry, in British America, with sixty warriors he made strong efforts to form a peace treaty. After impressing them with the scalp dance, Little Crow spoke of the efforts the "Big Knives" were making to catch him, in very desponding tones, though he asserted the power of his warriors, and said though "he considered himself as good as a dead man, they should fight awhile yet." He spoke of the Government proceedings against himself and the condemned Sioux. He did "not complain that they were refused a tract of land on which to settle, which would place them under British protection," but would "be glad of a little ammunition to kill Americans with." This, Governor Dallas decidedly refused; to which he replied, "it made no difference, he had plenty." The people becoming tired of his insolence, Gov. Dallas ordered him and his followers to trouble them no more with their presence.[97]

They are back to their "winter quarters," dissen-

[97]Occasional reference to Little Crow's activities in the north during the spring of 1863 was made by the Minnesota

284

LITTLE CROW

sions arising. Many are sick of the war—some never having been engaged in it, having gone off with them because they were Indians, and supposed all Indians doomed, if caught. Standing Buffalo had never favored the war, neither had Sweet Corn; they wanted to make peace, and were determined to deliver themselves up as soon as assured by the President that no harm should come to them.

press. On April 23 the St. Paul *Pioneer* reported that "Little Crow with a party has frequented the neighborhood of Long Lake, on the Missouri, about 125 miles above Fort Pierre, and a little South-west of Devil's Lake. White Lodge, with another party has been at Painted Wood, in the same neighborhood. The balance have been at Devil's Lake, during the winter. Delegations from these Indians have been frequently to St. Joseph and Pembina, and one party of seventy visited Fort Garry, with the design of obtaining arms and ammunition from the British traders, but we are happy to say that they were refused, and the most sincere friendship and sympathy was manifested by our British neighbors for us in our troubles." This visit to Fort Garry (the future Winnipeg), and the unsatisfactory interview with Alexander Grant Dallas, then the Hudson's Bay Company's governor for Rupert's Land, occurred about the first of June, and resulted in an interesting account of Little Crow, printed in the St. Paul *Pioneer* from the *World:* "He is about fifty years of age—of medium height and spare figure. Of course, he has high cheekbones—what Indian was ever known without them? Face thin and cadaverous, and he has suffered much from sickness; he is now far from being in full health. At Fort Garry, the other day, in his council with Governor Dallas, his chief-ship was dressed in a black cloth coat, velvet collar. He had a breech-clout of fine blue cloth, and around his waist a costly shawl served the purpose of a sash. Another shawl was converted into a turban. Deer skin leggins and the usual moccasins completed the costume. He had discarded the rifle, and flourished an elegant seven-shooter . . . "

The return of thieving parties elated Little Crow, for they had been very successful; he resolved to redeem his fallen fortunes in that direction. Ten months before, a mighty nation bowed to his nod; he was rich in booty, his soul feasting on the blood of the slain. Now, taking his little son, he descends to petty horse stealing, accompanied by less than twenty followers. We know naught of his wanderings, of his fastings and weariness, of his despondency and his howlings over his sad prospects, as he passes to the seat of his former raid! Little Crow, one year before boasting of his might, is almost alone, a wanderer avoiding the presence of those whose life he lately sought; with retribution upon his track.

Chapter LXII

The Ransomed

MORE than two months of weary marches—of sleepless nights and terrible anxiety—constantly watched by weasel-eyed captors, of savage abuse from which their women hearts recoiled—of hunger and cold, and the worn captives of Shetak memory reached the banks of the Missouri river far to the southwest. The little girls had been allowed sometimes to ride on the two poles dragged behind the horse, but otherwise had received inhuman treatment. Little Tilla Everett, only eight years old, was one time struck on the head by a squaw with a heavy stake, from the effects of which she was a long time insensible, and none expected her to recover, or that she would ever find her father, if he still lived.

All the hellish ingenuity of their nature seemed taxed to invent some new torture, the details of which would make the blood curdle. Both the women were *enciente* when taken, and were obliged to submit to the vile embraces, one of five and the other of three of these monsters, till abortion followed; and even then there was scarce a suspension of suffering. Mrs. Dooley [Laura Duly] was four times sold—for a horse, again for a blanket, and once for a bag of shot. Her little girl, six years old, was sold for a gold watch, and again for two yards of cloth.

The most menial service was exacted, and severe abuse meted to the mothers, who endeavored to keep their helpless ones constantly beside them, and receive the blows instead of them. But there came a time when even this was forbidden. Mrs. Julia Wright was ordered to go for water. The child of two years cried for its mother, when it was beaten by a squaw and then turned over to a male brute who went out behind the tent and killed it before the mother's return.

One Indian boasted of going to a house where a woman was making bread—the mother of a child which lay in the cradle—that he split the woman's head open with a tomahawk, and then placed the babe in the hot oven, keeping it there till baked to death, when he beat its brains out against the wall. This is corroborated by whites who have been at the house where it happened.

When we reflect that these women and children fell into the hands of such monsters, we wonder at their final escape, or at their enduring powers. Thank heaven for the rescue!

On the last day of October, 1862, when love of life had fled—their emaciated bodies scarcely covered by the shreds of clothing left them—their first joy since their captivity was in seeing a party of white men floating down the river. The Indians, finding they could not inveigle them on shore, commenced hostile demonstrations, when the hopes of the women sank. At the risk of life, however, they made them-

selves seen and heard. Major Charles E. Galpin, for
it was he with a small party of men returning to his
trading post, from this day devoted all his soul to this
object, and directed that no effort be spared for their
ransom.[98] The persons whose hearts were filled with
gratitude to him who secured them protection at
Fort Randall were Mrs. Wright and daughter, Mrs.
Dooley and daughter, Misses Rosanna and Ellen Ireland, and Tilla Everett, the only member of her family
spared to her father. Of this Mr. Everett remained
for months in ignorance, suffering from wounds in
the hospital at Mankato. When the press announced
the ransom of his child, he started to find his lost one.
At last they met. She rushed to his wide open arms,

[98]Isaac V. D. Heard, *History of the Sioux War,* pp. 99-102,
gives an account of this captivity and the affecting eventual
reunion of Everett and his daughter. Charles E. Galpin's role
in the rescue of the prisoners is related by Charles P. Barbier,
"Recollections of Ft. La Framboise in 1862 and the Rescue of
Lake Chetak Captives," *South Dakota Historical Collections,*
1922, vol. 11, pp. 232-242. (Barbier was the father-in-law of
John P. Williamson, son of Stephen Riggs's fellow missionary.) Another account is by John Pattee, then Captain in the
Fourteenth Iowa Infantry; see *South Dakota Historical Collections,* 1910, vol. 5, pp. 283-290, and the accompanying note by
Doane Robinson, p. 350. Some contemporary official docu-
mentation may be found in 37th Congress, 3rd Session,
House Executive Document 1 [Serial 1157], pp. 519-523. Galpin
was en route down from Fort Benton or Fort Stuart with a
party of miners, and met the Santees about November 15,
perhaps owing his own escape to the fact that his wife was a
full-blooded Sioux. The actual ransom of the captives was
effected by Sioux of the Fool Soldier band, who gained possession of them on the evening of November 20 and brought
them into Fort Pierre on the morning of the 24th.

and was in tearless silence folded to his throbbing heart. They who saw it wept, but the scene was too sacred for words. In the moment of almost delirious joy they half forgot what heart and flesh had suffered. May the world deal gently by all these sufferers.

Chapter LXIII

The Indian Expedition

CAMP Pope, where the troops under command of Brig. Gen. Sibley were ordered to report, was at the mouth of Red Wood river, so late the theatre of the terrible massacres which inaugurated the war in Minnesota.

For weeks activity and bustle prevailed, in anticipation of a three months' campaign—no small undertaking. The Brigade Commissary, Capt. Wm. H. Forbes, who had suffered the loss of some forty thousand dollars in the great raid, evinced his usual energy, ability and good sense, that no want of calculation in him would bring failure. Two hundred and twenty-five wagons were loaded with well packed provisions, and in due time, all was ready.

On the ninth of June the monotony of camp life was interrupted by the arrival of Gen. Sibley. All were anxious to be on the move. Every domestic circle in the State was more or less personally interested in the success of the expedition. Its officers, from the Lieutenants to the General commanding, were from our own hearth stones. The troops were our own, fathers, brothers and sons of Minnesota.

Gen. Sibley, with the great energy which had characterized his life now bent all powers to this purpose —to forever free the beautiful northwest from the assassins against whom this expedition was planned.

Scarcely had the excitement attendant on his arrival subsided, when the strong man "bows himself and weeps," as only a bereaved father can. The first tidings from home brings the sad message of a daughter's death, smitten by disease. But all things in camp reminded him of the responsibility of his position, and he must gird him for duty.

On the 16th of June, 1863, the expedition took up the line of march for Dakota territory. The entire force numbered about four thousand men, distributed as follows: Sixth Regiment, Col. Crooks, eight hundred and sixty men; Seventh Regiment, Col. Marshall, seven hundred and forty men; Tenth Regiment, Col. Baker, five hundred and seventy-eight men (three companies had been detailed for special duty); Cavalry, Col. McPhail, eight hundred and six men; and Capt. Jones' Battery, one hundred and forty men and eight guns.

Gen. Sibley's Staff was organized as follows:

Capt. R. C. Olin, Acting Adjutant General.

Capt. C. B. Atchinson [Atchison], Assistant Commissary of musters, and Acting Ordnance officer.

Captain Douglas Pope, Aid-de-Camp.

Captain Edward Corning, Quartermaster.

Captain Wm. H. Forbes, Commissary.

George H. Spencer, Chief Clerk of Commissary Department.

Captain Wm. H. Kimball, Quartermaster's Assistant, assigned to special duty as pioneer in charge of pontoon trains.

Lieutenant Joseph R. Putman, Aid-de-Camp.

F. J. Holt Beever, A. St. Clair Flandrau, and Archibald Hawthorne, Aid-de-Camps, with rank of Second Lieutenant.

Seventy scouts, half of whom were volunteer Indians, and a majority of the balance half-breeds, were with the expedition—in command of Major J. R. Brown, J. G. McCleod, and Wm. J. Dooley [Duly], who were to act as chiefs of scouts, each half to serve on alternate days, and precede the expedition. The position of Rev. S. R. Riggs was changed from chaplain to interpreter, yet he acted in the first as before, and with all the temptations around him proved his trust in that Being who alone can deliver from the evils of vice.

For transportation of commissary stores there were two hundred and twenty-five wagons; for ordnance, twenty; pontoons, eleven; and battery, two;—for camp equipage of thirty-eight companies, nineteen; quartermaster's department and medical supplies, seventeen; regimental headquarters, eight; headquarters of the expedition, two. Surgeon Alfred Wharton received the appointment of medical director.

The sale of intoxicating liquors was prohibited; notwithstanding, those who so desired found their canteens re-filled whenever they had been emptied. —Strange and mysterious are the genii of this prince of evil!

Thus the well organized force was on the move, a train of five miles in length, formidable enough in appearance to awe the whole Sioux nation, and of courage and daring equal to any danger or effort.

The setting out was most unpropitious. Such a season of drouth was never known in the West. The prairies were literally parched, and all the sloughs and little streams dry. The fierce prairie winds were like the siroccos of the desert, withering every green thing. Clouds of dust, raised by this immense column, would blind the eyes, choke the throat and blacken the faces of the men, so that they looked more like colliers than soldiers. In time, wagons and provision boxes fell in pieces, and much time was spent in making secure those uninjured. Both men and animals suffered for water, but the health of the men was not seriously affected. On the 19th, Mr. Riggs, writing from Camp Baker, one mile above the ruins of Hazlewood Mission Station, says:

"We have travelled three days, and have made about thirty miles from Camp Pope. The teams are all very heavily loaded, so heavy, indeed, that although we all wish for rain to make the earth rejoice, yet if that rain should come, it might very seriously affect the progress of this command at present. But the green grass is so dried up that fires run on the prairie wherever it was not burned last fall. And the streams of water too, are falling, so that we shall be obliged to keep near to the larger rivers or lakes, to obtain a supply of water for these 4,000 men, and as many animals.

"Our soldiers have marched, carrying their knapsacks, their blankets and their guns, an average of ten miles a day, which, with the immense train we have, in its present state, is thought as much as can reasonably be calculated upon. Yesterday morning, while the train was crossing the Yellow Medicine, I obtained from the General a squad of scouts and orderlies and came on to gather currants in the deserted gardens of the Missions. We found, and brought away with us a quantity of the pie-plant. These are the last remnants of civilization to be found in this direction. I gathered a few pinks and other flowers from my own garden at Hazlewood. Some of the men brought in lettuce, which they found in the gardens of the Agency.

"It is to me quite saddening to look on the desolation which the outbreak has made in the land. Seeing them again, has more deeply impressed me with the exceeding folly as well as sin of the Dakotas. By that one wicked act they have forever deprived themselves of homes in this beautiful land. But there is a Providence that shapes the destinies of people as well as individuals, brings good out of evil, and makes the wrath of man to praise HIM."

On the Sabbath day the standard rested from its march. This arrangement was, on the first Sabbath, made by the Commanding General, unless in cases of urgent necessity. We endorse the sentiment of Mr. Riggs, that on the low ground of temporal economy they would find it profitable. "We shall march further," he says, "week after week, by resting on God's day, than we should by marching through the seven. But there is a higher view of this subject: If God be with us in this campaign, we shall make it a success; if God be not with us, we shall fail of accomplishing the desired objects. And one way to secure the presence and assistance of God, is to 'remember the Sabbath day, to keep it holy.'"

Chapter LXIV

Death of General Little Crow

ON the third of July, 1863, a boy and his father were performing important service to their country—a service which will immortalize the name of Lampson.

Mr. Lampson lived at Hutchinson, a town which suffered much in the troubles of 1862, since which everybody had been on watchful lookout for retaliation, and seldom went unarmed any distance from town. Mr. L. and his son Chauncey were six miles in the country on this eventful day, when they discovered two Indians *picking berries* in an "opening" in the woods. Bushes and scattering poplars were interspersed, so that the Indians did not discover the two pair of eyes upon them. Mr. L. determined to make sure of his game before announcing his presence, so he crept forward among the vines and rested his gun against the tree they climbed. He fired, his shot taking effect, as evinced by the loud yell. His victim fell to the ground severely wounded. Not knowing the number of Indians, Mr. L. thought best to retreat a little, where he could obtain the shelter of some bushes.

The wounded Indian crept after him, when the two Indians and Chauncey Lampson, who was concealed from their view, fired simultaneously. Chauncey's ball killed the wounded Indian, and the other sprang to his horse and rode away. A ball from the Indian's rifle whistled close to his cheek, while one from the other's gun struck his father on the left shoulder blade, making a slight flesh wound.

Mr. Lampson dropped when struck, and his son, supposing him killed, fearing a large force of Indians near, having no more ammunition, and not daring to approach his father to obtain more, beat a hasty retreat for town.

He arrived at ten o'clock in the evening, when the news flew like fire on the prairie. An army squad, with a number of the citizens, were soon marching to the scene of conflict, while others started in other directions to warn the citizens; others still went to Lake Preston for a squad of cavalry, who were guided to the spot before daylight and relieved "Mr. Injun" of his scalp. *Mark this, reader, this was the first scalp for which the twenty-five dollars reward was claimed, the first Sioux scalp taken by white man* in 1863.

When found by the company guided to the spot by young Lampson, the body of the Indian had been straightened, new moccasins put upon his feet, and his blanket carefully adjusted, as no dead "Injun" could do it. This led to the conviction that these were not alone.

We will not leave the reader to suppose that the elder Lampson "laid him down to die," from the slight though unpleasant wound he had received. With the courage which characterized his first movement, he crawled into the bushes, reloaded his gun, drew his revolver, and waited for the foe. None coming, he profited by the cover of night to come forth from concealment. Divesting himself of his white garments, that they might not prove a fatal mark, and taking a circuitous route, he reached home about two o'clock on the morning of the "FOURTH."

On the return of the military squad with the citizen's coat, moccasins, and a number of trinkets found on the dead Indian, the programme of the day was changed by sending for the body, which was brought in about three o'clock in the afternoon. For two or three hours it was the centre of attraction. The coat was identified as one taken from the man murdered some distance from there, of which mention has been made. All who beheld, declared a striking resemblance between this Indian and Little Crow, only this one a shade lighter — the age about fifty. Both arms were withered and deformed by breaking and permanent displacement of the bones, the result of rough handling in past time. A strange coincidence, they thought, as this was the case with Little Crow. As the body was becoming offensive, they "dumped" him into a hole and left him, no tears of regret having fallen, and the Lampsons little dreaming the service they had rendered the State in ridding it of one for whom a government train five miles long was in pursuit.

The press published the facts as here related. In two weeks the news reached the camp of General Sibley. The striking coincidence, the minute description of the body, its resemblance to Little Crow, attracted the attention of the Commanding General, who had known him well for years, and he declared it to be none other than the arch-enemy. In this opinion Major Brown and Capt. Forbes concurred. Calling to the aid of their memories the Indian scouts and half-breeds, not one was known in the whole tribe who bore this resemblance in all the minutiæ to Little Crow. It was considered a strongly corroborative circumstance that the citizens of Hutchinson, who knew him, should detect this resemblance. This opinion was returned to the press, when investigation confirmed the fact that the *scalp of the terror-inspiring* LITTLE CROW *was a trophy at the historical rooms in the State Capital.*[99]

[99]Little Crow's scalp, skull, and the wrist bones of one arm are still preserved in the museum collections of the Minnesota Historical Society. Once a popular attraction, they have lost their fascination, and the curator, Mr. Alan R. Woolworth, advises me that they have not been displayed for many years. The account of Little Crow's demise related here is correct in most details, though his companion did not escape on horseback. Before the dead Indian was identified as Little Crow, an account of the incident was sent the St. Paul *Pioneer* of July 14, 1863, by a correspondent writing from Hutchinson five days earlier. By July 21 a correspondent with Sibley's camp, then at Camp Olin on the James River, Dakota Territory, could write, "The reported death of Little Crow is credited by the General, Major Brown, and Capt. Forbes, all of whom are personally acquainted with him . . . " The day after quoting this letter, on August 6, the *Pioneer* represented Sibley as having written Colonel Miller, "there is reason to believe that the Indian killed by Mr. Lampson and son, near Hutchinson, was Little Crow himself. I wrote you

A more marked instance of retribution, history does not record. The leader of the first Indian war which has scourged our State, in which for the first time white men felt the scalping-knife of the savage, now paying the forfeit, his own head furnishing the *first* scalp white man has ever taken!

The grave of Little Crow, which was only a hole dug for the offals of slaughtered cattle, being lightly covered, his head was soon exposed to view, and with a stick was sloughed from the body, where for several days it remained, the brains oozing out in the hot sun, when a more critical investigation was made. The teeth were found to be double set around the mouth, which was known to be the case with Little Crow; and now the offensive, worthless thing, suddenly magnified into importance, was carefully prepared in a strong solution of lime. The decaying body, almost devoid of flesh, was exhumed, placed in a

---

a few days since that he and nine men were reported absent on a war excursion below, and none of us who are acquainted with the Sioux can fix upon any Indian answering the description given of displaced bones and withered arms, but that noted rascal himself." For further comment, see W. W. Folwell, *A History of Minnesota*, vol. 2, pp. 283-286. Folwell is dispassionate enough, but in a still later time a president of the Minnesota Historical Society, Walter N. Trenerry, can raise the question: "The Shooting of Little Crow: Heroism or Murder?" (*Minnesota History*, September, 1962, vol. 38, pp. 150-153). Although not unmindful of conditions as they existed in 1863, Trenerry asks if it was right "to shoot an unsuspecting stranger peaceably stuffing his mouth with fresh raspberries."

box, and sunk in the river before passing into the anatomist's hands.[100]

[100]These remarks were mostly based on a letter from Captain J. W. Bond to Colonel Stephen Miller, Glencoe, August 16, 1863, printed in the St. Paul *Pioneer* four days later. It was Bond who collected the skull from a garden, then "in a large dinner-pot, filled with a strong solution of lime," his colonel "being desirous of presenting it to the Minnesota Historical Society." Other bones were being retrieved when he left Hutchinson. Bond said: "When brought to town on the morning of the 4th [of July], he was scalped and his features swollen; and, though partially recognized, the people thought it was so improbable that Little Crow should be *there*, that they still are positive that it is *not* the body of that celebrated chief. Those who knew him best, and had fed and cared for him the oftenest during many winters past, are the most so. I did not meet a person in the town—not even Chauncey Lampson—who thought it was his body. I did not think so myself till I returned, and read the statement of his son and other corroborative evidence."

Chapter LXV

Capture of Wo-wi-nap-a, Son of Little Crow

FIVE hundred miles northwest, at Camp Atchinson, not forty miles from Devil's lake,[101] the expedition train was divided, a portion remaining in camp with orders to root out the Indians, if any remained in that region. The other division, General Sibley at its head, had moved in a southwestern direction for the Missouri river, where the main body of the foe had fled.

Three companies in command of Capt. W. H. Burt went out from Camp Atchinson on the 28th [24th] of June to scour the region for a trail the scouts reported having seen the day before. Near the shores of Devil's lake on the 28th the trail was lost in a dried-up slough. In their search the head of an Indian was discovered instead, protruding from a clump of bushes.

One of the scouts approached and demanded his surrender. He threw down his gun, glad of the prospect of getting something to eat. The remains of a lean wolf were beside him, killed with his last charge of ammunition, and cooked for his last rations. He soon spoke to William Quinn, the half-breed inter-

[101]Camp Atchison (consistently spelled Atchinson by Mrs. McConkey) was an entrenched camp established in Dakota Territory beyond the Cheyenne River, nearly south of Devils Lake.

303

preter, by whom, and several others, he was recognized as the son of Little Crow. He was very much emaciated, and in great straits, not knowing whither to go or what to do. He had expected to find his people there, but not an Indian had he seen, and he would doubtless soon have starved to death. His head was full of vermin, at once shaven, and he was taken into camp to await the order of the Commanding General. We subjoin his statement, that the reader may compare it with the afore given circumstances at Hutchinson:[102]

"I am the son of Little Crow; my name is Wo-wi-nap-a [One Who Appeareth]; I am sixteen years old; my father had two wives before he took my mother; the first one had one son, the second one a son and daughter. The third wife was my mother. After taking my mother, he put away the first two. He had seven children by my mother, six of whom are dead, I am the only one living now. The fourth wife had five children born; do not know whether they died or not; two were boys and three were girls. The fifth wife had five children, three of whom are dead, two are living. The sixth wife had three children, all of

---

[102]These preliminary remarks are based on a communication from Major M. Cook to Colonel Miller, August 2, 1863, printed in the St. Paul *Pioneer,* August 13, 1863, together with the statement of Wo-wi-nap-a, interpreted by Joseph Demarais, Jr. Captain Burt had returned to Camp Atchison with his prisoner on August 1. As usual, Mrs. McConkey's version of the statement by Little Crow's son has slight variances in the wording.

them are dead, the oldest was a boy, the other two were girls. The last four wives were sisters.

"Father went to St. Joseph last spring. When we were coming back, he said he could not fight the white men, but would go below and steal horses from them and give them to his children, so that they could be comfortable, and then he would go away off.

"Father also told me that he was getting old, and wanted me to go with him to carry his bundles. He left his wives and other children behind. There were sixteen men and one squaw in the party that went below with us. We had no horses, but walked all the way down to the settlement. Father and I were picking redberries near Scattered lake, at the time he was shot. It was near night. He was hit the first time in the side, just above the hip. His gun and mine were lying on the ground. He took up my gun and fired it first and then fired his own. He was shot the second time while firing his own gun. The ball struck the stock of his gun and then hit him in the side, near the shoulders. This was the shot that killed him. He told me that he was killed, and asked me for water, which I gave him. He died immediately after. When I heard the first shot fired I laid down, and the man did not see me before father was killed.

"A short time before father was killed, an Indian named Hi-a-ka [Hi-u-ka], who married the daughter of my father's second wife, came to him. He had a horse with him, also a gray colored coat, that he had taken from a man whom he had killed, to the north of where father was killed. He gave the coat to father, telling him he would need it when it rained, as he had no coat with him. Hi-a-ka said he had a horse now, and was going back to the Indian country.

"The Indians who went down with us, separated. Eight of them and the squaw went north; the other eight went further down I have not seen any of them since. After father was killed, I took both guns and the ammunition, and started for Devil's lake, where I expected to find some of my friends. When I got to Beaver Creek, I saw the tracks of two Indians, and at Standing Buffalo's village saw where the eight Indians who had gone first had crossed.

"I carried both guns as far as Shayenne river, where I saw two men. I was scared, and threw my gun and ammunition down. After that, I travelled only in the night, and as I had no ammunition to kill anything to eat, I had not strength enough to travel fast. I went on until I arrived near Devil's lake, when I stayed in one place three days, being so weak and hungry that I could go no farther. I had picked up a cartridge near Big Stone lake, which I still had with me, and loaded father's gun with it, cutting the ball into slugs. With this charge, I shot a wolf, ate some of it, which gave me strength to travel, and I went on up the lake, until the day I was captured, which was twenty-six days from the day my father was killed."

Sixteen years before the capture of Wo-wi-nap-a, the writer had been a guest at the house of Doctor Williamson, the missionary at Little Crow's village before its removal up the Minnesota Valley. When the novelty of a white woman's landing from a "fire canoe" had a little subsided, this then baby Chief, with others, was held up, that my unsophisticated admiration might be sealed with a kiss—the same pappoose I sometimes saw affectionately caressed by his father, a weakness on his part he would prefer should have passed unnoticed. Like Joseph, he was the favorite son of his father, because his mother was loved more than all his wives. Wo-wi-nap-a returned with the expedition, and has since been in the guard house.[103]

[103]Wo-wi-nap-a was tried and sentenced to be hanged, but the sentence was never carried out. He grew up to be a Christian Indian who took the name "Thomas Wakeman," and founded the Y. M. C. A. among the Sioux; a son became a minister. See W. W. Folwell, *A History of Minnesota,* vol. 2, pp. 285-286. A photograph made soon after his capture is reproduced in *Minnesota History,* September, 1962, vol. 38, p. 153.

Chapter LXVI

Two Captive Boys

IN June, 1863, considerable sympathy was elicited in St. Paul by the arrival of two little boys, who had been in savage hands. Their ages were six and nine years, and to the good Catholic priest of St. Joe they owed their release. He had parted with all his worldly goods to effect this, then robbed himself of needful apparel to clothe them decently and comfortably.[104]

George Ingalls, the eldest of these boys, was, when the trouble commenced, living near Yellow Medicine. The family fled for the fort, but were seized by Indians, who sprang from a hole in the earth. Mr. Ingalls was killed, and his family made prisoners. His three daughters, sisters of young George, were carried off to the plains, suffering incredible hardships, till ransomed at the Agency on the Missouri river.

George was sometimes at Big Stone lake, in the same camp with a boy who forms the subject of another chapter. Finally they moved on to the north-

---

[104]Isaac V. D. Heard, *History of the Sioux War*, pp. 299-300, says that three boys were ransomed by the Catholic missionary at St. Joseph, Father Germaine (and Mrs. McConkey amends her statement to the same effect in Chapter LXVIII). A horse was given for the two younger boys, and a horse and two blankets for the eldest. This happened sometime prior to June 3, when Father Germaine wrote to a friend at Pembina to tell of ransoming the boys.

west, towards Devil's lake, where the Indian forces were to concentrate for the winter.

My reader will recollect little Jimmy Scott of Old Crossing, who submitted to his captors, as his grandmother bade him, whom we now again introduce, having passed through such suffering and hardship as to remember little else, even the name of his grandmother. The poor child would cry most piteously when questioned. Both physical and mental powers seemed seriously affected by the ordeal through which he had passed.

The boys say they never suffered for food, but the quality was not the most desirable, much of the time only buffalo meat. They suffered much from intense cold during the winter, in the bleak winds from the lake, and there was much misery in the severe drudgery. The Indian women who played mother to them were sad to part with them, and seemed unwilling to do so until plead with by the boys themselves. Little Jimmy cried bitterly on the neck of his Indian mother when he "kissed her good-bye."

May friends be so kind, the healing balm so gently applied to bitter memories, that this experience be no serious drawback on their future lives.

Chapter LXVII

Thrilling Adventures of Mr. Brackett and Death of Lieutenant Freeman

THE monotony of Camp Atchinson was interrupted on the evening of August 2, by the appearance of an emaciated figure who fell to the ground in sheer weakness and exhaustion. He was picked up and carried into a tent, and recognized as George E. Brackett of Minneapolis, beef contractor of the expedition, who had gone with the main body.[105]

He had, with Lieutenant Ambrose Freeman of St. Cloud, when about sixty miles out, left the main column for a day's adventure. Five miles away, they overlooked the country from a range of hills, when they saw several of the scouts not far away. Passing a fairy-like lake, three graceful antelopes tempted a shot. One was wounded, which Lieut. Freeman followed, giving his horse in charge of Mr. Brackett. This drew them from their course, though the train was in sight several miles distant. Seeing the scouts on the other side of the lake, curiosity led them on, through fresh evidences of Indians near.

These dangers passed, they shaped their course towards the train. On the lookout for the enemy, they

[105]The narrative that follows is derived from a correspondent writing from "Camp Atcheson, 105 miles northwest of Fort Abercrombie, near Lake Jessie, Dakota Terr., August 1, 1863," printed in the St. Paul *Pioneer,* August 14, 1863.

discovered three objects who they decided to be *real* Indians, following up the train. Each made preparations to meet the other, and crept around the bluff. A surprise ensues, when they recognize in each other friends of the same party. One of these scouts was Chaska, already well known.

Just at this time a large squad of men were noticed on the bluff nearly three miles away, at the same time a squad of cavalry, as they supposed, started toward them. The scouts turned off to the lake to water their horses. The cavalry and themselves in motion perceptibly lessened the distance between them, and no doubt existed but that Gen. Sibley's full command was on the other side of the hill.

Judge of the surprise when fifteen Indians, deceptively bearing a flag of truce, charged upon them. They yelled to the scouts and rode toward them, but Lieut. Freeman was shot with an arrow through the back, and another Indian fired at Mr. Brackett, who escaped the ball by clinging to the neck of his horse. At the same time Chaska, from the top of a knoll, let fly at the Indians. Lieut. Freeman sat on his horse till they had passed in the rear of the scouts, when he remarked, "I am gone," and fell. He asked for water, which was given, slightly changed his position, and was gone.

The Indians were all around them, but fell back as the daring scouts rode toward them, ready to fire. This respite gave Mr. Brackett a chance to get the Lieutenant's rifle and revolver before he followed the scouts, and to overtake them while his pursuers waited to catch the horse from which his comrade had just fallen. This done, with loud and triumphant yells they start on again, and after a race of four miles, the fleeing party are completely surrounded. All jumped from their horses. The faithful Chaska, more intent on the safety of his friend than his own, saw him safely hid in the bushes, then went forward to meet his red brethren. This was the last Mr. Brackett saw of the scouts, but lay with his rifle cocked while the Indians quarreled which should have his horse. But for this they would doubtless have searched out his hiding place.

The afternoon was now far spent. In a half hour, after the Indians had left in a circuitous course round a marsh, probably to avoid pursuit, Mr. Brackett crawled out from the rushes, and with the sun to his back travelled for two hours. Thus he did for two days, and hid in a marsh at night. After the third day he began diligent search for the trail, which he struck on the afternoon of the fifth day, about twelve miles from where he left the train, and about seventy from Camp Atchinson. A man of ordinary caliber would have yielded to despondency and died. Not so with the hero of this adventure.—Though subsisting on frogs, birds and cherries for five days, his feet worn with constant travel, his forehead blistered by the scorching sun, and sleeping every night with only his nether garment for a covering, his indomitable energy enabled him to go on, though when he reached the camp, he could not have held out another day. The remainder of this adventure we give in Mr. Brackett's own words:

"About ten miles before reaching Camp A, I sat down to rest, and had such difficulty in getting under weigh again, that I determined to stop no more, feeling sure that once again down, I should never be able to regain my feet unaided. I entered the camp near the camp fire of a detachment of the 'Pioneers' (Capt. Jonathan Chase's Company of the Ninth Minnesota Infantry), and fell to the ground, unable to raise again. But, thank God! around that fire were sitting some St. Anthony friends, among whom were Messrs. Mc-Mullen and Whittier, attached to that company, who kindly picked me up, and carried me to my tent.

"I lost my coat, hat and knife in the fight on the first day. I took Lieut. F.'s knife, and with it made moccasins of my boot-legs, my boots so chafing my feet in walking that I could not wear them. These moccasins were constantly getting out of repair, and my knife was as much needed to keep them in order for use, as to make them in the first place. But just before reaching the trail of the expedition on the fifth day, I lost Lieut. F.'s knife. This loss I felt at the time decided my fate, if I had much farther to go, but kind Providence was in my favor, for almost the first object that greeted my eyes upon reaching the trail, was a knife, old and worn to be sure, but priceless to me. This incident some may deem a mere accident, but let such an one be placed in my situation at that time, and he would feel with me, that it was a boon granted by the Great Giver of good. On the third day, about ten miles from the river spoken of, I left Lieut. F.'s rifle on the prairie, becoming too weak to carry it longer, besides it had already been so damaged by rain that I could not use it. I wrote upon it that Lieut. F. had been killed, and named the course I was then pursuing. I brought the pistol into Camp Atchinson.

"While wandering, I lived on cherries, roots, bird's eggs, young birds and frogs, caught by hand, all my ammunition but one cartridge having been spoiled by the rain on the first day. That cartridge was one for Smith's breech loading carbine, and had a gutta percha case. I had also some waterproof percussion caps in my portmonaie. I took one-half the powder in the cartridge, and a percussion cap, and with the pistol and some dry grass, started a nice fire, at which I cooked a young bird, something like a loon, and about the size. This was on the second night. On the fourth, I used the remainder of the cartridge in the same way, and for a like purpose. The rest of the time I ate my food uncooked, except some hard bread (found at the fourth camp mentioned above), which had been fried and then thrown into the ashes. I have forgotten one sweet morsel (and all were sweet and very palatable to me), viz: some sinews spared by the wolves from a buffalo carcass. As near as I am able to judge, I travelled in seven days at least two hundred miles. I had ample means for a like journey in civilized localities, but for the first time in my life, found gold and silver coin a useless thing. My bootleg moccasins saved me; for a walk of ten miles upon such a prairie, barefooted, would stop all further progress of any person accustomed to wear covering upon the feet. The exposure at night, caused, more particularly, by lying in low and wet places in order to hide myself, was more prostrating to me than scarcity of food. The loneliness of the prairies, would have been terrible in itself, without the drove of wolves that, after the first day, hovered, in the day-time, at a respectable distance, and in the night time howled closely around me, seemingly sure that my failing strength would soon render me an easy prey. But a merciful Providence has spared my life, by what seems now, even to myself, almost a miracle."

Mr. Brackett speaks in the highest terms of Chaska. He feels that he owes his life to him, by his firing in the first encounter, and rushing toward him in the second, which enabled him to hide.

Lieutenant Ambrose Freeman was a native of Virginia, and for seven years a resident of St. Cloud, Minnesota, where his wife and five children waited his return. He bore an unblemished character, and was best loved and respected where longest known. His character in civil, accompanied him in military life, and no man in the expedition could have been more generally regretted. His body was recovered and buried at Camp Sibley, near the Big Mound, where a great battle with the Indians was fought soon after his fall.

Chapter LXVIII

The Captive John Julien

THE subject of this chapter was one of the three boys ransomed by the kind-hearted Catholic priest at St. Joe. His captivity was of ten months' duration, but there is less of misery in it than of the other boys. John Julien was cook for the government laborers at Big Stone lake at the time of the savage onset.[106] He escaped and hid in the woods until he supposed the danger passed, then thought he would find out if possible the fate of his employers. He was made prisoner by an Indian who lived near, with the intent of protecting till he could set him at liberty. His name is Eu-kosh-nu, "man with short hair." He took no part in the massacres, and taking the boy across the lake, sent him off alone. He found the enemy were on his track, brought the boy back, and for several days kept him concealed at his own lodge.

Then he allowed him to go with his own son to the lake. No sooner was he seen than a vicious Indian, who had deeply drank of the extermination spirit, took aim at his heart, and then ran off, supposing his pistol had performed its intent.

[106]Compare Chapter XVIII and Note 48, where Anton Manderfield is observed to give the name of the 16-year-old cook as John Schmerch, a boy from Beaver Creek. Manderfield is doubtless correct, for the St. Paul *Pioneer*, May 27, 1863, refers to him (before his release) as a German who was taken prisoner at Big Stone Lake, about eighteen years of age.

His little Indian companion ran and told his father, who came at once, carried him to his house, washed and dressed his wounds, and made him as comfortable as he could in his comfortless tepee. Then he took down his gun, declaring he would shoot Hut-te-ste-mi, who had shot the white boy. This, John in his forgiving spirit overruled; so he put up his gun and went forth, hatchet in hand, to demand the pistol, which he smashed upon a stone, thus inciting the anger of the would-be murderer and endangering his own life.

Eu-kosh-nu dare not be found at his own house, and to protect his captive, had him taken to his cousin's, about half a mile distant. Good care was given to his wound during the five days he remained there, and the ball extracted from his side.

One month later, thirty lodges were struck, and the occupants fell in with Little Crow's party, who having been ousted in battles, had started for Devil's lake, in the north of Dakota Territory, where it was their intent to mass their forces after receiving all the assistance from other tribes they could get.

The wounded, suffering captive must go with them. He walked the first day, as his captor had no way for him to ride. Seeing he could not hold out another day, the man gave him to his relative, who protected him at Big Stone lake. He rode in the wagon of his new owner the rest of the way, and was with him during the remainder of his captivity.

Instead of remaining at Devil's lake, a portion of this party passed on to the Missouri river, among whom was John Julien. The cold had become intense, and the snow was deep; still these savage wanderers continue to move on, following the windings of the river, till an encampment of Yanktons five hundred lodges strong falls in their way. They rested and feasted on buffalo meat for five days, when they were joined by Little Crow with sixty lodges, with whom they remained during the rest of the winter.

None of these were stationary. The Yanktons broke camp and went in one direction, Little Crow's camp in another. The latter was very desirous to make peace with the Arickarees (commonly known as the Rees), and obtain their assistance in his campaign against the whites. Little Crow compelled the captive boy to go in front when his delegation went forward to meet the delegation of Rees, that if trouble ensued he might be first to suffer. The object of the embassy being known, there followed a shaking of hands and the smoking of pipes. But scarcely had the Rees reached the protection of their own people when they commenced firing. There was among them a peace and an anti-peace party, the latter the strongest, and of course over-ruling the former. Our little hero was again wounded in the fleshy part of his leg. Eight Sioux were killed, and one squaw, during the battle, which lasted from noon till sundown. Little Crow was completely routed, and retreated toward where he had wintered, forty miles distant. This was the last of April.[107]

The wounded boy tried hard to keep up. After running five miles, his leg became too painful to proceed, and he hid himself to avoid the enemy. At dark, however, he followed, and after travelling all night and the following day, reached the Sioux camp.

Little Crow again bends his steps towards Devil's lake, for the first five days entirely destitute of food. Fifty miles above Devil's lake,————the trader from St. Joseph, met them with a parley for their furs, for which they received provisions and blankets. This trader carried the tidings of this boy's captivity, as also two others then at other points, to St. Joe, when the priest arranged for him to buy them.

The owner of the boy was reluctant to sell; he preferred to take him to the settlement and deliver him up, in proof of his friendship for the whites. He had exacted nothing unreasonable, had not required him

[107]The report cited in the preceding note, "official information" received in St. Paul of the arrival at Fort Abercrombie on the 19th instant of "Joseph Demerois," a son of the post interpreter, who had come from St. Joseph via Devils Lake, includes the following: "Mr. Demerois states that Little Crow had been engaged in a fight with the Rees, and was defeated—they refused to join him. He had eight killed and several wounded. Among the killed was Petit Frise and his son. A German [youth] who was taken prisoner at Big Stone Lake, was wounded in the leg . . . " The informant had left Devils Lake on May 9, at which time "there were encamped about 600 teepees of Indians, or about eighteen hundred warriors, with Little Crow at their head."

to work, and when he sold a pony for a cap, coat, vest, pants, three shirts, a pair of stockings and a blanket, he clothed his captive with them instead of himself. The other Indians would not accede to his wish to go to the settlement, and thinking that Gen. Sibley would not come into the neighborhood, he finally consented to sell him. On the 13th of June he reached St. Joseph, received by the priest and kindly cared for while he remained, and then sent to St. Paul, where he arrived the 17th of September, with the hope of a speedy reunion with the remnant of his family.

Chapter LXIX

Progress of the Expedition

SLOWLY but surely plodded on the gigantic train. Little or no rain had visited them, and there fell scarcely a drop of dew to relieve the aridity of the earth. The heat was much of the time one hundred degrees or more, and the hot air, when filled with dust, was almost unendurable. The same rear fire followed the expedition now, as during the previous fall. It is easy to find fault, reclining at ease in one's home; but not so easy to perform a great and important work and meet the impatient demand of the public.

The objects of the expedition were kept constantly in view. The release of the prisoners was accomplished. The punishment of guilty parties followed, so far as the action of the General commanding was concerned, and over three hundred murderers were condemned to death. That they were not executed was no fault of his. *The supreme law of the army forbids the execution of any sentence of court martial without the sanction of the President of the United States.*

Unmoved by the clamor of fault-finders, the expedition was pushing on, though never an Indian had they seen. At last they come upon their trail — tent poles and camp fire remains and other signs evince their nearness—as they advance toward the Missouri.

Days—weeks passed, and no tidings came from the column to the anxious outer world; and nothing was known of them at Camp Atchinson. But they were far from being laggards in the field, and were in the heart of the enemy's country, determined to mete to the foe the justice they merited. Every man worked as if success depended alone on him.

At last Col. Marshall brings tidings that three engagements have taken place, in which the enemy, more than two thousand strong, the largest Indian force ever giving battle, had been routed with heavy loss and driven in terror across the Missouri river.

Col. Marshall left the expedition after one day on the return march, and rode nearly four hundred miles in seven days, much of the way without an escort and only two scouts.[108] The main features of the battles we leave to the report of the commanding officer. Some items, however, not therein mentioned, may not be uninteresting.

The great Sioux camp, when discovered by our forces, were in consultation for proposing terms of peace, instigated by Standing Buffalo, who had declared his intention to deliver himself up, whenever

[108]The lack of news from Sibley's column is exaggerated. The St. Paul *Pioneer* on August 13 printed a letter from Camp Atchison dated August 2, with news of Sibley's whereabouts as of July 22; and on August 15 the *Pioneer* printed the news from the Indian Expedition "brought down by Lieutenant Colonel Marshall," whose rapid traveling was praised. The news included that of the Battle of Big Mound, the Battle of Stone Lake, and the death of Lieutenant Beever.

opportunity offered to do so. All but eight daring, reckless young braves consented, who mounted their horses and rode swiftly away. A party followed to bring them in, and had just come up with them on the hill overlooking the camp of white men. The scouts went up to parley, and several messages were returned from them to individuals, among which was a special request from Standing Buffalo to George Spencer, to "come over and see him." George lacked no confidence in the chief, but something whispered to him, "go not up." Several of the men followed the scouts, and even shook hands with Indian acquaintances.—Among these was Doct. Josiah S. Weiser from Shakopee, Surgeon of the Mounted Rangers; but scarcely had he spoken to one, when one of the determined eight shot him through the heart. He fell from his horse and never spoke again. The scouts returned the fire, when the Indians fell back behind the ridge, firing as they went. One Solon Stevens, of Mankato, was slightly wounded by a spent ball, which had passed through a rubber blanket rolled up on his saddle. All peace overtures were now at an end. Those who had encouraged a surrender "fell in" to save themselves from their own people. Standing Buffalo, still persistent in his peace principles, ran away to the north, where he remained many weeks.

The fighting propensities of the savages were roused, and their war-whoop rang through all the prairie air. It was three o'clock in the afternoon of July 24, 1863, when Gen. Sibley ordered his troops forward. A terrible thunder storm shook the earth and sent a bolt of lightning into their midst, killing one man and his horse instantly. For three hours the contest raged, when the savages fled in confusion. The mounted regiment of Col. McPhail pressed on in pursuit, while the infantry, having marched from early morn till three o'clock before engaging the enemy, went into camp.

An unhappy mistake (such will occur in military circles as in well regulated families) has furnished food for calumny. We think it due the General commanding to set the facts before the world in their true light, obtained from one who *heard* the order, and received and executed an auxiliary.

Why was not the advantage gained at the first battle followed up, and the Indians more severely punished? We reply, such was the design. We have seen Col. McPhail's cavalry, supported by the Seventh infantry under Lieut. Col. Marshall, in pursuit of the fleeing foe, to be followed by the main column. But no man can accomplish impossibilities. They had marched that day forty miles before engaging the enemy. The scouts had just reported finding the enemy's trail when Captain Forbes of the Commissary Department rode to the front to say that the teams were giving out, and they were near the only water reported for several miles. Accordingly they went into camp.

"You ride to Col. McPhail—tell him not to pursue the enemy after dark, but to act discretionary as to a bivouac on the prairie," was the verbal order given by Gen. Sibley to Lieut. Beever, who volunteered to deliver it. This was followed by another to the Chief Clerk of the Commissary Department "to start three days' rations to reach the advancing force early in the morning." Five loaded teams were on the way by eleven o'clock that night, but when one mile out stragglers were met, and finally the entire pursuing force. The order had been misunderstood, and its most important phraseology delivered in a positive "return to camp." The regret of its bearer was too poignant for censure. He frankly admitted the mistake to his comrades, and awaited his opportunity to do so before the world. He sleeps in the shadow of the woods in which he met his fate, and cannot exonerate the man on whom an envious world throws the blame, who suffers the tongue of calumny rather than cast it on a worthy dead man.

They have repulsed the enemy in three battles, killing a large number, and driving him across the Missouri river, between which and the expedition's encampment was a mile of dense forest, interspersed with a heavy growth of prickly ash, the most impenetrable of all northern undergrowth. Forbidding as were the circumstances, Col. Crooks called for volunteers to follow him there. After thoroughly shelling the woods, and scouring the "bottom," they drew rein at its shore, and drank from the sweet though turbid stream, truly refreshing after having naught for many days but brackish water. They were fired on from the opposite shore, but the balls fell harmlessly into the river.

It is inquired why this last engagement was not the finale of the war, and why they were not followed across the river?

We have shown the nature of the ground. In the language of another, "white men cannot fight naked, and draw their subsistence from the lakes, woods and prairies, as the Indians can." They must have their baggage wagon and provision train. Men and animals were well nigh exhausted when they reached the Missouri: besides, the stores were scarcely sufficient for return rations. They would have had great difficulty getting the teams through the forest, and three days' time would have been consumed in crossing, which would have given the enemy three days' start, else they would have been all this time exposed to their fire.

"White people," says Mr. Riggs, "are superior to an Indian in a thousand things, but fighting is not one of them. Our big guns, and our long range muskets and our better drills, give us an advantage over them. But in fleeing and fighting, fighting and fleeing, they are our superiors. Moreover; they cover a retreat most beautifully. If any one supposes it is an easy matter to annihilate these Arabs of the desert, let him try it. Perhaps he will come back a wise man." Some ask, he says, "why Gen. Sibley did not kill more Indians?" We reply, "they would not stay to be killed."

Every man claims the privilege of deciding how a campaign should be conducted, and the qualification of its General. A free country guarantees this right, however great the injustice.

We find no more successful campaigns against the Indians than those of Gen. Sibley; and all in it with whom we have conversed agree that all was done which human wisdom and human energy could do. Let us not forget the vast power and the forty millions expended in unsuccessful attempts to drive the Seminoles from their swamp retreats in Florida. Time and an overruling Providence will work all right. The name of Henry H. Sibley will live on when those of his calumniators will be lost in oblivion.[109]

[109]Mrs. McConkey heaps praises on Sibley notwithstanding he was a Democrat, "a loyal, conscientious one, we have no doubt," and she herself "a wool-dyed Republican," as she says in a passage here omitted.

Chapter LXX

The Capture of a Teton

ON the morning of the 28th of July, just as Gen.
Sibley's command was breaking camp at Stony
lake, they were attacked by Indians, and after three
hours of sharp fighting repulsed the foe, who fled
toward the Missouri. Mr. Spencer, under the escort
of scouts, left the main column and discovered a
solitary pony grazing about a mile to the left. As they
approached, a dark, motionless object was seen lying
upon the ground. Some one cried out, "It's an old
buffalo robe"; but as one stooped to pick it up, it
sprang from the earth, and bounded off like a deer.
Some thirty shots were fired, all hitting the robe, but
the Indian kept on with the same zigzag course,
and a constant motion of the robe from side to side.

At last Pierre Bottineau, the chief guide, reined
up, put a revolver to his head, and fired, but he
dodged. He now dropped the robe and threw up
both hands. The robe was literally riddled with balls,
but not a scratch was on his person, and he had enlisted the admiration of his captors for his gallant
bearing. He was unarmed, save with a knife stuck in
his belt, which he threw away on being ordered to
do so. He was placed behind one of the scouts and
brought before General Sibley. He extended his hand
in friendly salute, which was not taken. With stern
eye upon him, the General questioned him closely,

till satisfied with the truth of his statement, when they shook hands. He belonged to the Teton band, one of the largest divisions of the Dakota nation, living west of the Missouri river. His father was one of the head chiefs, and the son had come on a visit to the Yanktonians. Learning they were to have a fight with the "Long Knives," curiosity led him on to see it. He retired with the repulsed Indians, but coming to good grass, stopped to let his pony graze, and, wrapping himself in his robe, laid down to rest and was fast asleep before he knew it. Thus the scouts had come upon him.

For the five days that he remained prisoner General Sibley caused him to be treated according to his rank, as heir-apparent to the chieftainship. He became strongly attached to Mr. Riggs, and seldom left his side. Mr. Spencer says, "he was not more than twenty years old, and his was as fine a specimen of the human form, as he ever beheld."

When the return order was given, General Sibley wrote a letter to his father commending the wisdom of his refusing to take up the tomahawk against the whites, saying he wished them to know that the whites were a merciful people, and though his son had been captured, he had spared his life, and permitted him to return to his own people. This was no doubt a stroke of good policy, as the death of this young Teton would have exasperated his tribe.

A few days after the dismissal of the young Teton, a party of miners, rich in gold dust washed from the deposits of Idaho [Montana], were descending the Missouri, at the very spot where our men went down to drink. Indians were all around, ready to spring from the weeds and bushes, and the young Teton, desiring peace, rushed toward them, holding the letter to his father over his head. But they understood not and shot him dead. They were at once surrounded, and, though fighting desperately and killing more than twice their number, every man was killed, and all the rich avails of toil fell into the spoiler's hands.

Chapter LXXI

Death of Lieut. Beever

WHILE Col. Crooks and his regiment were at the river, General Sibley, becoming aware of the proximity of Indians, executed an order for their return to camp, which the daring Lieutenant Beever volunteered to deliver. He was unmolested by the way, and though desired by Col. Crooks to remain until the men should be formed, and return under their protection, he was too true a soldier to disregard the discretionary order of a superior officer. Midway the trail forked in several directions—unfortunately, he took the wrong one.

Col. Crooks returned, and for several hours his absence was not noticed. Night had fallen upon the encampment before inquiry arose. No little alarm was created when it was known that he had not been seen.

The sudden disappearance of one in universal favor cast a gloom over the camp. Thursday, July 30, Gen. Sibley sent out eleven companies under Col. Crooks to make thorough reconnaissance of the woods, and if possible, find his body and that of private Nicholas Miller, who was missed the same day. The latter had said, before going out, that "*he wanted a shot.*" He was found scalped, not far from Lieut. Beever, but whether the same encounter terminated both lives will ever be unknown.

A short distance from where Lieut. Beever lay were two pools of blood, proving that he had not yielded his life without a recompense. His horse had been shot through the head, and three arrows were in his back, and a ball had passed through his body, but the finale had been the blow from a tomahawk. He was a "good shot"—had with him two revolvers carrying eleven balls, which had doubtless found lodgment, the dead or wounded Indians having been carried off by their comrades.

The remains were duly deposited in as good a coffin as could be obtained, and with his body servant as chief mourner, followed by almost the entire command, placed in his prairie grave near that of Doctor Weiser, to rest till the "graves give up their dead."

This event was one of the saddest connected with the campaign. Frederick J. Holt Beever was an English gentleman of means and education, travelling for his health and improvement. His love of adventure led him to embrace the opportunity offered by the expedition for seeing the western prairies, and he was attached to General Sibley's staff as volunteer Aid-de-camp. He was a jovial, social man, brave, energetic and reliable, and in his lowly bed rests well.[110]

[110]A long letter from "Sweetser," dated Camp Missouri River, July 31, 1863, and printed in the St. Paul *Pioneer,* August 15, 1863, besides telling of the military actions mentioned in the preceding note, relates the circumstances of Beever's death and furnishes some facts about his unusual life. An Englishman of aristocratic and wealthy family, he was said

to have taken high honors at Oxford, served in the Crimean War, and traveled over much of the United States, a superior photographer with "a splendid apparatus which he intended to have brought with the expedition." He had come to Wisconsin to hunt, a little more than a year earlier, and offered his services to Sibley when the campaign was being organized, so that a place was assigned him on the staff.

Chapter LXXII

Terminus of the Campaign

IN obedience to the order given below, the campaign was ended, and on Saturday morning, Aug. 1, commenced retracing their steps towards civilization:

"To the Officers and Soldiers of the Expeditionary forces in camp:

"It is proper for the Brigadier-General commanding to announce to you that the march to the west and south is completed, and that on to-morrow the column will move homewards, to discharge such other duties connected with the objects of the expedition, on the way, as may from time to time present themselves.

"In making this announcement, Gen. Sibley expresses also his high gratification that the campaign has been a complete success. The design of the Government in chastising the savages, and thereby preventing, for the future, the raids upon the frontier, has been accomplished. You have routed the miscreants who murdered our people last year, banded, as they were, with the powerful Upper Sioux, to the number of nearly 2,000 warriors, in three successful engagements, with heavy loss, and driven them, in confusion and dismay, across the Missouri river, leaving behind them all their vehicles, provisions and skins designed for clothing, which have been destroyed. Forty-four bodies of warriors have been found, and many others concealed or taken away, according to the custom of these savages, so that it is certain they lost in killed and wounded, not less than from one hundred and twenty to one hundred and fifty men. All this has been accomplished with the comparatively trifling loss on our part of three killed and as many wounded. You have marched nearly six hundred miles from St. Paul, and the powerful bands of the Dakotas, who have hitherto held undisputed possession of the great prairies, have succumbed to your valor and discipline, and sought safety in flight. The intense heat and drought have caused much suffering, which you have endured without a murmur. The companies of the 6th, 7th, 9th and 10th regiments of Minnesota Volunteers, and of the 1st regiment Minnesota Mounted Rangers, and the scouts of the battery, have amply sustained the reputation of the State by their bravery and endurance, amidst unknown dangers and great hardships. Each has had the opportunity to distinguish itself against a foe at least equal in numbers to itself.

"It would be a gratification if these remorseless savages could have been pursued and literally extirpated, for their crimes and barbarities merited such a full measure of punishment; but men and animals are alike exhausted after so long a march, and a further pursuit would only be futile and hopeless. The military results of the campaign have been completely accomplished, for the savages have not only been destroyed in great numbers, and their main strength broken, but their prospects for the future are hopeless indeed, for they can scarcely escape starvation during the approaching winter.

"It is peculiarly gratifying to the Brigadier-General commanding, to know that the tremendous fatigues and manifold dangers of the expedition thus far, have entailed so small a loss of life in his command. A less careful policy than that adopted, might have effected the destruction of more of the enemy, but that could only have been done by a proportional exposure on our part and the consequent loss of many more lives, bringing sorrow and mourning to our homes. Let us, therefore, return thanks to a merciful God for his manifest interposition in our favor, and for the success attendant upon our efforts to secure peace to the borders of our own State, and of our neighbors and friends in Dakota Territory, and as we proceed on our march toward those most near and dear to us, let us be prepared to discharge other duties which may be imposed upon us during our journey, with cheerful and willing hearts.

"To the Regimental and company officers of his command, the Brigadier-General commanding tenders his warmest thanks for their co-operation and aid on every occasion during the progress of the column through the heart of an unknown region, inhabited by a subtle and merciless foe.

"For the friends and families of our fallen comrades we have our warmest sympathies to offer in their bereavement.

"General Sibley takes this occasion to express his appreciation of the activity and zeal displayed by the members of his staff, one and all.

"By command of

"BRIGADIER-GENERAL SIBLEY."

The night previous to leaving, several shots were fired into camp by prowling Indians, who on the following morning made their appearance to the number of thirty or forty, determined to annoy where they could do nothing more.

Chapter LXXIII

Official Report of Brigadier General Henry H. Sibley to Maj. Gen. Pope[111]

MAJOR:—My last dispatch was dated 21st ultimo, from Camp Olin, in which I had the honor to inform Major General Pope, that I had left one-third of my force in an intrenched position at Camp Atchinson, and was then one day's march in advance, with 1,400 infantry and 500 cavalry, in the direction where the main body of the Indians were supposed to be. During the three following days, I pursued a course somewhat west of south, making fifty miles, having crossed the James river and the great coteau of the Missouri. On the 24th, about 1 P. M., being considerably in advance of the main column, with some of the officers of my staff, engaged in looking out for a suitable camping ground, the command having marched steadily from 5 A. M., some of my scouts came to me at full speed, and reported that a large camp of Indians had just before passed, and great numbers of warriors could be seen upon the prairie two or three miles distant. I immediately corralled my train upon

[111]This dispatch was dated Camp Carter, Bank of James River, August 7, 1863; see *Minnesota in the Civil and Indian Wars,* vol. 2, pp. 297-304; technically, it was addressed to Major J. F. Meline, Assistant Adjutant General, Department of the North West, Sibley's detailed, still unpublished, journal of this campaign is preserved in the National Archives among the records for the Department of the North West.

the shore of a salt lake near by, and established my camp, which was rapidly intrenched by Col. Crooks, to whom was entrusted that duty, for the security of the transportation in case of attack, a precaution I had taken whenever we encamped for many days previous.—While the earthworks were being pushed forward, parties of Indians, more or less numerous, appeared upon the hills around us, and one of my half-breed scouts, a relative of "Red Plume," a Sissiton chief, hitherto opposed to the war, approached sufficiently near to converse with him. "Red Plume" told him to warn me that the plan was formed to invite me to a council with some of my superior officers, to shoot us without ceremony, and then attack my command in great force, trusting to destroy the whole of it.

The Indians ventured near the spot where a portion of my scouts had taken position, three or four hundred yards from our camp, and conversed with them in an apparently friendly manner, some of them professing a desire for peace. Surgeon Joseph [Josiah] Weiser, of the First Minnesota Mounted Rangers, incautiously joined the group of scouts, when a young savage, doubtless supposing from his uniform and horse equipments that he was an officer of rank, pretended great friendship and delight at seeing him; but when within a few feet, treacherously shot him through the heart. The scouts discharged their pieces at the murderer, but he escaped, leaving his horse behind. The body of Dr.

Weiser was immediately brought into camp, unmutilated, save by the ball that killed him. Dr. Weiser was universally esteemed, being skillful in his profession, and a kind and courteous gentleman.

This outrage precipitated an immediate engagement. The savages in great numbers, concealed by the ridges, had encircled those portions of the camp not flanked by the lake referred to, and commenced an attack.

Col. Samuel McPhail, with two companies, subsequently reenforced by others as they could be spared from other points, was directed to drive the enemy from the vicinity of the hill where Dr. Weiser was shot, while those companies of the 7th Regiment under Lieut. Col. William R. Marshall and Major George Bradley, and one company of the 10th Regiment, under Capt. Alonzo J. Edgerton, was dispatched to support them. Taking with me a six-pounder under the command of Lieut. John C. Whipple, I ascended the hill towards "Big Mound," on the opposite side of the ravine, and opened fire with spherical case shot upon the Indians who had obtained possession of the upper part of the large ravine, and of the smaller ones tributary to it, under the protection of which they could annoy the infantry and cavalry without exposure on their part.

This flank and raking fire of artillery drove them from these hiding places into the broken prairie, where they were successively dislodged from the ridges, being utterly unable to resist the steady advance of the 7th Regiment and the Rangers, but fled before them in confusion. While these events were occurring on the right, the left of the camp was also threatened by a formidable body of warriors. Col. William Crooks, whose regiment the (6th), was posted on that side, was ordered to deploy part of his command as skirmishers and to dislodge the enemy. This was gallantly done, the Col. directing in person the movements of one part of his detached force, and Lieut. Col. John T. Averill of the other, Major Robert N. McLaren remaining in command of that portion of the regiment required as part of the camp guard.

The savages were steadily driven from one strong position after another, under a severe fire, until, feeling their utter inability to contend longer with our soldiers in the open field, they joined their brethren in one common flight. Upon moving forward with my staff, to a commanding point which overlooked the field, I discovered the whole body of Indians, numbering from one thousand to fifteen hundred, retiring in confusion from the combat, while a dark line of moving objects on the distant hills indicated the locality of their families. I immediately dispatched orders to Col. McPhail, who had now received an accession of force from other companies of his Mounted Regiment, to press on with all expedition and fall upon the rear of the enemy, but not to continue the pursuit after nightfall, and Lieut. Col. Marshall was directed to follow and support him with the companies of the 7th, and Captain Edgerton's company of the 10th, accompanied by one six-pounder, and one section of Minnesota howitzers under Captain John Jones.

At the same time, all the companies of the 6th and 10th regiments, except two from each which were left as a camp guard, were ordered to rendezvous, and to proceed in the same direction, but they had so far to march from their respective posts, before arriving at the point occupied by myself and staff, that I felt convinced of the uselessness of their proceeding farther, the other portions of the pursuing force being some miles in the advance, and I accordingly directed their return to camp.

The cavalry gallantly followed the Indians, and kept up a running fight until nearly dark, killing and wounding many of their warriors, the infantry under Lieut. Col. Marshall being kept at a double quick in their rear. The order to Col. McPhail was improperly delivered, as requiring him to return to camp, instead of leaving it discretionary with him to bivouac in the prairie. Consequently he retraced his way with his weary men and horses, followed by the still more wearied infantry, and arrived at the camp early the next morning, as I was about to move forward with the main column. Thus ended the battle of the Big Mound.

The severity of the labor of the entire command may be appreciated, when it is considered that the engagement only commenced after the day's march was nearly completed, and that the Indians were chased at least twelve miles, making altogether full forty miles performed without rest.

The march of the cavalry, of the 7th regiment, and of "B" company of the 10th regiment, in returning to camp after the tremendous efforts of the day, is almost unparalleled, and it told so fearfully upon men and animals that a forward movement could not take place until the 26th, when I marched, at an early hour. Colonel Baker had been left in command of the camp (named by the officers Camp Sibley), during the engagement of the previous day, and all the arrangements for its security were actively and judiciously made, aided as he was by that excellent officer, Lieut. Colonel Samuel P. Jennison, of the same regiment.

Upon arriving at the camp from which the Indians had been driven in such hot haste, vast quantities of dried meat, tallow and buffalo robes, cooking utensils, and other indispensable articles were found concealed in the long reeds around the lake, all of which were, by my direction, collected and destroyed. For miles along the route, the prairie was strewn with like evidences of a hasty flight. Col. McPhail had previously advised me that beyond Dead Buffalo lake, as far as the pursuit of the Indians had continued, I would find neither wood nor water. I consequently established my camp on the border of that lake, and very soon afterwards parties of Indians made their appearance, threatening an attack. I directed Capt.

Jones to repair with his section of six-pounders, supported by Capt. Chase, with his company of pioneers, to a commanding point, about six hundred yards in advance, and I proceeded there in person. I found that Col. Crooks had taken position with two companies of his regiment, commanded by Captain and Lieut. [Hiram P. and William] Grant, to check the advance of the Indians in that quarter. An engagement ensued at long range, the Indians being too wary to attempt to close, although greatly superior in numbers. The spherical case from the six-pounders soon caused a hasty retreat from that locality, but perceiving it to be their intention to make a flank movement on the left of the camp, in force, Capt. Oscar Taylor, with his company of Mounted Rangers, was dispatched to retard their progress in that quarter. He was attacked by the enemy in large numbers, but manfully held his ground until recalled, and ordered to support Lieut. Colonel Averill, who, with two companies of the 6th regiment, deployed as skirmishers, had been ordered to hold the savages in check.

The whole affair was ably conducted by these officers, but the increasing numbers of the Indians, who were well mounted, enabled them, by a circuitous route, to dash towards the extreme left of the camp, evidently with a view to stampede the mules herded on the shore of the lake.

This daring attempt was frustrated by the rapid motions of the companies of Mounted Rangers, commanded by Captains Eugene M. Wilson and Peter B. Davy, who met the enemy and repulsed them with loss, while Maj. McLaren, with equal promptitude, threw out along an extended line, the six companies of the 6th regiment, under his immediate command, thus entirely securing that flank of the camp from further attacks. The savages, again foiled in their designs, fled with precipitation, leaving a number of their dead upon the prairie—and the battle of Dead Buffalo lake was ended.

On the 27th, I resumed the march, following the trail of the retreating Indians until I reached Stony lake, where the exhaustion of the animals required me to encamp, although grass was very scarce.

The next day, the 28th, took place the greatest conflict between our troops and the Indians, so far as numbers were concerned, which I have named the battle of "Stony Lake." Regularly alternating each day, the 10th regiment, under Col. J. H. Baker, was in the advance and leading the column, as the train toiled up the long hill. As I passed Col. Baker, I directed him to deploy two companies of the 10th as skirmishers. Part of the wagons were still in the camp under the guard of the 7th regiment, when, as I reached the top of the ridge in advance of the 10th regiment, I perceived a large force of mounted Indians moving rapidly upon us. I immediately sent orders to the several commands promptly to assume their positions, in accordance with the programme of the line of march; but this was done, and the whole long train, completely guarded at every point, by the vigilant and able commanders of the regiments, and of corps, before the order reached them. The 10th gallantly checked the advance of the enemy in front, the 6th and cavalry on the right, and the 7th and cavalry on the left, while the six-pounders and two sections of mountain howitzers, under the efficient direction of their respective chiefs, poured as rapid and destructive fire from as many different points. The vast number of Indians enabled them to form two-thirds of a circle, five or six miles in extent, along the whole line of which they were seeking for some weak point upon which to precipitate themselves. The firing was incessant and rapid from each side, but so soon as I had completed the details of the designated order of march, and closed up the train, the column issued in line of battle upon the prairie, in the face of the immense force opposed to it, and I resumed my march without any delay. This proof of confidence in our own strength completely destroyed the hopes of the savages and completed their discomfiture. With yells of disappointment and rage, they fired a few parting volleys, and then retreated with all expedition. It was not possible, with our jaded horses, to overtake their fleet and comparatively fresh ponies.

This was the last desperate effort of the combined Dakota bands, to prevent a farther advance, on our part, towards their families. It would be difficult to estimate the number of warriors, but no cool and dispassionate observer would probably have placed it at a less figure than from 2,200 to 2,500. No such concentration of force has, so far as my information extends, ever been made by the savages of the American Continent.

It is rendered certain, from information received from various sources, (including that obtained from the savages themselves, in their conversations with our half-breed scouts), that the remnant of the bands who escaped with Little Crow, had successively joined the Sissitons, the Cut Heads, and finally the "Yank-ton-ais," the most powerful single band of the Dakotas, and together with all these, had formed one enormous camp, of nearly, or quite, ten thousand souls.

To assert that the courage and discipline displayed by officers and men, in the successive engagements with this formidable and hitherto untried enemy, were signally displayed, would but ill express the admiration I feel for the perfect steadiness and the alacrity with which they courted an encounter with the savage foe. No one, for a moment, seemed to doubt the result, however great the preponderance against us in numerical force. These wild warriors of the plain had never been met in battle, by American troops, and they have ever boasted that no hostile army, however numerous, would dare to set foot upon the soil of which they claim to be the undisputed masters. Now that they have been thus met, and their utmost force defied, resisted, and utterly broken and routed, the lesson will be a valuable one, not only in its effect upon these particular bands, but upon all the tribes of the Northwest.

When we went into camp, on the banks of Apple river, a few mounted Indians could alone be seen. Early next morning, I dispatched Col. McPhail with the companies of the Mounted Rangers, and the two six-pounders, to harass and retard the retreat of the Indians across the Missouri river, and followed with the main column, as rapidly as possible; we reached the woods, on the border of that stream, shortly after noon, on the 28th; but the Indians had crossed their families, during the preceding night, and it took but a short time for the men to follow them, on their ponies. The hills, on the opposite side, were covered with the men, and they had probably formed the determination to oppose our passage of the river, both sides of which were here covered with a dense growth of underbrush and timber, for a space of more than a mile.

I dispatched Col. Crooks, with his regiment, which was, in turn, in the advance, to clear the river of Indians, which he successfully accomplished, without loss, although fired upon, fiercely, from the opposite side. He reported to me that a large quantity of transportation, including carts, wagons, and other vehicles, had been left behind in the woods.

I transmitted, through Mr. Beever, a volunteer Aid on my Staff, an order to Col. Crooks, to return to the main column, with his regiment, the object I had in view, in detaching him, being fully attained. The order was received, and Mr. Beever was entrusted with a message, in return, containing information desired by me, when, on his way to headquarters, he unfortunately took the wrong trail, and was, the next day, found where he had been set upon and killed by an outlying party of the enemy. His death occasioned much regret to the command, for he was esteemed by all for his devotion to duty, and for his modest and gentlemanly deportment.

A private of the 6th regiment, who had taken the same trail, was also shot to death with arrows, probably by the same party.

There being no water to be found on the prairie, I proceeded down the Missouri to the nearest point on Apple river, opposite Burnt Boat Island, and made my camp. The following day, Col. Crooks, with a strong detachment of eleven companies of infantry and dismounted cavalry, and three guns, under the command of Capt. John Jones, was dispatched to destroy the property left in the woods, which was thoroughly performed, with the aid of Lieut. Jones, and a portion of the Pioneer Corps. From one hundred and twenty to one hundred and fifty wagons and carts were thus disposed of. During this time, the savages lay concealed in the grass, on the opposite side of the river, exchanging occasional volleys with our men. Some execution was done upon them, by the long range arms of the infantry and cavalry, without injury to any one of my command.

I waited two days in camp, hoping to open communication with General Sully, who, with his comparatively fresh mounted force, could easily have followed up and destroyed the enemy we had so persistently hunted.

The long and rapid marches had very much debilitated the infantry, and as for the horses of the cavalry, and the mules employed in the transportation, they were utterly exhausted.

Under the circumstances, I felt that this column had done everything possible, within the limits of human and animal endurance, and that a further pursuit would not only be useless, as the Indians could cross and recross the river in much less time than could my command, and thus evade me, but would necessarily be attended with the loss of many valuable lives.

For three successive evenings, I caused the cannon to be fired, and signal rockets sent up, but all these elicited no reply from General Sully, and I am apprehensive he has been detained by insurmountable obstacles. * The point struck by me on the Missouri, is about forty miles, by land, below Fort Clark, in

*While Gen. Sibley was pushing his forces to the Southwest, General Sully was moving up the Missouri, to cut off the retreat of the fleeing foe; and on the 4th of September surprised four hundred of their lodges, fought and dispersed them with a loss of fifty men, killing more than twice that number of the enemy—capturing provisions, furs, horses, and ammunition, and regaining a large amount of property taken the previous year. [H.M.]

latitude forty-six degrees forty-two minutes—longitude, one hundred degrees thirty-five minutes.

The military results of the expedition have been highly satisfactory. A march of nearly six hundred miles from St. Paul has been made, in a season of fierce heats and unprecedented drouth, when even the most experienced voyageurs predicted the impossibility of such a movement; a vigilant and powerful, as well as confident, enemy was found, successively routed in three different engagements, with a loss of at least one hundred and fifty killed and wounded of his best and bravest warriors, and his beaten forces driven in confusion and dismay, with the sacrifice of vast quantities of subsistence, clothing, and means of transportation, across the Missouri river, many, perhaps most of them, to perish miserably in their utter destitution, during the coming fall and winter.

These fierce warriors of the prairie have been taught by dear bought experience, that the long arm of the government can reach them in their most distant haunts, and punish them for their misdeeds; that they are utterly powerless to resist the attacks of a disciplined force, and that but for the interposition of a mighty stream between us and them, the utter destruction of the great camp containing all their strength was certain. It would have been gratifying to us all, if the murdering remnant of the Medawakanton and Wak-paton bands could have been extirpated, root and branch, but as it is, the bodies of many of the most guilty have been left on the prairie, to be devoured by wolves and foxes.

I am gratified to be able to state that the loss sustained by my column in actual combat was very small. Four men of the cavalry were killed, and four wounded, one, I fear, fatally. One private of the same regiment was killed by lightning, during the first engagement, and Lieut Freeman of company "D" also of the Mounted Rangers, a valuable officer, was pierced to death by arrows, on the same day, by a party of hostile Indians, while, without my knowledge, he was engaged in hunting at a distance from the main column. Bodies of the dead were interred with funeral honors, and the graves secured from desecration by making them in the semblance of ordinary rifle pits.

It would give me pleasure to designate by name all those of the splendid regiments and corps of my command who have signalized themselves by their gallant conduct, but as that would really embrace officers and men, I must content myself by bringing to the notice of the Major General commanding, such as came immediately under my observation.

I cannot speak too highly of Colonels Crooks and Baker, and Lieut. Colonel Marshall, commanding respectively the 6th, 10th and 7th regiments, Minnesota Volunteers, and of Lieut. Colonels Averill and Jennison, and Majors McLaren and Bradley, and of the line officers and men of these regiments. They have deserved well of their country and of their State. They were ever on hand to assist me in my labors, and active, zealous, and brave in the performance of duty.

Of Col. McPhail, commanding the Mounted Rangers, and of Majors John H. Parker and Orrin T. Hayes, and the company officers and men generally, I have the honor to state, that as the cavalry was necessarily more exposed and nearer the enemy than the other portions of the command, so they alike distinguished themselves by unwavering courage and splendid fighting qualities.

The great destruction dealt out to the Indians is mostly attributable to this branch of the service, although many were killed or disabled by the Artillery and Infantry also.

Captain Jones and his officers and men were ever at their posts, and their pieces were served with much skill and effect.

To Captain Jonathan Chase of the Pioneers and his invaluable company, the expedition has been greatly indebted for service in the peculiar line for which they were detailed.

Captain William R. Baxter's company H, of the 9th regiment, having been attached to the 10th regiment, as a part of its organization temporarily, upheld its high reputation for efficiency, being the equal in that regard of any other company.

The Surgical Department of the expedition was placed by me in charge of Surgeon Alfred Wharton, as Medical Director, who has devoted himself zealously and efficiently to his duties.

In his official report to these head-quarters, he accords due credit to the Surgeons and Assistants of the several regiments present with them. Of the members of my own staff I can affirm that they have been equal to the discharge of the arduous duties imposed upon them.

Captain Rollin C. Olin, my Assistant Adjutant General, has afforded me great assistance, and for their equal gallantry and zeal may be mentioned Captains Pope and Atchinson, Lieutenants Pratt and Hawthorn, and Captain Fox [*i.e.,* E. St. Julien Cox], temporarily attached to my staff, his company having been left at Camp Atchinson.

The Quartermaster of the expedition, Captain Corning, and Captain Kimball, Assistant Quartermaster, in charge of the pontoon train, have discharged their laborious duties faithfully and satisfactorily; and for Captain Forbes, Commissary of Subsistence, I can bear witness that but for his activity, attention, and business capacity, the interests of the Government would have suffered much more than they did, by the miserable state in which many of the packages containing subsistence stores, were found.

Chief Guides, Major J. R. Brown and Pierre Bottineau, have been of the greatest service by their experience and knowledge of the country; and the Interpreter, Rev. Mr. Riggs, has also rendered much assistance in the management of the scouts. The scouts generally, including the Chiefs McLeod and

Duly, have made themselves very useful to the expedition, and have proved themselves faithful, intrepid and intelligent.

I have the honor to transmit herewith the reports of Colonels Crooks, Baker, and Lieut. Colonel Marshall, commanding respectively the 6th, 10th and 7th regiments of Minnesota Volunteers, and of Colonel McPhail, commanding 1st regiment Minnesota Mounted Rangers.

I am, Major, very respectfully,
Your obedient servant,
H. H. SIBLEY,
Brig. General Commanding

Chapter LXXIV

Official Report of Brigadier General Alfred Sully

Head-quarters Indian Expedition Camp at
Mouth of Little Sheyenne River,
Sept. 11th, 1863.

MAJOR: The last report I had the honor to send
you was from the mouth of the Little Sheyenne river,
bearing date August 16, 1863; since which time my
movements have been too rapid and the danger of
sending any communication such that it has been
impossible for me to do so. I therefore have the honor
to report my movements from last report up to
date.[112]

On the morning of the 19th, the steamer I was
waiting for with supplies finally arrived. She was immediately unloaded, and all the baggage of the officers and men of the command was sent down by her
to the depot at Ft. Pierre, together with every man
who was in the least sick or not well mounted. By
this I reduced my force considerably, and was enabled to transport, with the wretched mules, that
had been furnished me, about three days' rations and

[112]Sully, who took a column up the Missouri River that was
supposed to cooperate with Sibley's, had to contend with
various delays, and in the end operated independently, as
described. His various official reports, with other documents
of great interest, extending into 1864, are printed in *South
Dakota Historical Collections,* 1916, vol. 8, pp. 109-525.

forage enough to keep these transportation animals alive, depending on grass I might find, to feed the cavalry and artillery horses. Luckily for me, I found the grazing north much better than I had dared to hope for.

On the 20th, were visited by one of the most terrific rain and hail storms I have seen. This stampeded some of my animals and a few were lost—they swam across the Missouri—and it also destroyed a quantity of my rations in the wagons, thereby causing me some delay in the march; but I succeeded in getting off the afternoon of the 21st, and marched up the Little Sheyenne about eleven miles, the road being very heavy. The next day we marched only seven miles, camping on a slough on the prairie without wood. The next day we marched in a north-westerly direction to the outlet of Swan lake. On the 24th, we marched due north, eighteen miles, and encamped on a small creek, called Bois Cache. Here we came into the buffalo country, and I formed a hunting party for the command, which I had soon to disband, as they disabled more horses than buffalo. We continued our march north about twenty-two miles and reached a small stream called Bird Archie [Ache] creek. This day the hunters succeeded in killing many buffalo, and reported that they saw Indians near the Missouri.

Early on the morning of the 28th, I sent out a small scouting party, who captured two squaws and some children and brought them into me. These Indians reported that Gen. Sibley had had a fight near the head of Long lake, and that they were on their way to the Agency at Crow creek, but were lost, and were alone; but the scouts found tracks of lodges going up the Missouri. I therefore immediately detailed companies F and K of the 2d Nebraska cavalry, under command of Captain D. La Boo, ordering them to go to the Missouri, and follow up the trail, with orders to capture some Indians if possible and bring them in, so that I might get information; if they could not do that, to kill them and destroy the camps. I continued the march with the rest of the command that day, passing through large herds of buffalo, and was obliged to make a march of thirty-five miles before I could reach water. The weather was very hot, and it was night before we reached camp on the Beaver river.

On the 27th, I started late, having had some difficulty in crossing the river, making a march of five miles still in a northerly direction, and encamped on another branch of the same river. Company K of the 2d Nebraska joined me this day, having been separated from the other company. The next day we had to make some deviations to the west, on account of hills and sloughs, and made the outlet of Long lake, a march of about twenty miles. On the way we saw numerous signs of Indians in large numbers having been recently there, and found an old lame Indian concealed in the bushes, who was well known by many of the men of the command as having for some years resided near Sioux city. He had the reputation of being what is called a "good Indian." He stated that "his horse had been taken away from him and that he had been left there." He looked almost starved to death. He gave me the following details, which have since mostly turned out to be correct: he stated "Gen. Sibley had fought the Indians at the head of Long lake, fifty miles north-east from me, some weeks ago; that he followed them down to the mouth of Apple creek; that the Indians attacked him on the way, and that there was some skirmishing.

"At Apple creek, Sibley had another fight, and that in all the fights, about fifty-eight Indians were killed; that Gen. Sibley fortified his camp at Apple creek, and after a while returned to James river; that a few days after Gen. Sibley left, the Indians, who had their scouts out watching, recrossed the Missouri, and while doing so, discovered a Mackinaw boat on its way down. They attacked the boat, fought the entire day until sundown, sunk her, and killed all on board—twenty-one men, three women and some children; that before she was sunk, the fire from the boat killed ninety-one Indians, and wounded many more; that a small war party followed Sibley some days, returned with the report that he had crossed the James river; then some of the Indians went north; the larger portion, however, went towards the head of Long lake; and that he thought a portion of them encamped on the Missouri river west of me."

The report was so much in keeping with the Indian mode of warfare, that though it came from an Indian, I was led to give it some consideration, particularly the part that stated the Indians, after watching Sibley's return, recrossed, when all danger was over, and went back to their old hunting grounds. Besides, the guides who were acquainted with the country, stated that "a large body of Indians could not live on the other side long, without going a great distance west; that always at this season of the year the Indians camped on the Coteau, near the tributaries of the James, where the numerous lakes or springs kept the grass fresh; here the buffalo were plenty, and the lakes and streams full of fish; and that here they prepared their meat for the winter, moving to the Missouri where the fuel was plenty to winter." I therefore determined to change my course towards the east, to move rapidly, and go as far as my rations would allow.

I felt serious alarm for the safety of Capt. LaBoo, who had but fifty men with him, and who had already been out over two days without rations. I encamped here for the next day, and sent out four companies of the 2d Nebraska and of the 6th Iowa, under command of Major J. W. Pearman, 2d Nebraska, to hunt him up, and see if there were any Indians on the Missouri. The next day, however, Capt. LaBoo's company returned, having made a march of one hundred and eighty-seven miles, living upon what buffalo and game they could kill, scouring the country to my left, overtaking the camp of ten lodges he was sent after, destroying them, but seeing no Indians.

This same day (29th), I sent two companies of the 6th Iowa to the mouth of Apple creek. They reported, on their return, that they found the fortified camp of Gen. Sibley, his trail, and his return trail towards the east; that they could see no signs of there having been any fight there, nor could they see the Mackinaw boat reported by the old Indian. This detachment was under command of Captain D. W. C. Cram, 6th Iowa. The battalion of Major Pearman joined me before starting, having seen nothing, and, after a march of above ninety miles, through a country with no wood whatever, but with good grass and plenty of lakes, of the most abominable water. On the 3d of September, we reached a lake, where, on the plains near by, were the remains of a very large number of buffalo killed, some quite recently. Here I encamped, to wait the reports of the commands I had out, during the march, who, every day, discovered fresh signs of Indians, their lodge trails spread over the country, but all moving towards a point known to be a favorite haunt of the Indians. I had this day detailed one battalion of the 6th Iowa, Maj. Albert E. House commanding, and Mr. Frank LaFramboise, as guide, to keep ahead of me five miles, and, in case they saw a small band of Indians, to attack them, or take them prisoners. If they should find a large band, too large to successfully cope with, to watch the camp at a distance, and send back word to me, my intention being to leave my train under charge of a heavy guard, move up in the night time, so as to surround them, and attack them at daybreak. But, for some reason, satisfactory to the guide, he bore off much to my left, and came upon the Indians, in an encampment of over four hundred lodges, some say six hundred, in ravines, where they felt perfectly secure, being fully persuaded that I was still on my way up the Missouri. This is what the Indian prisoners say. They also state that a war party followed me on my way up, in hopes of stampeding me; but this they could not do. I marched with great care, with an advance guard and flankers; the train in two lines, sixty paces apart; the troops on each side; in front and centre, myself, with one company and the battery; all the loose stock was kept between the lines of wagons. In this way, I lost no animals on the campaign, except some few, about a dozen, that got out of camp at night. Nor did the Indians, during all the trip, ever attack me, or try to stampede me.

Major House, according to my instructions, endeavored to surround and keep in the Indians until word could be sent me; but this was an impossibility with his 300 men, as the encampment was very large, mustering at least 1,200 warriors. This is what the Indians say they had; but I, as well as everybody in the command, say over 1,500. These Indians were partly Santees from Minnesota, Cut-heads from the Coteau, Yanktonais and Blackfeet, who belong on the other side of the Missouri; and, as I have since learned, Unkapapas, the same party who fought General Sibley, and destroyed the Mackinaw boat. Of this I have unmistakable proof, from letters and papers found in camp, and on the persons of some of the Indians, besides relics of the Minnesota massacre; also from the fact that they told Mr. La Framboise, the guide, when he was surrounded by about 200 of them, that "they had fought Gen. Sibley, and they did not see why the whites wanted to come and fight them, unless they were tired of living, and wanted to die." Mr. La Framboise succeeded in getting away from them, after some difficulty, and ran his horse a distance of more than ten miles, to give me information, Major House, with his command, still remaining there. He reached me a little after four o'clock. I immediately turned out my command. The horses, at the time, were out grazing. At the sound of the bugle, the men rushed, with a cheer, and in a very few minutes, saddled up and were in line. I left four companies, and all the men who were poorly mounted, in the camp, with orders to strike the tents and corral the wagons, and starting off with the 2d Nebraska on the right, the 6th Iowa on the left, one company of the 7th Iowa, and the battery in the centre, at a full gallop, we made the distance of over ten miles in much less than an hour.

On reaching near the ground, I found that the enemy were leaving and carrying off what plunder they could. Many lodges, however, were still standing. I ordered Col. R. W. Furnas, 2d Nebraska, to push his horses to the utmost, so as to reach the camp, and assist Major House in keeping the Indians corraled. This order was obeyed with great alacrity, the regiment going over the plains at a full run. I was close upon the rear of the regiment with the 6th Iowa. The 2d Nebraska took the right of the camp, and was soon lost in a cloud of dust, over the hills. I ordered Col. D. S. Wilson, 6th Iowa, to take the left, while I, with the battery, one company of the 7th Iowa, Capt. A. J. Millard, and two companies of the 6th Iowa, Major Ten Broeck commanding, charged through the centre of the encampment. I here found an Indian chief, by the name of Little Soldier, with some few of his people. This Indian has always had the reputation of being a "good Indian," and friendly. I placed them under guard, and moved on. Shortly after, I met with the notorious chief, Big Head, and some of his men. They were dressed for a fight, but my men cut them off. These Indians, together with some of their warriors, mustering about thirty, together with squaws, children, ponies and dogs, gave themselves up, numbering over 120 human beings. About the same time, firing began, about a half a mile from me, ahead, and was kept up, becoming more and more brisk, until it was quite a respectable engagement. A report was brought to me (which proved to be false), that the Indians were driving back some of my command. I immediately took possession of the hillocks near by, forming line, and placing the battery in the centre, on a high knoll. At this time, night had about set in, but still the engagement was briskly kept up, and in the melee it was hard to distinguish my line from that of the enemy. The Indians made a very desperate resistance, but finally broke and fled, pursued in every direction by bodies of my troops. I would here state, that the troops, though mounted, were armed with rifles, and, according to my orders, most of them dismounted and fought afoot, until the enemy broke, when they re-mounted and went in pursuit. It is to be regretted that I could not have had an hour or two more of daylight, for I feel sure, if I had, I could have annihilated the enemy. As it was, I believe I can safely say, I gave them one of the most severe punishments that the Indians have ever received. [Battle of White Stone Hill]. After night set in, the engagement was of such a promiscuous nature, that it was hard to tell what results would happen; I therefore ordered all the buglers to sound the "rally," and building large fires, remained under arms, during night, collecting together my troops.

The next morning, early (the 4th), I established my camp on the battle field, the wagon train, under charge of Major Pearman, 2d Nebraska, having, in the night, been ordered to join me, and sent out strong scouting parties, in different directions, to scour the country, to overtake what Indians they could; but in this they were not very successful, though some of them had some little skirmishes.

They found the dead and wounded in all directions, some of them miles from the battle field; also immense quantities of provisions, baggage, &c., where they had apparently cut loose their ponies from "travailles," and got off on them; also numbers of ponies and dogs, harnessed to "travailles," running all over the prairie. One party that I sent out, went near to the James river, and found there, eleven dead Indians. The deserted camp of the Indians, together with the country all around, was covered with their plunder. I devoted this day, together with the following (the 5th), to destroying all this property, still scouring the country. I do not think I exaggerate in the least, when I say that I burned up over four or five hundred thousand pounds of dried buffalo meat, as one item, besides three hundred lodges and a very large quantity of property, of great value to the Indians. A very large number of ponies were found dead and wounded on the field; besides a large number were captured. The prisoners (some 130) I take with me below, and shall report to you more specially in regard to them.

The surgeon of the 2d Nebraska regiment, Dr. Bowen, who has shown a great energy and desire to attend to his duties during the campaign, started out during the night of the engagement with a party of fifteen men, to go back to the old camp to procure ambulances. But as they did not return on the morning of the second day, I knew he was either lost or captured. (He returned about noon of the second day.) I therefore sent out small scouting parties in every direction to hunt them up. One of these fell into an ambuscade, by which four of the party were killed and the rest driven in. I immediately sent out five companies of the 2d Nebraska regiment, Colonel Furnas in command, who, after a long march, found the Indians had fled. They succeeded, however, in overtaking three concealed in some tall grass, whom they killed. The fight has been so scattered, the dead Indians have been found in so many different places, that it is impossible for me to give an accurate report of the number killed of the enemy. I, however, think I am safe in reporting it at 100. (I report those that were left on the field and that my scouting parties found.)

During the engagement, for some time, the 2d Nebraska, afoot and armed with rifles, and there are among them probably some of the best shots in the world, were engaged with the enemy at a distance not over sixty paces, pouring on them a murderous fire in a ravine where the enemy were posted. The slaughter, therefore, was immense. My officers and the guides I have with me think one hundred and fifty will not cover their loss. The Indian reports make it two hundred. That the General may know the exact locality of the battle-field, I would state that it was, as near as I could judge, fifteen miles west of James river, and about half way between the latitudes of Bonebut and headwaters of Elm river, as laid down on the government map. The fight took place near a hill called by the Indians White Stone Hill.

In conclusion, I would state that the troops of my command conducted themselves well; and though it was the first that nearly all of them had ever been in, they showed that they are of the right material, and that in time, with discipline, they will make worthy soldiers. It is to be regretted that we lost so many valuable lives as we did, but this could not be helped; the Indians had formed a line of battle with good judgment, from which they could only be dislodged by a charge. I could not use my artillery without greatly endangering the lives of my own men; if I could, I could have slaughtered them.

I send you, accompanying, the reports of Colonel Wilson, 6th Iowa, and Colonel Furnas, 2d Nebraska, also official reports of killed and wounded, and take this occasion to thank both those officers for their good conduct and the cheerfulness with which they obeyed my orders on the occasion. Both of them had their horses shot in the action. I would also request permission to state that the several members of my staff rendered me every possible assistance.

On the morning of the 6th, I took up my line of march for Fort Pierre. If I could have remained in that section of country some two or three weeks, I might have accomplished more; but I was satisfied by the reports of my scouts that the Indians had scattered in all directions; some toward the James river; some, probably the Blackfeet, to recross the Missouri, and a part of them went north, where they say they have friends among the half-breeds of the north. My rations were barely sufficient with rapid marches to enable me to reach Fort Pierre. The animals, not only the *teams* I have already reported to you as worthless, but also the cavalry horses, showed the effect of rapid marching and being entirely without grain.

I brought with me all the prisoners I had, and tried to question them to gain some information. The men refused to say much, except that they are all "good Indians," and the other bad ones joined their camp without their will.

Their squaws, however, corroborate the report I have already given you in regard to the destruction of the people on board the Mackinaw boat and the fights with General Sibley, in which these Indians had a part. They also state that the Indians, after recrossing to this side of the Missouri, sent a party to follow Sibley until he went to the James river, then returned to their camp on Long lake to procure a large quantity of provisions and other articles they had "cached" there, and then came to the camp where I met them.

After marching about one hundred and thirty miles we reached the mouth of the Little Sheyenne on the 11th, where I found the steamboat I had ordered to be there on the 8th instant. It was lucky she was there, for without the grain she brought up I could not have brought my empty wagons back. For some miles north of Sheyenne and Pierre, the grass is about all gone. I placed my wounded on the boat, and as many empty wagons as she could carry. I am afraid the loss of horses and mules will be considered very great, but it could not be helped. When I found it *impossible* for the rear guard to get an animal along, I had it killed, to prevent its falling into the hands of the enemy.

Very respectfully, your ob't serv't,

ALF. SULLY,

Brigadier General Commanding.

P. S.—By actual count, the number of my prisoners is one hundred and fifty-six—men thirty-two, women and children one hundred and twenty-four. I would also beg leave to say that in the action, I had of my command between six hundred and seven hundred men actually engaged. My killed number, as far as ascertained, twenty; wounded, thirty-eight.

Very respectfully, your ob't serv't,

ALF. SULLY,

Brigadier General Commanding.

Chapter LXXV

The Death of Chaska

AMONG most of the Indian tribes of the Northwest there exists a tie or degree of relationship,
when entered into by two or more persons in good
faith, which is more binding than any other known
to the savage race. It is considered by them far more
sacred than the matrimonial tie. It is the tie of comradeship! A man may, on any pretext whatever,
throw away his wife and take another, if he chooses,
but to his comrade he is firmly bound until death
separates them. Nothing is considered more base or
cowardly than to desert one's comrade in the hour
of danger.

"Most white persons residing in the Indian country endeavor to select some Indian who is possessed
of courage, intelligence and a good hunter, and who
also can exert some influence over the band to which
he belongs, for a comrade; knowing that in whatever
situation he may be placed, it is in the power of his
Indian friend to materially assist him.

"All Indian traders have comrades upon whom
they rely to exert their influence to prevent the other
Indians from trading their furs and skins with any
one else, and to come up and pay their debts, which,
as a general thing, they are not very prompt in doing.
The Indian who stands in this relation to a trader,
expects some valuable present from his 'ko-da' or

friend, for his valuable service, and not unfrequently does he give in return the best he can afford—such as a horse, or his money when he receives his annuities, &c. But the circumstances of the two being taken into consideration, the Indian generally has the best of the bargain, for he is poor, and though he returns present for present, his offerings of friendship are of so little value, generally, that at the end of the year he is greatly your debtor. This tie involves the most implicit confidence in each other, and the idea of deceiving one's friend in any respect whatever, is held most dishonorable."

A compact like the foregoing had long existed between Wa-kin-yan-ta-wa (which means in English His Thunder), or Chaska, as more familiarly known to the whites, and George H. Spencer; and very valuable has the reader seen the workings of this tie to have been. The compact was formed in 1851 at Little Crow's Village, then located six miles below St. Paul. Though an uncultivated Indian, he possessed much intelligence, and was a young man of pleasing manners and address, rather good looking, with great energy of mind. In 1857 he accompanied Little Crow and several of the Chiefs to Washington, relative to making a treaty for a portion of their Reservation. He was distinguished for bravery on the war path and had taken the scalps of seven Chippewas, and also killed one of his own tribe in revenge for the death of a brother. For several years he had held the position of "Head Soldier" to Little Crow. But when

he refused to join in the war against the whites,
ire of his chief was raised against him. The tie
comradeship was stronger than the tie of chieftain
ship.

When in 1860 his comrade built his trading house
on Big Stone lake, Chaska insisted on going with
him, for, said he, "though you may risk yourself
there, I will not risk you alone with those wild, strange
Indians." So with wife and children he went, and
remained till he deemed it safe to leave him. From
such rare specimens have the noble attributes ascribed
to the Indian character been drawn. He was alike
unmindful of persuasion or threats, when, in 1862,
the horrid massacres commenced. We will not say
that there was no leavening influence, nor wholly un-
mixed with selfishness—but it was not the predominating idea.

When his comrade was shot, we have seen how
Chaska at the risk of his own life saved him, taking
him to his own lodge, washing and dressing his
wounds, and caring for him with all the love of a
brother. We have seen him active in forming the
friendly camp, and getting the prisoners into it. We
have seen him surrendering himself to General Sibley
for the crime of being an Indian, with a desire of being acquitted before the world of complicity in the
horrid massacres and war which followed. We have
seen him avowing a readiness to comply with any
terms which should elevate him to the dignity of the
white man's standard of man.

I am not pleased to see you in your blanket," said
en. Sibley.

"Then I will wear it no more," was the prompt
reply.

From that day Chaska was, to all intents and purposes a white man. In the expedition he was very
valuable as a scout, and a universal favorite. We have
seen him, just before the first battle with the Sioux,
saving the life of Mr. Brackett, and in the fight con-
ducting himself with great bravery. At the Missouri
river we hear him trying to persuade his friend to
return to camp, urging as a reason, I "do not like the
way things look here." While they were yet speaking came a shower of bullets from the opposite
shore. Even then, Lieut. Beever had received the
fatal arrow shot, and the woods must have been full
of the foe.

The journey westward was completed. The order
for return had been read, and on the first of August
faces were turned homeward. Mr. Spencer says, "on
the second, we rode along, talking pleasantly of the
future, he telling me how he would like to be situated
on a small piece of land near me, and congratulating
himself that his trouble was over, and that he would
soon be restored to the bosom of his family. Alas, for
my friend! he now sleeps tranquilly near the turbid
waters of the Missouri, under the shadows of our in-
trenchments. Savage though he was, he was a noble
man!"

On the evening of the second day, he went round to his friend's tent, where he was always welcome, and supped with him. He spoke of having captured a pack of furs, which he desired taken home in a wagon of the Commissary Department; and for this purpose returned to the tent about nine o'clock then in apparent health went to his own quarters for the night. Immediately after, he was taken ill. His comrade hastened to his bedside to find him senseless—dying. He talked wildly, and predicted a thunder storm such as should shake the earth and blind the people with its light, the day he should be put into the ground, and it was as he predicted. He never once recognized the friend whose life he had saved, and closed his eyes at 11 o'clock the same evening, at the age of thirty-two. There were strong suspicions that poison was the cause of his death, but there was no time for investigation. The following morning, August 3, Mr. Spencer says, "we laid his body in a rifle pit, concealing it, as best we could, to prevent the enemy from finding it, and opening the grave. He leaves a wife and two interesting children, to mourn his untimely end."[113]

[113]The letter by "Sweetser" cited in Note 110 includes a paragraph: "I have to report, before closing this somewhat desultory letter the sudden death of Chaska, one of our Chief Indian scouts. He died last night after a sickness of only a few minutes. He has done noble work for the expedition, and will long be remembered for his faithfulness, sagacity, and loyalty to the whites. It was Chaska . . . who saved the life of George Spencer during the troubles of last fall."

Chapter LXXVI

Home Again

JOY animated the hearts and enlivened the steps of the men. Their weary out-marches were ended, and all had left loved ones at home. Every man in that long column had acted well his part, without which its history would be incomplete. A cautious and wise policy had been pursued, when a daring, dashing, reckless leadership would have brought irretrievable disaster to the expedition. Comparatively few casualties had occurred. God had been with them, and nearly all were returning healthier, stronger, and wiser than when they left. Devout thanksgiving arose as the distance lessened between them and all held most dear. They had left their homes when June's fresh roses shed fragrance on their way —had wandered through dry and parched regions— had met and driven the enemy, and now on the first flush of autumn's golden tints, return; making it, if not a complete, *a great success.* A halo of glory enshrouds these veterans of the prairies. Booming cannon announces their approach, and glad hearts bound with joy as they go forth to welcome their return. Mothers, wives and children wait with open arms to receive them. Only a few look in vain for those who had gone forth so full of life, of courage, and hope!*

*The column was decreased but seven. [H.M.]

Home Again

A halo of glory encircles the brow of the commanding. High in the confidence of the ▓ and better fitted for the work assigned him thar other man — erect in manhood's glory he star. Greatness has been thrust upon Nature's noblema. and fittingly he has worn it.

When a few hundred citizens around the region of St. Anthony's Falls desired to be recognized as the Territory of Minnesota, no more fitting person was found to represent their interests in Congress. When this vast territory took upon itself the privilege of State rights, its first elected Governor was Henry H. Sibley. Retiring to private life, as a true citizen he always served its interests; and when called to this most important military post, he girded on the armor. Promotion followed till he ranked among the higher military powers of the nation. Surrounded by this halo of earthly glory, he draws near the spot where memory has delighted to linger. But he is a man, with the heart of a man. The tramp of the "pale horse" has been heard in his dwelling, and has carried away his angel Mary and his only son Frank of eleven years, to a land where brighter and perpetual sunshine falls. And here, at his own hearth-stone — here, grateful for its remaining blessings — here, while he plans for the finale of the war — till the last echo of the Dakotas' war-whoop shall have died on the ear — here, with the mellowing influences of home loves, we leave him.

INDEX

Index

The Lakeside Classics